Letts

11+

Success

for CEM

Practice Test Papers

4 test papers

- **Comprehension**

- **Verbal Reasoning**

- **Maths**

- **Non-Verbal Reasoning**

Get started

Faisal Nasim

 **Audio**

Contents

Guidance notes for parents

What your child will need to sit these papers

- A quiet place to sit the exam
- A clearly visible clock
- A way to play the audio download
- A pencil and an eraser
- A piece of paper

Your child should not use a calculator for any of these papers.

How to invigilate the test papers

It is recommended that your child sits Test A (with a 15-minute break between Papers 1 and 2) and then sits Test B in the same way at a later date. Don't help your child or allow any talking. Review the answers with your child and help improve their weaker areas.

Step 1: Cut out the answers and keep them hidden from your child.

Step 2: Cut out the answer sheet section. Your child should write their full name on top of the first answer sheet. Give them the question paper booklet. They must not open the paper until they are told to do so by the audio instructions.

Step 3: Start the audio.

Step 4: Ask your child to work through the practice questions before the time starts for each section. An example is already marked on each section of the answer sheet. Your child should mark the answer sheet clearly and check that the practice questions are correctly marked.

Step 5: Mark the answer sheet. Then, together with your child, work through the questions that were answered incorrectly. When working through the Non-Verbal Reasoning sections, ensure you have the question papers open to help explain the answers to your child.

How your child should complete the answer sheet

Your child MUST NOT write their answers on the question paper; they must use the answer sheet. They should put a horizontal line through the boxes on the answer sheet. To change an answer, your child should fully erase the incorrect answer and then clearly select a new answer. Any rough workings should be done on a separate piece of paper.

The audio instructions

Both papers have audio instructions in order to prepare your child to listen and act upon them. Audio instructions are at the start, during and at the end of the sections. Audio warnings on the time remaining will be given at varying intervals. Your child should listen out for these warnings.

The symbols at the foot of the page

Written instructions are at the foot of the page. Your child MUST follow these instructions:

Continue working

Stop and wait for instructions

Your child can review questions within the allocated time, but must not move on to the next section until they are allowed to do so.

The instructions and examples at the beginning of the section

In the instructions, your child should look for: the time allowed; how many questions there are; and how to complete the answers.

Examples are at the beginning of every section to show the type of question included in a particular section. The example questions will be worked through as part of the audio instructions.

How to work out your child's overall score for each Test

Each question is worth one mark. For the purpose of marking, each test is split into two subject areas:

1) Maths (which includes Numeracy and Problem Solving) & Non-Verbal Reasoning

2) English (which includes the remaining sections).

For each test follow these steps to calculate your child's overall score:

1) Add up your child's scores for each of the two subject areas in both papers and note them in the blue boxes on the next page.

   For example, Test A Paper 1: 33 for English and 28 for Maths & Non-Verbal Reasoning and in Test A Paper 2: 29 for English and 30 for Maths & Non-Verbal Reasoning.

2) Add together both your child's total scores in English and then add together both your child's total scores in Maths & Non-Verbal Reasoning. Fill in each total in the blue boxes on the next page.

   For example: For English $33 + 29 = 62$ and for Maths & Non-Verbal Reasoning $28 + 30 = 58$.

3) Take your child's total English score and divide it by the maximum total English score (as shown in the table on the next page) and then multiply that figure by 100 to give you a percentage. Repeat this process for Maths & Non-Verbal reasoning.

   For example: English: $62 \div 92 \times 100 = 67\%$

   Maths & Non-Verbal Reasoning: $58 \div 79 \times 100 = 73\%$

4) Now add both percentages together and divide by 2 to give you your child's overall score for one test.

   For example $67 + 73 = 140 \div 2 = 70\%$

5) Repeat the steps above to calculate your child's overall score for Test B.

Test A	Subject	Your child's score	Maximum score
Test A Paper 1	English		49
Test A Paper 1	Maths & Non-Verbal Reasoning		36
Test A Paper 2	English		43
Test A Paper 2	Maths & Non-Verbal Reasoning		43
		Your child's total English score	Maximum total English score
			92
		Your child's total Maths & Non-Verbal Reasoning score	Maximum total Maths & Non-Verbal Reasoning score
			79

Your child's English percentage score	Your child's Maths & Non-Verbal Reasoning percentage score	Your child's overall score

Test B	Subject	Your child's score	Maximum score
Test B Paper 1	English		49
Test B Paper 1	Maths & Non-Verbal Reasoning		37
Test B Paper 2	English		38
Test B Paper 2	Maths & Non-Verbal Reasoning		48
		Your child's total English score	Maximum total English score
			87
		Your child's total Maths & Non-Verbal Reasoning score	Maximum total Maths & Non-Verbal Reasoning score
			85

Your child's English percentage score	Your child's Maths & Non-Verbal Reasoning percentage score	Your child's overall score

Please note: Your child should be aiming for an overall score of at least 70-75% in each Test. If your child does not score a good mark, focus on the areas where your child did not perform well and continue practising under timed conditions.

Once your child feels confident with these papers, move on to the Letts 11+ *Get ahead practice test papers.*

Get Started

Test A Paper 1

Instructions

1. Ensure you have pencils and an eraser with you.

2. Make sure you are able to see a clock or watch.

3. Write your name on the answer sheet.

4. Do not open the question booklet until you are told to do so by the audio instructions.

5. Listen carefully to the audio instructions given.

6. Mark your answers on the answer sheet only.

7. All workings must be completed on a separate piece of paper.

8. You should not use a calculator, dictionary or thesaurus at any point in this paper.

9. Move through the papers as quickly as possible and with care.

10. Follow the instructions at the foot of each page.

11. You should mark your answers with a horizontal line, as shown on the answer sheet.

12. If you want to change your answer, ensure that you rub out your first answer and that your second answer is clearly more visible.

13. You can go back and review any questions that are within the section you are working on only. You must await further instructions before moving on to another section.

Symbols and Phrases used in the Tests

 Instructions

 Time allowed for this section

 Stop working and await instructions

 Continue working

Comprehension

 ## INSTRUCTIONS

 YOU HAVE 9 MINUTES TO COMPLETE THE FOLLOWING SECTION.

YOU HAVE 10 QUESTIONS TO COMPLETE WITHIN THE TIME GIVEN.

EXAMPLES

Comprehension Example

South Africa is becoming an increasingly popular holiday destination. People from all over the world are being attracted by its natural beauty, cosmopolitan cities and diverse wildlife. Cape Town, the capital of South Africa, is especially popular. The city is dynamic and exciting and has a rich history and culture. It is also home to the stunning Table Mountain, which you can ascend on foot or by cable car.

Example 1

Which of the following is not mentioned as a reason why people are attracted to South Africa?

A   Natural beauty
B   Excellent food
C   Cosmopolitan cities
D   Diverse wildlife

The correct answer is B. This has already been marked in Example 1 in the Comprehension section of your answer sheet.

Practice Question 1

What is the name of the mountain in Cape Town?

A   Cape Mountain
B   Africa Mountain
C   Table Mountain
D   Leopard Mountain

The correct answer is C. Please mark this in Practice Question 1 in the Comprehension section of your answer sheet.

STOP AND WAIT FOR FURTHER INSTRUCTIONS

Read the passage below and then answer the questions that follow.

An extract from: **The Chocolate Revolution** *by Roald Dahl*

Today, chocolate-guzzling begins when a child is about five and goes on until the guzzler is 12. After which, with the advent of puberty, there is a gradual decline in consumption. Things were different when I was young. I grew up in the 20s and the chocolate revolution had not begun. There were very few delicious chocolate bars to tempt us. That's why sweet shops were called sweet shops and not chocolate shops.

When I was young, there was Cadbury's Bournville and Dairy Milk. There was the Dairy Milk Flake (the only great invention so far) and Whipped Cream Walnut, and there were also four different flavours of chocolate-coated Marshmallow Bar (vanilla, coffee, rose, lemon).

Consequently, we were much more inclined to spend our money on sweets and toffees or on sherbet-suckers, gobstoppers, liquorice bootlaces and aniseed balls – we did not mind that the liquorice was made from rats' blood and the sherbet from sawdust. They were cheap and to us, they tasted good.

Then came the revolution and the entire world of chocolate was suddenly turned upside down in the space of seven glorious years. Here is a summary of what happened.

- 1876: Chocolate was first used by the Spaniards, Italians and French in the early 17th century but only as a drink. Then, in 1876, a Swiss chap called Peters mixed chocolate powder with sugar and condensed milk and made a solid bar. Chocolate as we know it was invented.

- 1905: Cadbury got in on the act and began production of milk bars, starting with Dairy Milk.

- 1920: The first speciality chocolate bar, the Dairy Milk Flake, was invented. This was a milestone, the first time any manufacturer had seriously played with chocolate in their inventing rooms.

- 1928: Cadbury's Fruit and Nut bar popped up on the scene.

From 1930 to 1937 virtually all the great classic chocolate bars were invented and they are still on the best seller list.

- 1930: Frys invented the Crunchie.

- 1933: Black Magic appeared in boxes and, for some reason, it is still a best seller.

- 1935: The wonderful Aero was introduced.

(1) According to the author, when does a person's chocolate consumption begin to decline?

    A   Before their tenth birthday
    B   After their fifth birthday
    C   Never
    D   On the arrival of puberty

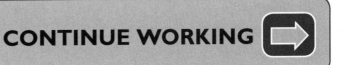

CONTINUE WORKING

(2) Why were shops called 'sweet shops' and not 'chocolate shops'?

A   Because chocolate had not yet been invented
B   Because shops didn't like to sell chocolate
C   Because they sold mainly sweets rather than chocolate
D   Because chocolate was forbidden

(3) Which of these types of chocolate is not mentioned by the author?

A   Dairy Milk
B   Whipped Cream Walnut
C   Bounty Bar
D   Marshmallow Bar

(4) According to the passage, which of the following did the author spend his money on?

Option 1: gobstoppers
Option 2: sherbet-suckers
Option 3: Skittles
Option 4: aniseed balls

A   Options 1 and 3 only
B   Options 2 and 4 only
C   Options 1, 2 and 4 only
D   All of the above

(5) What does the author suggest that liquorice was made from?

A   Sawdust
B   Black rubber
C   Rats' blood
D   Powdered sugar

(6) According to the author, how long did it take to transform the chocolate industry?

A   One year
B   Seven years
C   A decade
D   Twenty years

CONTINUE WORKING ⬛➡

(7) What was chocolate first used for?

A   To make medicine
B   To make drinks
C   To make salty snacks
D   To make walls

(8) From which country did the inventor of modern chocolate originate?

A   Switzerland
B   France
C   Spain
D   Italy

(9) What does the word 'wonderful' mean?

A   Feeble
B   Destructive
C   Amazing
D   Fortunate

(10) In which year was the Fruit and Nut bar invented?

A   1920
B   1928
C   1930
D   1933

STOP AND WAIT FOR FURTHER INSTRUCTIONS ⊗

Shuffled Sentences

 INSTRUCTIONS

 YOU HAVE 8 MINUTES TO COMPLETE THE FOLLOWING SECTION.

YOU HAVE 15 QUESTIONS TO COMPLETE WITHIN THE TIME GIVEN.

EXAMPLES

Example 1

The following sentence is shuffled and also contains one unnecessary word. Rearrange the sentence correctly in order to identify the unnecessary word.

wake under before must sunrise up we.

A	B	C	D	E
up	before	under	wake	sunrise

The correct answer is C. This has already been marked in Example 1 in the Shuffled Sentences section of your answer sheet.

Practice Question 1

The following sentence is shuffled and also contains one unnecessary word. Rearrange the sentence correctly in order to identify the unnecessary word.

very girl quickly the ran throw.

A	B	C	D	E
quickly	girl	the	ran	throw

The correct answer is E. Please mark this in Practice Question 1 in the Shuffled Sentences section of your answer sheet.

STOP AND WAIT FOR FURTHER INSTRUCTIONS

Each sentence below is shuffled and also contains one unnecessary word.
Rearrange each sentence correctly in order to identify the unnecessary word.

(1) boy eaten the the apple ate.

A	B	C	D	E
boy	the	apple	eaten	ate

(2) years old Sarah eight was ate.

A	B	C	D	E
ate	was	years	eight	old

(3) sped road flight car along the the.

A	B	C	D	E
road	car	flight	along	sped

(4) animals crops the grew his farmer.

A	B	C	D	E
crops	animals	his	grew	farmer

(5) lots we timing homework of had.

A	B	C	D	E
had	homework	we	timing	lots

(6) desk lifted was made the of wood.

A	B	C	D	E
desk	lifted	of	wood	made

(7) the most students enjoyed dislike of the course.

A	B	C	D	E
most	course	of	dislike	students

CONTINUE WORKING ⟶

8 made to many mistakes too she.

A	B	C	D	E
made	to	she	mistakes	too

9 gaze the through wind forest the blew.

A	B	C	D	E
forest	blew	the	wind	gaze

10 and Noah family his open friends loved.

A	B	C	D	E
friends	family	and	open	loved

11 quickly boy the young into ran.

A	B	C	D	E
quickly	the	boy	young	into

12 capability inhabitants city's upset were the.

A	B	C	D	E
were	capability	the	inhabitants	upset

13 can prevent exercise illness figure help frequent.

A	B	C	D	E
prevent	illness	exercise	figure	frequent

14 the jury summarised lawyer four the case for the.

A	B	C	D	E
four	jury	case	summarised	lawyer

15 attacked suffer fellow his inmates prisoner the.

A	B	C	D	E
inmates	fellow	attacked	suffer	prisoner

STOP AND WAIT FOR FURTHER INSTRUCTIONS ⊗

Numeracy

 INSTRUCTIONS

 YOU HAVE 6 MINUTES TO COMPLETE THE FOLLOWING SECTION.

YOU HAVE 13 QUESTIONS TO COMPLETE WITHIN THE TIME GIVEN.

EXAMPLES

The questions within this section are not multiple choice. Write the answer to each question on the answer sheet by selecting the correct digits from the columns provided.

Example 1

Calculate the answer to the following:

12 + 42

The correct answer is 54. This has already been marked in Example 1 in the Numeracy section of your answer sheet.

Practice Question 1

Calculate the answer to the following:

55 – 47

The correct answer is 8. Please mark this in Practice Question 1 in the Numeracy section of your answer sheet. Note that a single-digit answer should be marked with a 0 in the left-hand column, so mark 08 on your answer sheet.

STOP AND WAIT FOR FURTHER INSTRUCTIONS

(1) Calculate the answer to the following:

17 + 56

CONTINUE WORKING

(2) Calculate the answer to the following:

$120 \div 2$

(3) Calculate the answer to the following:

$54 - 7 + 9$

(4) Calculate the mode of the following data:

5, 7, 43, 12, 5, 12, 19, 21, 5, 6, 54

(5) Which number should replace the '?' in the following sequence?

14, 21, 29, 36, ?, 51

(6) How many minutes are there in $1\frac{1}{6}$ hours?

(7) What is the value of X in this equation?

$15 + X = 31 - 12$

(8) What is the remainder when 75 is divided by 8?

(9) How many months are there in half a decade?

(10) Which of these is not a multiple of 8?

40, 65, 88, 24, 56

(11) How many different factors does the number 36 have?

(12) I think of a number, multiply it by 2 and then divide it by 3. My answer is 8.

What number did I think of?

(13) What is the mean of these numbers?

12, 18, 10, 4

STOP AND WAIT FOR FURTHER INSTRUCTIONS ⊗

Problem Solving

 INSTRUCTIONS

 YOU HAVE 8 MINUTES TO COMPLETE THE FOLLOWING SECTION.

YOU HAVE 10 QUESTIONS TO COMPLETE WITHIN THE TIME GIVEN.

EXAMPLES

Example 1

Calculate the answer to the following:

Tom buys a chocolate bar for £1·50. He pays with a £5 note.
How much change does he receive?

A £1·50	**B** £3	**C** £3·50
D £4	**E** £5	

The correct answer is C. This has already been marked in Example 1 in the Problem Solving section of your answer sheet.

Practice Question 1

Sarah eats $\frac{1}{4}$ of a pizza.

What fraction of the pizza remains?

A $\frac{1}{2}$	**B** $\frac{1}{3}$	**C** $\frac{2}{5}$
D $\frac{3}{4}$	**E** $\frac{5}{6}$	

The correct answer is D. Please mark this in Practice Question 1 in the Problem Solving section of your answer sheet.

STOP AND WAIT FOR FURTHER INSTRUCTIONS ⊗

Calculate the answers to the following.

(1) Peter leaves home at 10 a.m. and returns at 12:30 p.m.
For how many minutes is Peter away from home?

A 120 minutes   **B** 90 minutes   **C** 180 minutes
D 100 minutes   **E** 150 minutes

(2) A man drives a truck at an average speed of 48 kilometres per hour.
What distance does the man cover if he drives for 3 hours?

A 148 km   **B** 96 km   **C** 144 km
D 100 km   **E** 150 km

(3) Sandra collects coins. In June, she collected 45 coins. In July, she collected 66 coins.
In August, she collected 34 coins.
How many coins did she collect in total in June, July and August?

A 79   **B** 145   **C** 48
D 142   **E** 100

(4) There are 44 sweets in a box. Ravi eats one quarter of them.
How many sweets are left in the box?

A 44   **B** 0   **C** 22
D 11   **E** 33

(5) Simon buys 2 packets of crisps. Each packet costs 22p. He pays with a £1 coin.
How much change does Simon receive?

A £0·22   **B** £0·44   **C** £0·78
D £0·56   **E** £0·88

(6) Shape A is a regular hexagon with a perimeter of 54 cm.
What is the length of one side of Shape A?

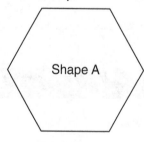

Shape A

Not drawn to scale

A 54 cm   **B** 12 cm   **C** 9 cm
D 6 cm   **E** 27 cm

CONTINUE WORKING ⇨

7 A bowl of sweets is shared between Tim and Robert using a ratio of 3:2.
If Robert receives 12 sweets, how many does Tim receive?

A 18   **B** 12   **C** 5
D 6   **E** 8

8 How many lines of symmetry does this shape have?

A 0   **B** 1   **C** 2
D 3   **E** 4

9 560 people attended a concert, rounded to the nearest 10. What is the largest possible
number of people that could have attended the concert?

A 560   **B** 550   **C** 565
D 555   **E** 564

10 The price of a dress is reduced by 20% in a sale. If the original price was £40, what is the
sale price?

A £40   **B** £36   **C** £24
D £32   **E** £8

STOP AND WAIT FOR FURTHER INSTRUCTIONS ⊗

Synonyms

INSTRUCTIONS

 YOU HAVE 7 MINUTES TO COMPLETE THE FOLLOWING SECTION.

YOU HAVE 24 QUESTIONS TO COMPLETE WITHIN THE TIME GIVEN.

EXAMPLES

Example 1

Select the word that is most similar in meaning to the following word:

push

A	B	C	D	E
shallow	shove	tug	hollow	cry

The correct answer is B. This has already been marked in Example 1 in the Synonyms section of your answer sheet.

Practice Question 1

Select the word that is most similar in meaning to the following word:

imitate

A	B	C	D	E
cover	copy	grow	live	irritate

The correct answer is B. Please mark this in Practice Question 1 in the Synonyms section of your answer sheet.

STOP AND WAIT FOR FURTHER INSTRUCTIONS

For each row, select the word from the table that is most similar in meaning to the word above the table.

(1) allow

A	B	C	D	E
forbid	aloud	permit	drive	made

(2) blank

A	B	C	D	E
blink	preserve	full	admit	empty

(3) cunning

A	B	C	D	E
swimming	clever	evil	foolish	cold

(4) false

A	B	C	D	E
frozen	falter	feign	untrue	dislike

(5) glad

A	B	C	D	E
happy	injure	give	upset	grown

(6) huge

A	B	C	D	E
high	minuscule	undue	mortify	enormous

(7) loyal

A	B	C	D	E
leave	dishonest	faithful	fortitude	lawn

(8) rowdy

A	B	C	D	E
timid	fortunate	shrouded	noisy	rouse

CONTINUE WORKING ⇨

9 polite

A	B	C	D	E
politician	holy	rude	aggressive	courteous

10 quick

A	B	C	D	E
sick	slow	lenient	heart	rapid

11 rare

A	B	C	D	E
royal	scarce	mercy	steak	abundant

12 real

A	B	C	D	E
reel	arson	duplicate	genuine	phoney

13 abandon

A	B	C	D	E
alert	home	call	leave	remain

14 rich

A	B	C	D	E
pauper	clothes	wealthy	house	money

15 rude

A	B	C	D	E
gentle	impolite	commerce	prude	argue

16 safe

A	B	C	D	E
sail	protect	dangerous	damage	secure

CONTINUE WORKING ⇨

17 tired

A	B	C	D	E
energetic	tyres	cosy	friendly	drowsy

18 weak

A	B	C	D	E
injury	week	fashion	feeble	powerful

19 answer

A	B	C	D	E
season	ignore	wager	reply	violent

20 behave

A	B	C	D	E
motion	act	admirable	behaviour	play

21 classify

A	B	C	D	E
secret	honour	categorise	spy	social

22 condemn

A	B	C	D	E
praise	help	restrict	criticise	pilot

23 dubious

A	B	C	D	E
singular	doubtful	perfect	double	sure

24 conflict

A	B	C	D	E
harmony	joke	clash	discussion	connive

STOP AND WAIT FOR FURTHER INSTRUCTIONS ⊗

Non-Verbal Reasoning

 ## INSTRUCTIONS

 YOU HAVE 7 MINUTES TO COMPLETE THE FOLLOWING SECTION.

YOU HAVE 13 QUESTIONS TO COMPLETE WITHIN THE TIME GIVEN.

EXAMPLES

COMPLETE THE SQUARE Example 1

Which figure on the right should replace the blank square in the pattern?

 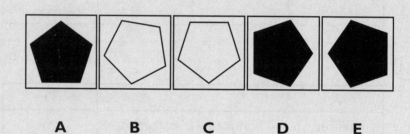

      A   **B**   **C**   **D**   **E**

The correct answer is D. This has already been marked in Example 1 in the Non-Verbal Reasoning section of your answer sheet.

COMPLETE THE SQUARE Practice Question 1

Which figure on the right should replace the blank square in the pattern?

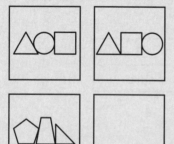 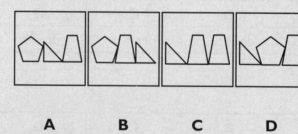

      A   **B**   **C**   **D**   **E**

The correct answer is A. Please mark this in Practice Question 1 in the Non-Verbal Reasoning section of your answer sheet.

CONTINUE WORKING

REFLECTION Example 2

Select how the following shape or pattern would appear when reflected in the dashed line.

| **A** | **B** | **C** | **D** |

The correct answer is C. This has already been marked in Example 2 in the Non-Verbal Reasoning section of your answer sheet.

REFLECTION Practice Question 2

Select how the following shape or pattern would appear when reflected in the dashed line.

 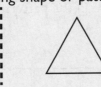

| **A** | **B** | **C** | **D** |

The correct answer is C. Please mark this in Practice Question 2 in the Non-Verbal Reasoning section of your answer sheet.

DIMENSION Example 3

Select how the following 3D figure would appear in a top-down, plan view.

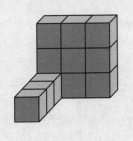 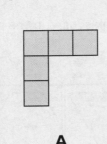 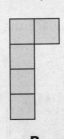 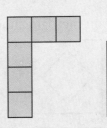 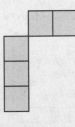

| **A** | **B** | **C** | **D** |

The correct answer is C. This has already been marked in Example 3 in the Non-Verbal Reasoning section of your answer sheet.

DIMENSION Practice Question 3

Select how the following 3D figure would appear in a top-down, plan view.

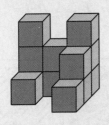 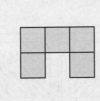 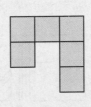 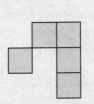 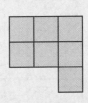

| **A** | **B** | **C** | **D** |

The correct answer is B. Please mark this in Practice Question 3 in the Non-Verbal Reasoning section of your answer sheet.

STOP AND WAIT FOR FURTHER INSTRUCTIONS

1 Which figure on the right should replace the blank square in the pattern?

2 Which figure on the right should replace the blank square in the pattern?

3 Which figure on the right should replace the blank square in the pattern?

4 Which figure on the right should replace the blank square in the pattern?

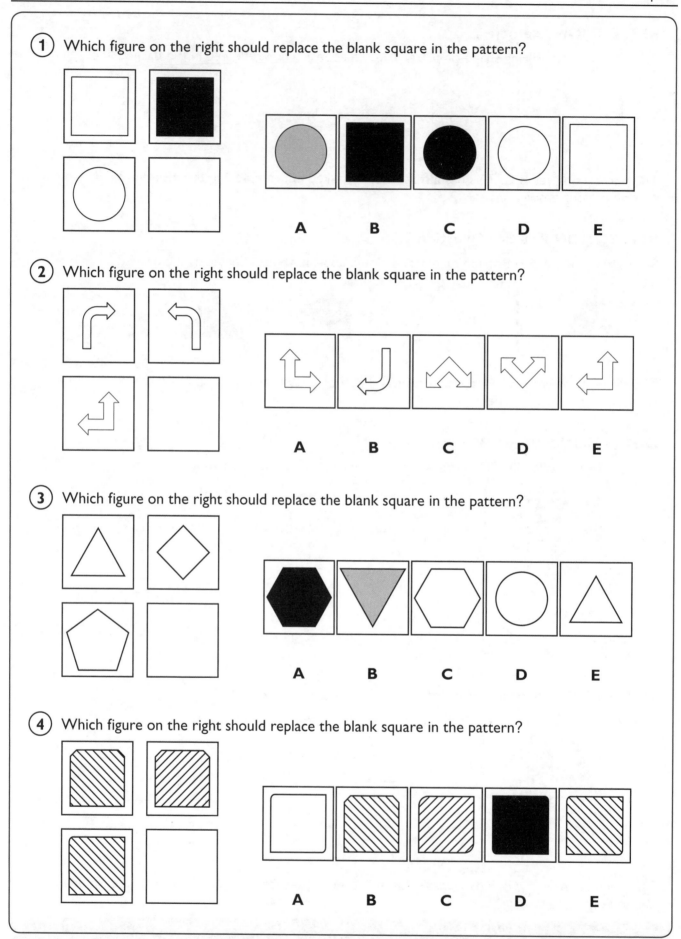

A   B   C   D   E

CONTINUE WORKING

5) Select how the following shape or pattern would appear when reflected in the dashed line.

6) Select how the following shape or pattern would appear when reflected in the dashed line.

7) Select how the following shape or pattern would appear when reflected in the dashed line.

8) Select how the following shape or pattern would appear when reflected in the dashed line.

9) Select how the following 3D figure would appear in a top-down, plan view.

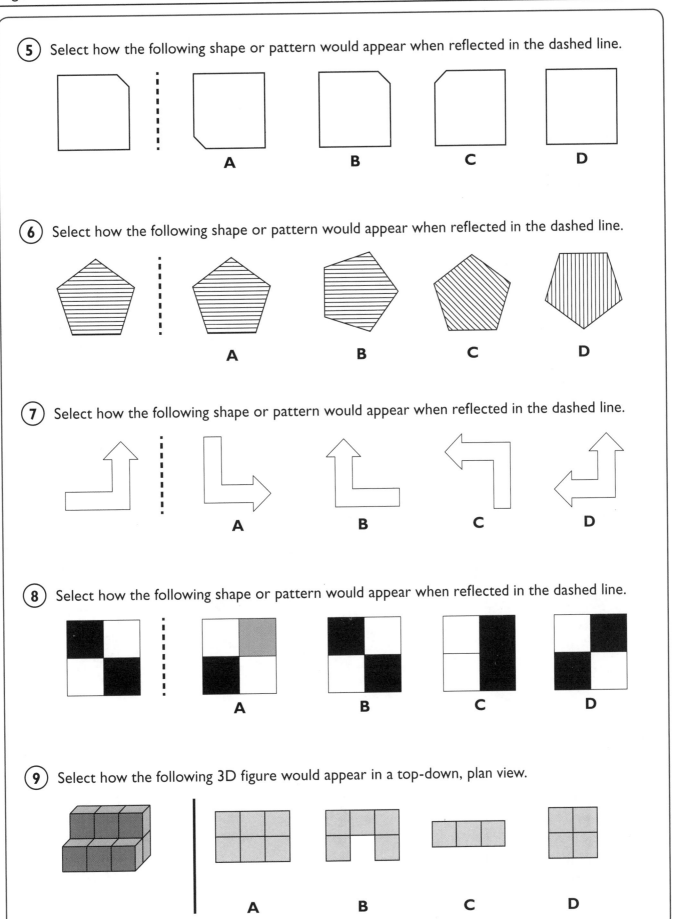

CONTINUE WORKING

(10) Select how the following 3D figure would appear in a top-down, plan view.

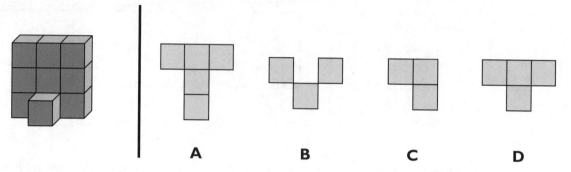

A   B   C   D

(11) Select how the following 3D figure would appear in a top-down, plan view.

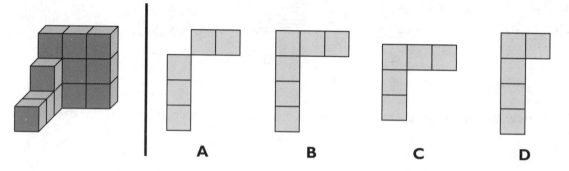

A   B   C   D

(12) Select how the following 3D figure would appear in a top-down, plan view.

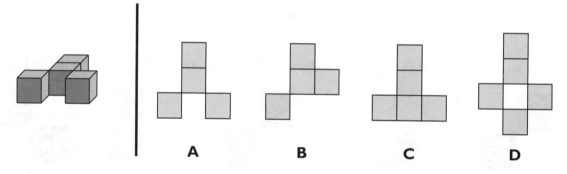

A   B   C   D

(13) Select how the following 3D figure would appear in a top-down, plan view.

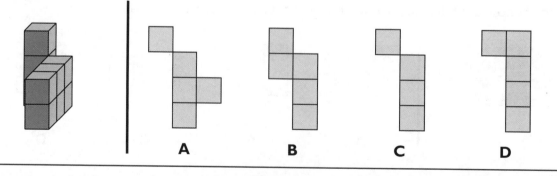

A   B   C   D

END OF PAPER

Get Started
Test A Paper 2

Instructions

1. Ensure you have pencils and an eraser with you.
2. Make sure you are able to see a clock or watch.
3. Write your name on the answer sheet.
4. Do not open the question booklet until you are told to do so by the audio instructions.
5. Listen carefully to the audio instructions given.
6. Mark your answers on the answer sheet only.
7. All workings must be completed on a separate piece of paper.
8. You should not use a calculator, dictionary or thesaurus at any point in this paper.
9. Move through the papers as quickly as possible and with care.
10. Follow the instructions at the foot of each page.
11. You should mark your answers with a horizontal line, as shown on the answer sheet.
12. If you want to change your answer, ensure that you rub out your first answer and that your second answer is clearly more visible.
13. You can go back and review any questions that are within the section you are working on only. You must await further instructions before moving on to another section.

Symbols and Phrases used in the Tests

 Instructions

 Time allowed for this section

 Stop working and await instructions

 Continue working

Problem Solving

 INSTRUCTIONS

 YOU HAVE 8 MINUTES TO COMPLETE THE FOLLOWING SECTION.

YOU HAVE 10 QUESTIONS TO COMPLETE WITHIN THE TIME GIVEN.

EXAMPLES

A $\frac{1}{2}$	B £3	C £3·50	D $\frac{3}{4}$	E $\frac{1}{3}$
F £1·50	G £5	H $\frac{2}{5}$	I £4	J $\frac{5}{6}$

Example 1

Select an answer to the question from the 10 different possible answers in the table above.

Tom buys a chocolate bar for £1·50. He pays with a £5 note.
How much change does he receive?

The correct answer is C. This has already been marked in Example 1 in the Problem Solving section of your answer sheet.

Practice Question 1

Sarah eats $\frac{1}{4}$ of a pizza.

What fraction of the pizza remains?

The correct answer is D. Please mark this in Practice Question 1 in the Problem Solving section of your answer sheet.

STOP AND WAIT FOR FURTHER INSTRUCTIONS

A 24 kph	**B** 2 hours	**C** £3·75	**D** 62	**E** $\frac{1}{3}$
F 74	**G** $\frac{1}{4}$	**H** 9 hours	**I** 27 kph	**J** £1·30

Several questions will follow for you to answer. Select an answer to each question from the 10 different possible answers in the table above. You may use an answer for more than one question.

(1) James goes to sleep at 10 p.m. and wakes up the following morning at 7 a.m.

For how long does James sleep?

(2) For breakfast, James eats 4 of the 12 eggs in his fridge.

What fraction of the total number of eggs in the fridge does James eat?

(3) James drives to work. The drive takes 30 minutes and covers a distance of 12 km.

What is James' speed in kilometres per hour (kph) during this drive?

(4) In James' company, there are a total of 97 men and 23 women.

How many more men are there in James' company than women?

(5) Before lunch, James has 12 meetings. Each meeting takes 10 minutes.

How long does James spend in meetings before lunch?

(6) A sandwich costs £2·50 and a drink costs £1·20.

James buys a sandwich and drink for lunch and pays with a £5 note.

How much change does James receive?

(7) James feels sleepy in the afternoon so he takes a nap for 20 minutes.

For what fraction of an hour does James take a nap?

(8) James earns £7·50 per hour.

How much does James earn in half an hour?

CONTINUE WORKING

(9) After work, James drives to the gym. The drive takes 20 minutes and covers a distance of 9 km.

What is James' speed in kilometres per hour (kph) during this drive?

(10) James brushes his teeth before going to bed every night.

He also brushes his teeth every morning.

How many times does James brush his teeth in August?

STOP AND WAIT FOR FURTHER INSTRUCTIONS ⊗

Cloze

 YOU HAVE 10 MINUTES TO COMPLETE THE FOLLOWING SECTION.

YOU HAVE 20 QUESTIONS TO COMPLETE WITHIN THE TIME GIVEN.

EXAMPLES

Example 1

Read the sentence below and select the most appropriate word from the table.

A	B	C	D	E
defeated	heaved	master	flow	politely

The skilful chess player easily (Q1) _____ his opponent.

Please select your answer to go in the place of (Q1) in the above sentence.

The correct answer is A. This has already been marked in Example 1 in the Cloze section of your answer sheet.

Practice Question 1

Read the sentence below and select the most appropriate word from the table.

A	B	C	D	E
crunching	eating	dreading	reading	shining

The sun was (Q2) _____ and there was not a single cloud in the sky.

Please select your answer to go in the place of (Q2) in the above sentence.

The correct answer is E. Please mark the answer E in Practice Question 1 in the Cloze section of your answer sheet.

STOP AND WAIT FOR FURTHER INSTRUCTIONS

Read the passage and select the most appropriate word from the table below by choosing the letter above the word. There are 10 questions. For example, Q1 is where you should put your answer to Question 1 on your answer sheet.

A	B	C	D	E
minutes	found	strong	adequate	absorbed

F	G	H	I	J
essential	deficiency	pills	directly	brittle

Vitamin D

Vitamin D is (Q1) _____ for maintaining healthy and
(Q2) _____ teeth and bones. Luckily, Vitamin D can be
(Q3) _____ by the body (Q4) _____ from sunlight.

On a clear summer's day, (Q5) _____ amounts of Vitamin D can be
produced by the body if you spend just ten (Q6) _____ per day outside.
However, in winter, this process can require up to two hours.

Therefore, many people suffer from a Vitamin D (Q7) _____ in winter.
This can cause their bones to become (Q8) _____ and can also trigger
mental illnesses such as depression.

Fortunately, Vitamin D can also be (Q9) _____ naturally in certain
foods such as butter and eggs. Some people also take (Q10) _____ and
supplements to boost their Vitamin D levels.

CONTINUE WORKING ⇨

Read the passage and select the most appropriate word from the table below by choosing the letter above the word. There are 10 questions. For example, Q11 is where you should put your answer to Question 11 on your answer sheet.

A	B	C	D	E
estimate	death	fought	crowned	morning

F	G	H	I	J
flee	forces	significant	army	attempts

The Battle of Hastings

The Battle of Hastings was (Q11) _____ in 1066 between the Norman (Q12) _____ of William the Conqueror and an English army led by King Harold Godwinson.

Historians (Q13) _____ that 15,000 soldiers took part in the battle. The two (Q14) _____ attacked each other from (Q15) _____ until evening. Finally, Harold was struck and killed by an arrow and the English began to (Q16) _____.

William was (Q17) _____ king later that year and ruled over England until his (Q18) _____ in 1087. The Battle of Hastings was a (Q19) _____ turning point in English history. Despite many (Q20) _____, no foreign army ever successfully managed to invade England after 1066.

STOP AND WAIT FOR FURTHER INSTRUCTIONS ⊗

Non-Verbal Reasoning

 INSTRUCTIONS

 YOU HAVE 8 MINUTES TO COMPLETE THE FOLLOWING SECTION.

YOU HAVE 15 QUESTIONS TO COMPLETE WITHIN THE TIME GIVEN.

EXAMPLES

SIMILARITY Example 1

The three figures given are similar in some way.

Work out how they are similar and select the figure that goes with them.

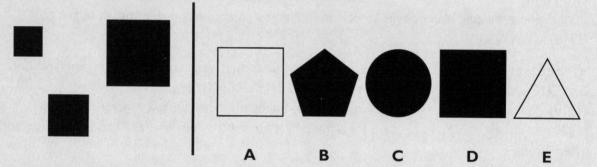

The correct answer is D. This has already been marked in Example 1 in the Non-Verbal Reasoning section of your answer sheet.

SIMILARITY Practice Question 1

The three figures given are similar in some way.

Work out how they are similar and select the figure that goes with them.

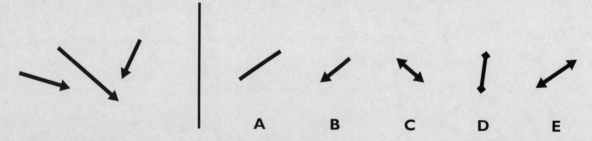

The correct answer is B. Please mark this in Practice Question 1 in the Non-Verbal Reasoning section of your answer sheet.

CONTINUE WORKING

CUBE NET Example 2

Look at the cube net below. Select the only cube that could be formed from the net.

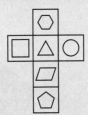

A   B   C   D

The correct answer is B. This has already been marked in Example 2 in the Non-Verbal Reasoning section of your answer sheet.

CUBE NET Practice Question 2

Look at the cube net below. Select the only cube that could be formed from the net.

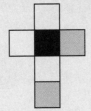 

A   B   C   D

The correct answer is C. Please mark this in Practice Question 2 in the Non-Verbal Reasoning section of your answer sheet.

COMPLETE THE SEQUENCE Example 3

Select the correct picture from the row on the right in order to finish the incomplete sequence on the left.

A   B   C   D   E

The correct answer is A. This has already been marked in Example 3 in the Non-Verbal Reasoning section of your answer sheet.

COMPLETE THE SEQUENCE Practice Question 3

Select the correct picture from the row on the right in order to finish the incomplete sequence on the left.

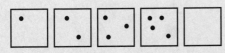

A   B   C   D   E

The correct answer is D. Please mark this in Practice Question 3 in the Non-Verbal Reasoning section of your answer sheet.

STOP AND WAIT FOR FURTHER INSTRUCTIONS

(1) The three figures given are similar in some way. Work out how they are similar and select the figure that goes with them.

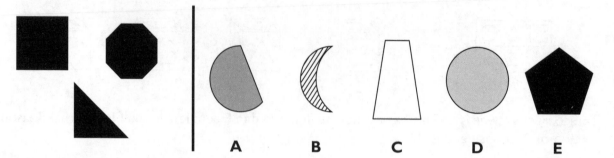

| A | B | C | D | E |

(2) The three figures given are similar in some way. Work out how they are similar and select the figure that goes with them.

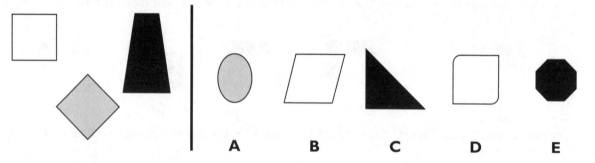

| A | B | C | D | E |

(3) The three figures given are similar in some way. Work out how they are similar and select the figure that goes with them.

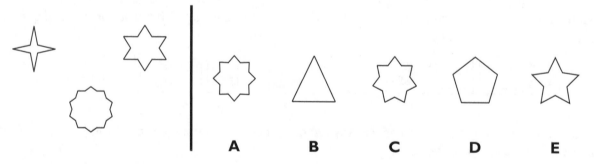

| A | B | C | D | E |

(4) The three figures given are similar in some way. Work out how they are similar and select the figure that goes with them.

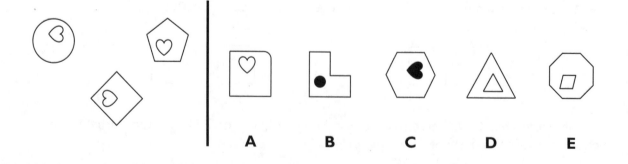

| A | B | C | D | E |

CONTINUE WORKING ⇨

(5) The three figures given are similar in some way. Work out how they are similar and select the figure that goes with them.

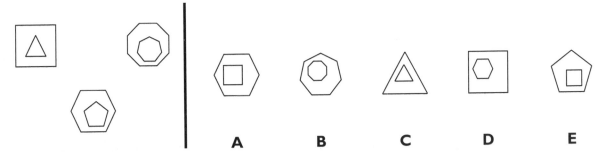

(6) Look at the cube net below. Select the only cube that could be formed from the net.

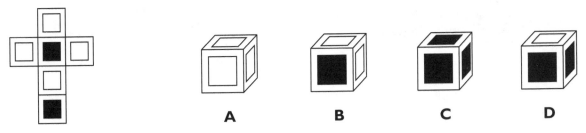

(7) Look at the cube net below. Select the only cube that could be formed from the net.

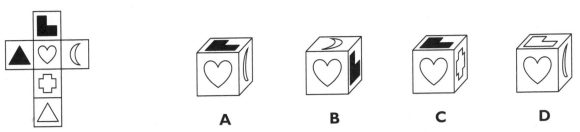

(8) Look at the cube net below. Select the only cube that could be formed from the net.

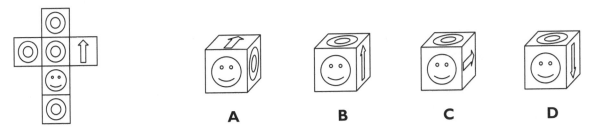

(9) Look at the cube net below. Select the only cube that could be formed from the net.

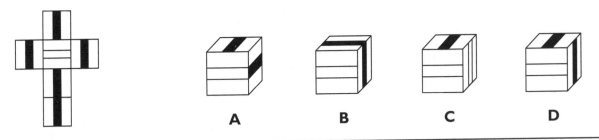

CONTINUE WORKING ⇨

(10) Look at the cube net below. Select the only cube that could be formed from the net.

A　　**B**　　**C**　　**D**

(11) Select the correct picture from the row on the right in order to finish the incomplete sequence on the left.

A　　**B**　　**C**　　**D**　　**E**

(12) Select the correct picture from the row on the right in order to finish the incomplete sequence on the left.

A　　**B**　　**C**　　**D**　　**E**

(13) Select the correct picture from the row on the right in order to finish the incomplete sequence on the left.

A　　**B**　　**C**　　**D**　　**E**

(14) Select the correct picture from the row on the right in order to finish the incomplete sequence on the left.

A　　**B**　　**C**　　**D**　　**E**

(15) Select the correct picture from the row on the right in order to finish the incomplete sequence on the left.

A　　**B**　　**C**　　**D**　　**E**

STOP AND WAIT FOR FURTHER INSTRUCTIONS

Grammar & Spelling

 INSTRUCTIONS

 YOU HAVE 5 MINUTES TO COMPLETE THE FOLLOWING SECTION.

YOU HAVE 8 QUESTIONS TO COMPLETE WITHIN THE TIME GIVEN.

EXAMPLES

Example 1

Identify a homophone of the word 'night' from the words below.

A	B	C	D	E
knight	dark	bright	summer	light

The correct answer is A. This has already been marked in Example 1 in the Grammar & Spelling section of your answer sheet.

Practice Question 1

Select the correct prefix to give the opposite of the word 'believable'.

A	B	C	D	E
in	un	on	mis	pro

The correct answer is B. Please mark the answer B in Practice Question 1 in the Grammar & Spelling section of your answer sheet.

STOP AND WAIT FOR FURTHER INSTRUCTIONS

1 Identify a homophone of the word 'faint' from the words below.

A	B	C	D	E
fine	feint	recover	swoon	feign

2 What type of word is 'slowly'?

A	B	C	D	E
adjective	verb	pronoun	adverb	noun

3 Select the correct prefix to give the opposite of the word 'agreeable'.

A	B	C	D	E
up	dis	un	in	mis

4 Select the word below that is misspelt.

A	B	C	D	E
feed	phony	fish	phrozen	famous

5 Select the word below that is misspelt.

A	B	C	D	E
hollow	resauceful	smartly	pointed	hovered

6 Select the word below that is misspelt.

A	B	C	D	E
date	handy	calender	suffocate	describe

7 Select the word below that is misspelt.

A	B	C	D	E
timid	greatful	singular	social	tremor

8 Select the word below that is misspelt.

A	B	C	D	E
injured	seperate	politely	beseech	desperate

STOP AND WAIT FOR FURTHER INSTRUCTIONS ⊗

Antonyms

 YOU HAVE 5 MINUTES TO COMPLETE THE FOLLOWING SECTION.

YOU HAVE 15 QUESTIONS TO COMPLETE WITHIN THE TIME GIVEN.

EXAMPLES

Example 1

Which word is most opposite in meaning to the following word?

hot

A	B	C	D	E
follow	cold	freeze	ice	jelly

The correct answer is B. This has already been marked in Example 1 in the Antonyms section of your answer sheet.

Practice Question 1

Which word is most opposite in meaning to the following word?

below

A	B	C	D	E
attack	deep	lower	above	before

The correct answer is D. Please mark the answer D in Practice Question 1 in the Antonyms section of your answer sheet.

STOP AND WAIT FOR FURTHER INSTRUCTIONS

For each row, select the word from the table that is most opposite in meaning to the word above the table.

(1) after

A	B	C	D	E
later	summer	night	before	how

(2) handsome

A	B	C	D	E
beautiful	soldier	ugly	simmer	pretty

(3) winner

A	B	C	D	E
gold	loser	practice	first	shake

(4) insult

A	B	C	D	E
salty	foreign	attack	compliment	shine

(5) allow

A	B	C	D	E
aloud	hover	permit	grant	forbid

(6) lack

A	B	C	D	E
back	leisure	lesson	abundance	drought

(7) junior

A	B	C	D	E
young	jealous	parasite	doctor	senior

CONTINUE WORKING ➡

(8) kind

A	B	C	D	E
cruel	closed	clever	clear	conscious

(9) narrow

A	B	C	D	E
deep	broad	tight	river	thin

(10) always

A	B	C	D	E
often	hindrance	never	heighten	almost

(11) simple

A	B	C	D	E
fraught	complicated	pine	simply	police

(12) careful

A	B	C	D	E
hateful	caring	mindful	careless	protective

(13) general

A	B	C	D	E
gesture	horse	particular	cavalry	army

(14) peace

A	B	C	D	E
piece	harmony	tranquil	agitate	war

(15) artificial

A	B	C	D	E
art	mountain	natural	sky	powerful

STOP AND WAIT FOR FURTHER INSTRUCTIONS ⊗

Numeracy

INSTRUCTIONS

 YOU HAVE 9 MINUTES TO COMPLETE THE FOLLOWING SECTION.

YOU HAVE 18 QUESTIONS TO COMPLETE WITHIN THE TIME GIVEN.

EXAMPLES

Some questions within this section are not multiple choice. For these write the answer to each question on the answer sheet by selecting the correct digits from the columns provided.

Example 1

Calculate the answer to the following:

12 + 42

The correct answer is 54. This has already been marked in Example 1 in the Numeracy section of your answer sheet.

Practice Question 1

Calculate the answer to the following:

55 – 47

The correct answer is 8. Please mark this in Practice Question 1 in the Numeracy section of your answer sheet. Note that a single-digit answer should be marked with a 0 in the left-hand column, so mark 08 on your answer sheet.

STOP AND WAIT FOR FURTHER INSTRUCTIONS

(1) Calculate the answer to the following:

74 − 59

(2) Which number comes next in the following sequence?

17, 24, 30, 35, 39, ?

(3) Which of these numbers is not divisible by 3?

18, 15, 12, 33, 48, 27, 55

(4) How many quarters are there in $8\frac{3}{4}$?

(5) Calculate the value of X in the equation below.

$0 \cdot 5 = \dfrac{8}{X}$

(6) What is the remainder when 55 is divided by 11?

(7) How many millimetres are there in 4·8 cm?

(8) How much greater is $\dfrac{1}{4}$ of 60 than $\dfrac{1}{5}$ of 70?

(9) Linda has 7 red balls, 6 green balls, 5 yellow balls and 2 black balls.

What fraction of Linda's balls are not green?

A	B	C	D	E
$\dfrac{6}{20}$	$\dfrac{7}{10}$	$\dfrac{3}{5}$	$\dfrac{13}{20}$	$\dfrac{1}{2}$

(10) A circle has a radius of 32 cm.

What is the diameter of the circle?

A	B	C	D	E
8 cm	16 cm	32 cm	64 cm	72 cm

CONTINUE WORKING ⇨

(11) Calculate the median of the following numbers:

32, 45, 12, 98, 1, 74, 23, 43, 34

A	B	C	D	E
23	43	32	45	34

(12) I roll a fair die. What is the probability that I roll an even number?

A	B	C	D	E
$\dfrac{5}{6}$	$\dfrac{1}{2}$	$\dfrac{1}{3}$	$\dfrac{2}{3}$	$\dfrac{1}{6}$

(13) The coordinates of 3 vertices of a square are (2, 2), (2, 6) and (6, 2).

What are the coordinates of the 4th vertex of the square?

A	B	C	D	E
(6, 6)	(2, 4)	(6, 4)	(4, 2)	(3, 6)

(14) Calculate the answer to the following:

$\dfrac{1}{2} + \dfrac{1}{3}$

A	B	C	D	E
$\dfrac{1}{2}$	$\dfrac{7}{8}$	$\dfrac{2}{5}$	$\dfrac{5}{6}$	$\dfrac{1}{5}$

(15) Calculate the answer to the following:

$\dfrac{2}{3} \times \dfrac{1}{4}$

A	B	C	D	E
$\dfrac{3}{12}$	$\dfrac{2}{7}$	$\dfrac{1}{6}$	$\dfrac{1}{3}$	$\dfrac{1}{2}$

CONTINUE WORKING ⏵

(16) Calculate the answer to the following:

$\frac{1}{2} \div 3$

A	B	C	D	E
$\frac{1}{4}$	$\frac{1}{3}$	$\frac{1}{5}$	$\frac{3}{8}$	$\frac{1}{6}$

(17) The number D is three times larger than the number P.

The number F is twice as large as the number D.

Which expression shows the value of the number F in terms of P?

A	B	C	D	E
0P	2P	3P	$\frac{P}{2}$	6P

(18) The length of a rectangle is twice its width.

If the rectangle has a length of 7 cm, what is the perimeter of the rectangle?

A	B	C	D	E
7 cm	14 cm	3·5 cm	28 cm	21 cm

END OF PAPER

Get Started

Test B Paper 1

Instructions

1. Ensure you have pencils and an eraser with you.

2. Make sure you are able to see a clock or watch.

3. Write your name on the answer sheet.

4. Do not open the question booklet until you are told to do so by the audio instructions.

5. Listen carefully to the audio instructions given.

6. Mark your answers on the answer sheet only.

7. All workings must be completed on a separate piece of paper.

8. You should not use a calculator, dictionary or thesaurus at any point in this paper.

9. Move through the papers as quickly as possible and with care.

10. Follow the instructions at the foot of each page.

11. You should mark your answers with a horizontal line, as shown on the answer sheet.

12. If you want to change your answer, ensure that you rub out your first answer and that your second answer is clearly more visible.

13. You can go back and review any questions that are within the section you are working on only. You must await further instructions before moving on to another section.

Symbols and Phrases used in the Tests

 Instructions   Time allowed for this section   Stop working and await instructions   Continue working

Comprehension

INSTRUCTIONS

 YOU HAVE 9 MINUTES TO COMPLETE THE FOLLOWING SECTION.

YOU HAVE 10 QUESTIONS TO COMPLETE WITHIN THE TIME GIVEN.

EXAMPLES

Comprehension Example

South Africa is becoming an increasingly popular holiday destination. People from all over the world are being attracted by its natural beauty, cosmopolitan cities and diverse wildlife. Cape Town, the capital of South Africa, is especially popular. The city is dynamic and exciting and has a rich history and culture. It is also home to the stunning Table Mountain, which you can ascend on foot or by cable car.

Example 1

Which of the following is not mentioned as a reason why people are attracted to South Africa?

A   Natural beauty
B   Excellent food
C   Cosmopolitan cities
D   Diverse wildlife

The correct answer is B. This has already been marked in Example 1 in the Comprehension section of your answer sheet.

Practice Question 1

What is the name of the mountain in Cape Town?

A   Cape Mountain
B   Africa Mountain
C   Table Mountain
D   Leopard Mountain

The correct answer is C. Please mark this in Practice Question 1 in the Comprehension section of your answer sheet.

STOP AND WAIT FOR FURTHER INSTRUCTIONS

Read the passage below and then answer the questions that follow.

An extract from: **The Limpopo Academy of Private Detection**
by Alexander McCall-Smith

In Botswana, home to the No. 1 Ladies Detective Agency for the problems of ladies, and others, it is customary – one might say very customary – to enquire of the people whom you meet whether they have slept well. The answer to that question is almost inevitably that they have indeed slept well, even if they have not, and have spent the night tossing and turning as a result of the nocturnal barking of dogs, the activity of mosquitoes or the prickings of a bad conscience. Of course, mosquitoes may be defeated by nets or sprays, just as dogs may be roundly scolded; a bad conscience, though, is not so easily stifled. If somebody were to invent a spray capable of dealing with an uncomfortable conscience, that person would undoubtedly do rather well – but perhaps might not sleep as soundly as before, were he to reflect on the consequences of his invention. Bad consciences, it would appear, are there for a purpose: to make us feel regret over our failings. Should they be silenced, then our entirely human weaknesses, our manifold omissions, would become all the greater – and that, as Mma Ramotswe would certainly say, is not a good thing.

Mma Ramotswe was fortunate in having an untroubled conscience, and therefore generally enjoyed undisturbed sleep. It was her habit to take to her bed after a final cup of red bush tea at around ten o'clock at night. Mr. J.L.B. Matekoni, her husband and by common consent the finest mechanic in all Botswana, would often retire before her, particularly if he had had a tiring day at work. Mechanics in general sleep well, as do many others whose day is taken up with physically demanding labour. So by the time that Mma Ramotswe went to bed, he might already be lost to this world, his breathing deep and regular, his eyes firmly closed to the bedside light that he would leave for his wife to extinguish.

She would not take long to go to sleep, drifting off to thoughts of what had happened that day; to images of herself drinking tea in the office or driving her van on an errand; to the picture of Mma Makutsi sitting upright at her desk, her large glasses catching the light as she held forth on some issue or other. Or to some memory of a long time ago, of her father walking down a dusty road, holding her hand and explaining to her about the ways of cattle – a subject that he knew so well. When a wise man dies, there is so much history that is lost: that is what they said, and Mma Ramotswe knew it to be true. Her own father, the late Obed Ramotswe, had taken so much with him, but had also left much behind, so many memories and sayings and observations, that she, his daughter, could now call up and cherish as she waited for the soft arms of sleep to embrace her.

CONTINUE WORKING

1 In which country does this story take place?

A   Botswana
B   Nigeria
C   Africa
D   Morocco

2 According to the passage, which of the following questions is it usual to be asked?

A   'What did you eat?'
B   'How are your parents?'
C   'Did you sleep well?'
D   'How old are you?'

3 According to the passage, what is an effective way of dealing with mosquitoes?

A   Dousing them with buckets of water
B   Shooting them
C   Using sprays or nets
D   Befriending them

4 What is the purpose of a 'bad conscience'?

A   To ensure that our successes are not forgotten
B   To make us feel depressed
C   To cause us pain
D   To remind us to be remorseful for our mistakes

5 At what time did Mma Ramotswe drink her tea?

A   10 p.m.
B   3 p.m.
C   2:30 p.m.
D   11:30 p.m.

6 According to the passage, why do mechanics sleep well?

A   Because they are often lazy
B   Because they are tired from a hard day's work
C   Because they drink lots of tea
D   Because they go to bed very late

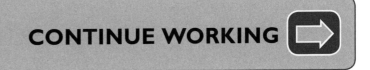

CONTINUE WORKING

(7) What did Mma Ramotswe think about before falling asleep?

Option 1: mechanical work that needed to be completed
Option 2: Mma Makutsi sitting at her desk
Option 3: drinking tea at home
Option 4: driving her vehicle

A   Options 1 and 3 only
B   Options 2 and 4 only
C   Options 1, 2 and 4 only
D   All of the above

(8) On which of the following subjects was Obed Ramotswe knowledgeable?

A   How to repair a car
B   How to tend to cows
C   How to run a law firm
D   How to deal with intruders

(9) What does the word 'extinguish' mean?

A   Detest
B   Protect
C   Smell
D   Quench

(10) What was Mma Ramotswe's relationship with her late father like?

A   They hated each other
B   They never met
C   They were unhappy
D   They were close

STOP AND WAIT FOR FURTHER INSTRUCTIONS ⊗

Shuffled Sentences

 ## INSTRUCTIONS

 YOU HAVE 8 MINUTES TO COMPLETE THE FOLLOWING SECTION.

YOU HAVE 15 QUESTIONS TO COMPLETE WITHIN THE TIME GIVEN.

EXAMPLES

Example 1

The following sentence is shuffled and also contains one unnecessary word. Rearrange the sentence correctly in order to identify the unnecessary word.

wake under before must sunrise up we.

A	B	C	D	E
up	before	under	wake	sunrise

The correct answer is C. This has already been marked in Example 1 in the Shuffled Sentences section of your answer sheet.

Practice Question 1

The following sentence is shuffled and also contains one unnecessary word. Rearrange the sentence correctly in order to identify the unnecessary word.

very girl quickly the ran throw.

A	B	C	D	E
quickly	girl	the	ran	throw

The correct answer is E. Please mark this in Practice Question 1 in the Shuffled Sentences section of your answer sheet.

STOP AND WAIT FOR FURTHER INSTRUCTIONS

Each sentence below is shuffled and also contains one unnecessary word.
Rearrange each sentence correctly in order to identify the unnecessary word.

1. were on in the many mistakes there book.

A	B	C	D	E
in	there	book	many	on

2. on rely friends can I my with.

A	B	C	D	E
with	rely	on	friends	can

3. the allowed the through of meat piece sliced butcher.

A	B	C	D	E
butcher	allowed	meat	of	piece

4. an the was delayed by watches half train hour.

A	B	C	D	E
delayed	half	watches	hour	train

5. here you always umbrella an punch should carry.

A	B	C	D	E
always	punch	umbrella	should	an

6. for worms searched bush the the in bird attacked.

A	B	C	D	E
worms	attacked	bird	bush	searched

7. the players unexpectedly match cancelled was football.

A	B	C	D	E
football	cancelled	was	players	match

8. cooked the sausage chef the on assume the grill.

A	B	C	D	E
assume	chef	grill	sausage	cooked

CONTINUE WORKING

(9) vegetables able fruit and must eat you day every.

A	B	C	D	E
fruit	eat	able	day	every

(10) life the doctor unable was woman's save the to permit.

A	B	C	D	E
permit	save	life	unable	doctor

(11) to hunt fly packs in hyenas tend.

A	B	C	D	E
fly	tend	packs	hyenas	hunt

(12) city farm is in favourite Rome Europe my.

A	B	C	D	E
my	city	Rome	in	farm

(13) are robe shoes very my fashionable new.

A	B	C	D	E
fashionable	robe	my	very	shoes

(14) glass shattered the persuade window instantly.

A	B	C	D	E
glass	shattered	instantly	persuade	window

(15) the the froze sun over mountains shone.

A	B	C	D	E
shone	mountains	froze	over	sun

STOP AND WAIT FOR FURTHER INSTRUCTIONS ⊗

Numeracy

 ## INSTRUCTIONS

 YOU HAVE 7 MINUTES TO COMPLETE THE FOLLOWING SECTION.

YOU HAVE 15 QUESTIONS TO COMPLETE WITHIN THE TIME GIVEN.

EXAMPLES

The questions within this section are not multiple choice. Write the answer to each question on the answer sheet by selecting the correct digits from the columns provided.

Example 1

Calculate the answer to the following: $12 + 42$

The correct answer is 54. This has already been marked in Example 1 in the Numeracy section of your answer sheet.

Practice Question 1

Calculate the answer to the following: $55 - 47$

The correct answer is 8. Please mark this in Practice Question 1 in the Numeracy section of your answer sheet. Note that a single-digit answer should be marked with a 0 in the left-hand column, so mark 08 on your answer sheet.

STOP AND WAIT FOR FURTHER INSTRUCTIONS ⊗

(1) How many weeks are there in half a year?

(2) Omar runs at a speed of 10 kph.

How many minutes will it take Omar to run 2·5 km?

CONTINUE WORKING

(3) Calculate the answer to the following:

$7 + (6 \times 9) - 3$

(4) What is $\frac{1}{4}$ of 256?

(5) Which number should replace the '?' in the following sequence?

12, 14, 11, ?, 10, 12, 9

(6) What is the perimeter of this equilateral triangle in centimetres?

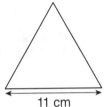

Not drawn to scale

11 cm

(7) Last year, Bob was 7 years old.

How old will Bob be in 3 years' time?

(8) There are 7 Kags in 1 Kog. There are 8 Kogs in 1 Kig. How many Kags are there in 1 Kig?

(9) How many more edges than faces does a cube have?

(10) Subtract four hundred and ninety-one from five hundred and seventy-nine.

(11) Kelly eats 3 meals per day. How many meals does Kelly eat in a fortnight?

(12) A jug contains $\frac{3}{4}$ of a litre of water. A cup has a capacity of 75 ml.

How many identical cups can be filled with the water in the jug?

(13) Tara showers once per day from 27th September to 2nd October, inclusive.

How many times does Tara shower in this period?

(14) A plastic button weighs 40 g. The total weight of identical plastic buttons in a basket is 0·8 kg.

How many plastic buttons are in the basket?

(15) How much greater is $\frac{1}{4}$ of 44 than $\frac{1}{3}$ of 33?

STOP AND WAIT FOR FURTHER INSTRUCTIONS

Problem Solving

 ## INSTRUCTIONS

 YOU HAVE 8 MINUTES TO COMPLETE THE FOLLOWING SECTION.

YOU HAVE 10 QUESTIONS TO COMPLETE WITHIN THE TIME GIVEN.

EXAMPLES

Example 1

Calculate the answer to the following:

Tom buys a chocolate bar for £1·50. He pays with a £5 note.
How much change does he receive?

A   £1·50   **B**   £3   **C**   £3·50   **D**   £4   **E**   £5

The correct answer is C. This has already been marked in Example 1 in the Problem Solving section of your answer sheet.

Practice Question 1

Sarah eats $\frac{1}{4}$ of a pizza.

What fraction of the pizza remains?

A $\frac{1}{2}$ **B** $\frac{1}{3}$ **C** $\frac{2}{5}$ **D** $\frac{3}{4}$ **E** $\frac{5}{6}$

The correct answer is D. Please mark this in Practice Question 1 in the Problem Solving section of your answer sheet.

STOP AND WAIT FOR FURTHER INSTRUCTIONS

Calculate the answers to the following.

(1) What is the sum of the 3 smallest positive prime numbers?

   A 0   **B** 1   **C** 6   **D** 9   **E** 10

CONTINUE WORKING

(2) A clock shows a time of 12:22 pm. The clock is 35 minutes fast.

What is the correct time?

A 12:57 p.m.   **B** 11:22 a.m.   **C** 11:45 p.m.   **D** 11:47 a.m.   **E** 12:45 p.m.

(3) What is the value of X in the equation below?

$4X + 3X = 54 - 2X$

A 9   **B** 8   **C** 7   **D** 6   **E** 5

(4) A ten-pence coin has a weight of 7 grams. Gill has £1 worth of ten-pence coins.

What is the total weight of Gill's coins?

A 7 g   **B** 14 g   **C** 20 g   **D** 35 g   **E** 70 g

(5) Fred drinks a litre of water every 3 days. How many days will 18 litres of water last him?

A 18 days   **B** 6 days   **C** 26 days   **D** 54 days   **E** 48 days

(6) Ken takes a test and gets 4 out of every 5 questions correct.

What percentage of the questions does Ken get correct?

A 40%   **B** 20%   **C** 80%   **D** 90%   **E** 75%

(7) Henry has a piece of string that measures 1·5 metres. He cuts the piece of string into 10 equal parts.

What is the total length of 3 of the parts?

A 20 cm   **B** 50 cm   **C** 90 cm   **D** 30 cm   **E** 45 cm

(8) Hannah is facing in a northwest direction. She turns 180° clockwise.

What direction is Hannah now facing?

A northeast   **B** southwest   **C** west   **D** southeast   **E** east

(9) What is the value of B on the number line here?

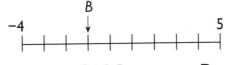

A −3   **B** 0   **C** 2·5   **D** −1   **E** 4

(10) 10 men take 3 hours to build Fence A.

How long would it take 20 men to build Fence A?

A 3 hours   **B** 6 hours   **C** 2 hours   **D** 1·5 hours   **E** 1 hour

STOP AND WAIT FOR FURTHER INSTRUCTIONS

Synonyms

 INSTRUCTIONS

 YOU HAVE 7 MINUTES TO COMPLETE THE FOLLOWING SECTION.

YOU HAVE 24 QUESTIONS TO COMPLETE WITHIN THE TIME GIVEN.

EXAMPLES

Example 1

Select the word that is most similar in meaning to the following word:

push

A	B	C	D	E
shallow	shove	tug	hollow	cry

The correct answer is B. This has already been marked in Example 1 in the Synonyms section of your answer sheet.

Practice Question 1

Select the word that is most similar in meaning to the following word:

imitate

A	B	C	D	E
cover	copy	grow	live	irritate

The correct answer is B. Please mark this in Practice Question 1 in the Synonyms section of your answer sheet.

STOP AND WAIT FOR FURTHER INSTRUCTIONS

For each row, select the word from the table that is most similar in meaning to the word above the table.

1 almost

A	B	C	D	E
nearly	again	swap	smooth	most

2 irritate

A	B	C	D	E
preserve	ignore	breathe	annoy	halt

3 begin

A	B	C	D	E
finish	commence	attack	break	house

4 useful

A	B	C	D	E
froth	useless	beneficial	immense	master

5 dash

A	B	C	D	E
crawl	sprint	stroke	hover	dream

6 demonstrate

A	B	C	D	E
fasten	demon	burn	hold	protest

7 unpleasant

A	B	C	D	E
pleasure	offer	disagreeable	march	pheasant

8 keen

A	B	C	D	E
seen	burst	element	eager	broken

CONTINUE WORKING →

9 essential

A	B	C	D	E
material	fundamental	potential	item	possible

10 ignore

A	B	C	D	E
eat	eager	small	disregard	joke

11 inspect

A	B	C	D	E
show	paw	examine	pretend	turn

12 jealous

A	B	C	D	E
shimmer	envious	hate	jelly	scowl

13 last

A	B	C	D	E
hammer	leave	shove	final	frighten

14 lethal

A	B	C	D	E
leather	growth	deadly	metre	hung

15 preserve

A	B	C	D	E
hound	point	poke	damage	maintain

16 gentle

A	B	C	D	E
gainful	harmful	mild	hoarse	grateful

CONTINUE WORKING ⇨

17 reflect

A	B	C	D	E
bellow	reflection	mirror	glass	lake

18 naked

A	B	C	D	E
branch	hope	tree	nail	bare

19 many

A	B	C	D	E
less	some	mane	growth	numerous

20 operate

A	B	C	D	E
opinion	illness	function	labour	surgery

21 miss

A	B	C	D	E
overlook	kill	vanish	drench	frown

22 compliment

A	B	C	D	E
attest	insult	input	praise	match

23 urgent

A	B	C	D	E
relaxed	pressing	ruffled	urge	shiver

24 supply

A	B	C	D	E
supple	cook	canoe	subtle	provide

STOP AND WAIT FOR FURTHER INSTRUCTIONS ⊗

Non-Verbal Reasoning

INSTRUCTIONS

 YOU HAVE 6 MINUTES TO COMPLETE THE FOLLOWING SECTION.

YOU HAVE 12 QUESTIONS TO COMPLETE WITHIN THE TIME GIVEN.

EXAMPLES

REFLECTION Example 1

Select how the following shape or pattern would appear when reflected in the dashed line.

                       A   **B**   **C**   **D**

The correct answer is C. This has already been marked in Example 1 in the Non-Verbal Reasoning section of your answer sheet.

REFLECTION Practice Question 1

Select how the following shape or pattern would appear when reflected in the dashed line.

                       A   **B**   **C**   **D**

The correct answer is C. Please mark this in Practice Question 1 in the Non-Verbal Reasoning section of your answer sheet.

CONTINUE WORKING ➡

LEAST SIMILAR Example 2

Select the figure that is least similar to other figures.

A   B   C   D   E

The correct answer is B. This has already been marked in Example 2 in the Non-Verbal Reasoning section of your answer sheet.

LEAST SIMILAR Practice Question 2

Select the figure that is least similar to other figures.

    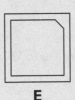

A   B   C   D   E

The correct answer is A. Please mark this in Practice Question 2 in the Non-Verbal Reasoning section of your answer sheet.

STOP AND WAIT FOR FURTHER INSTRUCTIONS

1. Select how the following shape or pattern would appear when reflected in the dashed line.

A   B   C   D

2. Select how the following shape or pattern would appear when reflected in the dashed line.

A   B   C   D

CONTINUE WORKING

(3) Select how the following shape or pattern would appear when reflected in the dashed line.

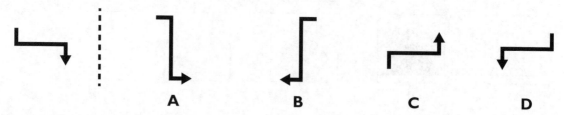

A   **B**   **C**   **D**

(4) Select how the following shape or pattern would appear when reflected in the dashed line.

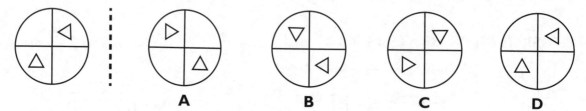

A   **B**   **C**   **D**

(5) Select how the following shape or pattern would appear when reflected in the dashed line.

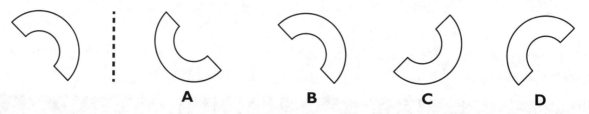

A   **B**   **C**   **D**

(6) Select how the following shape or pattern would appear when reflected in the dashed line.

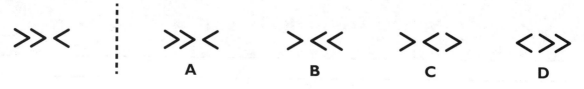

A   **B**   **C**   **D**

(7) Select the figure that is least similar to other figures.

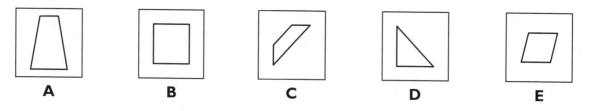

A   **B**   **C**   **D**   **E**

(8) Select the figure that is least similar to other figures.

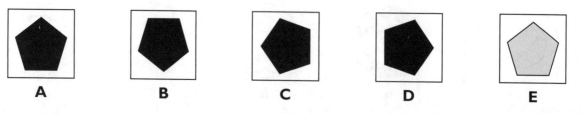

A   **B**   **C**   **D**   **E**

CONTINUE WORKING

9 Select the figure that is least similar to other figures.

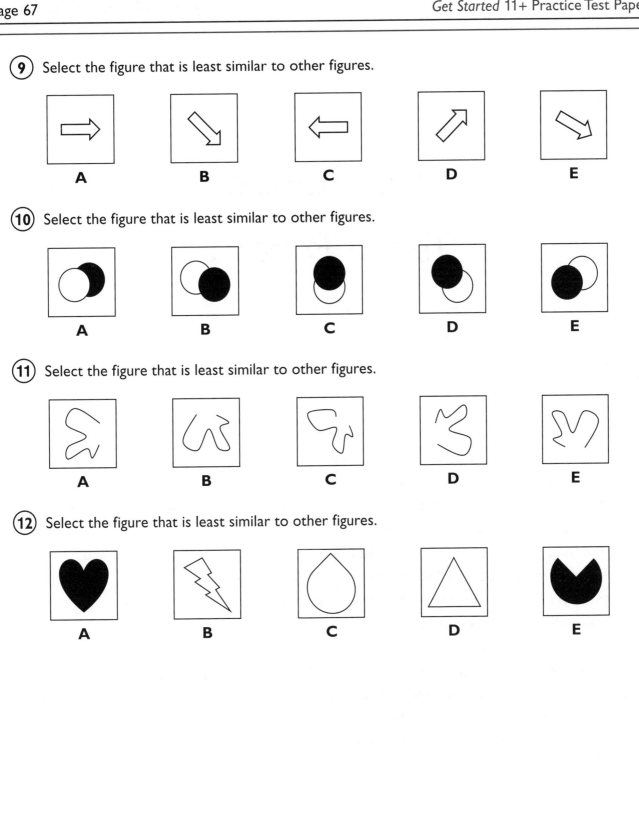

A	B	C	D	E

10 Select the figure that is least similar to other figures.

A	B	C	D	E

11 Select the figure that is least similar to other figures.

A	B	C	D	E

12 Select the figure that is least similar to other figures.

A	B	C	D	E

END OF PAPER

Get Started

Test B Paper 2

Instructions

1. Ensure you have pencils and an eraser with you.

2. Make sure you are able to see a clock or watch.

3. Write your name on the answer sheet.

4. Do not open the question booklet until you are told to do so by the audio instructions.

5. Listen carefully to the audio instructions given.

6. Mark your answers on the answer sheet only.

7. All workings must be completed on a separate piece of paper.

8. You should not use a calculator, dictionary or thesaurus at any point in this paper.

9. Move through the papers as quickly as possible and with care.

10. Follow the instructions at the foot of each page.

11. You should mark your answers with a horizontal line, as shown on the answer sheet.

12. If you want to change your answer, ensure that you rub out your first answer and that your second answer is clearly more visible.

13. You can go back and review any questions that are within the section you are working on only. You must await further instructions before moving on to another section.

Symbols and Phrases used in the Tests

 Instructions   Time allowed for this section   Stop working and await instructions   Continue working

Problem Solving

 INSTRUCTIONS

 YOU HAVE 12 MINUTES TO COMPLETE THE FOLLOWING SECTION.

YOU HAVE 15 QUESTIONS TO COMPLETE WITHIN THE TIME GIVEN.

EXAMPLES

A $\frac{1}{2}$	**B** £3	**C** £3·50	**D** $\frac{3}{4}$	**E** $\frac{1}{3}$
F £1·50	**G** £5	**H** $\frac{2}{5}$	**I** £4	**J** $\frac{5}{6}$

Example 1

Select an answer to the question from the 10 different possible answers in the table above.

Tom buys a chocolate bar for £1·50. He pays with a £5 note.
How much change does he receive?

The correct answer is C. This has already been marked in Example 1 in the Problem Solving section of your answer sheet.

Practice Question 1

Sarah eats $\frac{1}{4}$ of a pizza.

What fraction of the pizza remains?

The correct answer is D. Please mark this in Practice Question 1 in the Problem Solving section of your answer sheet.

STOP AND WAIT FOR FURTHER INSTRUCTIONS

A	£500	**B**	$\frac{5}{12}$	**C**	$\frac{1}{12}$	**D**	3 hours	**E**	200
F	525	**G**	£115	**H**	42 m	**I**	£12·50	**J**	14 m
K	400	**L**	$1\frac{1}{2}$ hours	**M**	$\frac{1}{4}$	**N**	80 m	**O**	8 hours

Several questions will follow for you to answer. Select an answer to each question from the 15 different possible answers in the table above. You may use an answer for more than one question.

(1) 500 students attend First Primary School. 40% of the students at the school are girls.

How many girls attend First Primary School?

(2) $\frac{1}{5}$ of the students at First Primary School have brown hair.

How many of the students at First Primary School do **not** have brown hair?

(3) Each student arrives at school at 8:30 a.m. and leaves at 4:30 p.m.

How long does each student spend at school?

(4) Maria attends First Primary School 5 days per week.

Each day, she spends £2·50 on bus fares to travel to and from school.

How much does Maria spend per week on bus fares to travel to and from school?

(5) $\frac{1}{2}$ of the students at First Primary School are 9, 10 or 11 years old.

$\frac{1}{4}$ of the students at First Primary School are 8 years old.

If I pick 1 student from First Primary School at random, what is the probability that they are not 8, 9, 10 or 11 years old?

(6) Each student at First Primary School has 4 gym classes per week. Each class lasts 45 minutes.

How long does each student spend in gym class per week?

(7) The sports field at First Primary School is rectangular in shape. It has a perimeter of 68 m and a length of 20 m.

What is the width of the sports field?

CONTINUE WORKING

(8) Each student at First Primary School spends £1 per day on lunch.

How much is spent on lunch per day by students at First Primary School?

(9) Each student at First Primary School spends 2 hours per day doing homework.

What fraction of a whole day does each student at First Primary School spend doing homework?

(10) The main school building is three times as long as the annexe building. The annexe building is twice as long as the school's car park garage.

If the car park garage is 7 m long, how long is the main school building?

(11) The students in Class A at First Primary School bake cookies and sell them at the School Fair. They sell large cookies for £2 and small cookies for £1. They sell 42 large cookies and 31 small cookies.

How much money do they make selling cookies?

(12) Henry lives 1·567 km away from First Primary School. Anish lives 1·487 km away from First Primary School.

How much further away from First Primary School does Henry live than Anish?

(13) The lunch break at First Primary School begins at 12:10 and ends at 13:40.

How long is the lunch break?

(14) $\frac{1}{4}$ of the students at First Primary School travel to school by bus. $\frac{1}{3}$ of the students at First Primary School travel to school by car. The rest of the students at First Primary School walk to school.

What fraction of the students at First Primary School walk to school?

(15) Next year, the number of students at First Primary School will increase by 5%.

How many students will attend First Primary School next year?

STOP AND WAIT FOR FURTHER INSTRUCTIONS

Cloze

 INSTRUCTIONS

 YOU HAVE 10 MINUTES TO COMPLETE THE FOLLOWING SECTION.

YOU HAVE 20 QUESTIONS TO COMPLETE WITHIN THE TIME GIVEN.

EXAMPLES

Example 1

Read the sentence below and select the most appropriate word from the table.

A	B	C	D	E
defeated	heaved	master	flow	politely

The skilful chess player easily (Q1) _____ his opponent.

Please select your answer to go in the place of (Q1) in the above sentence.

The correct answer is A. This has already been marked in Example 1 in the Cloze section of your answer sheet.

Practice Question 1

Read the sentence below and select the most appropriate word from the table.

A	B	C	D	E
crunching	eating	dreading	reading	shining

The sun was (Q2) _____ and there was not a single cloud in the sky.

Please select your answer to go in the place of (Q2) in the above sentence.

The correct answer is E. Please mark the answer E in Practice Question 1 in the Cloze section of your answer sheet.

STOP AND WAIT FOR FURTHER INSTRUCTIONS ⊗

Read the passage and select the most appropriate word from the table below by choosing the letter above the word. There are 10 questions. For example, Q1 is where you should put your answer to Question 1 on your answer sheet.

A	B	C	D	E
banks	built	cities	divided	parks

F	G	H	I	J
fascinating	families	torn	culture	travelling

Berlin

Berlin is the capital of Germany and one of the largest (Q1) _____ in Europe. It is located in the northeast of the country, close to the border with Poland. Lying on the (Q2) _____ of the River Spree, it has a population of approximately 3·6 million.

Berlin has a temperate climate and is full of forests, (Q3) _____, gardens and lakes. Locals love to spend warm summer evenings and weekends relaxing in the parks with their friends and family. The city prides itself on its emphasis on (Q4) _____ and it is home to many museums and opera houses.

The recent history of the city is (Q5) _____ and unique. Throughout the 1970s and 1980s, a wall (Q6) _____ the eastern and western parts of the city. This partition was (Q7) _____ almost overnight and (Q8) _____ from the east to the west of the city was forbidden. Therefore, many (Q9) _____ were separated for decades, only to be reunited when the wall was (Q10) _____ down in 1989.

CONTINUE WORKING ➡

Read the passage and select the most appropriate word from the table below by choosing the letter above the word. There are 10 questions. For example, Q11 is where you should put your answer to Question 11 on your answer sheet.

A	B	C	D	E
thirty	reservation	dish	husband	finally

F	G	H	I	J
writing	evening	forward	hungry	unacceptable

A Letter of Complaint

Dear Mr Jones,

I am (Q11) _____ to you to complain about the (Q12) _____ treatment I received in your restaurant last week. I do not usually like to make a fuss but the service I experienced at your establishment was atrocious. My (Q13) _____ and I had been very much looking (Q14) _____ to our meal. However, when we arrived we were told that there was no record of our (Q15) _____. This came as rather a shock as I had booked the table myself only a few days before.

We were (Q16) _____ seated after half an hour's wait but our orders were not taken for another (Q17) _____ minutes. By this time, we were ravenously (Q18) _____. Alas, the food was poor quality: my steak was overcooked and my husband's chicken (Q19) _____ was tasteless. The mood was spoiled and our (Q20) _____ was ruined. I sincerely hope you are able to address these issues so that future patrons of your restaurant are not made to suffer in the same manner.

Yours sincerely,

Mrs Butteridge

STOP AND WAIT FOR FURTHER INSTRUCTIONS ⊗

Non-Verbal Reasoning

 ## INSTRUCTIONS

 YOU HAVE 8 MINUTES TO COMPLETE THE FOLLOWING SECTION.

YOU HAVE 15 QUESTIONS TO COMPLETE WITHIN THE TIME GIVEN.

EXAMPLES

SIMILARITY Example 1

The three figures given are similar in some way.

Work out how they are similar and select the figure that goes with them.

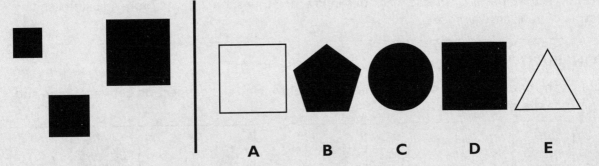

The correct answer is D. This has already been marked in Example 1 in the Non-Verbal Reasoning section of your answer sheet.

SIMILARITY Practice Question 1

The three figures given are similar in some way.

Work out how they are similar and select the figure that goes with them.

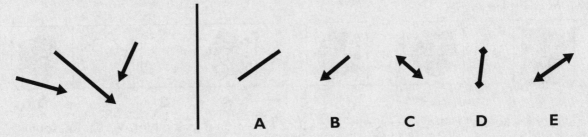

The correct answer is B. Please mark this in Practice Question 1 in the Non-Verbal Reasoning section of your answer sheet.

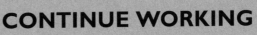 **CONTINUE WORKING**

CUBE NET Example 2

Look at the cube net below. Select the only cube that could be formed from the net.

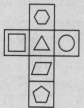

                            A   **B**   **C**   **D**

The correct answer is B. This has already been marked in Example 2 in the Non-Verbal Reasoning section of your answer sheet.

CUBE NET Practice Question 2

Look at the cube net below. Select the only cube that could be formed from the net.

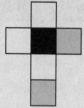

                            A   **B**   **C**   **D**

The correct answer is C. Please mark this in Practice Question 2 in the Non-Verbal Reasoning section of your answer sheet.

CONNECTION Example 3

Look at the two shapes on the left immediately below. Find the connection between them and apply it to the third shape.

 is to as is to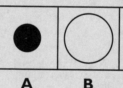

                                                     A   **B**   **C**   **D**

The correct answer is C. This has already been marked in Example 3 in the Non-Verbal Reasoning section of your answer sheet.

CONNECTION Practice Question 3

Look at the two shapes on the left immediately below. Find the connection between them and apply it to the third shape.

 is to as is to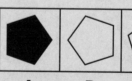

                                                     A   **B**   **C**   **D**

The correct answer is D. Please mark this in Practice Question 3 in the Non-Verbal Reasoning section of your answer sheet.

STOP AND WAIT FOR FURTHER INSTRUCTIONS

(1) The three figures given are similar in some way. Work out how they are similar and select the figure that goes with them.

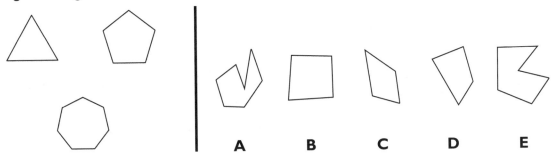

A   B   C   D   E

(2) The three figures given are similar in some way. Work out how they are similar and select the figure that goes with them.

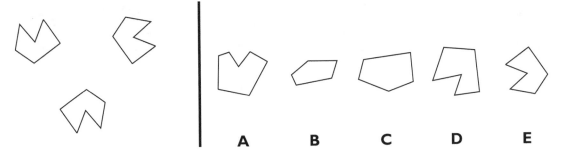

A   B   C   D   E

(3) The three figures given are similar in some way. Work out how they are similar and select the figure that goes with them.

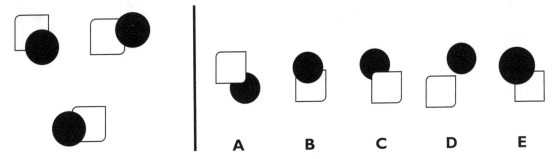

A   B   C   D   E

(4) The three figures given are similar in some way. Work out how they are similar and select the figure that goes with them.

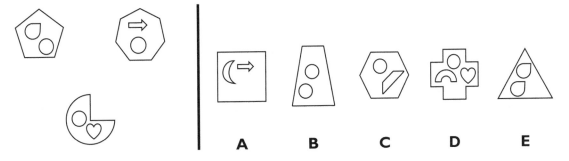

A   B   C   D   E

CONTINUE WORKING ⇨

5 The three figures given are similar in some way. Work out how they are similar and select the figure that goes with them.

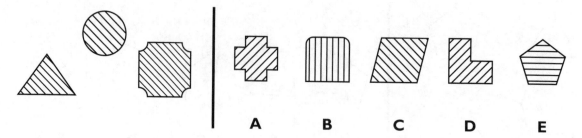

A   B   C   D   E

6 Look at the cube net below. Select the only cube that could be formed from the net.

A   B   C   D

7 Look at the cube net below. Select the only cube that could be formed from the net.

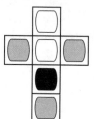

A   B   C   D

8 Look at the cube net below. Select the only cube that could be formed from the net.

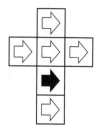

A   B   C   D

9 Look at the cube net below. Select the only cube that could be formed from the net.

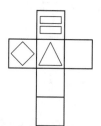

A   B   C   D

CONTINUE WORKING

10 Look at the cube net below. Select the only cube that could be formed from the net.

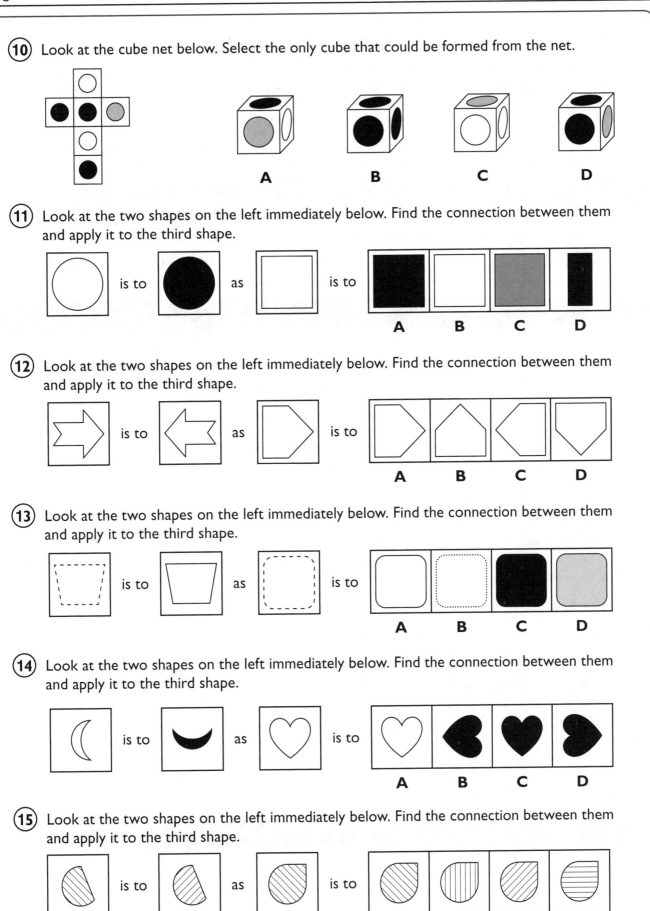

A　　　　B　　　　C　　　　D

11 Look at the two shapes on the left immediately below. Find the connection between them and apply it to the third shape.

is to　　　as　　　is to

A　　B　　C　　D

12 Look at the two shapes on the left immediately below. Find the connection between them and apply it to the third shape.

is to　　　as　　　is to

A　　B　　C　　D

13 Look at the two shapes on the left immediately below. Find the connection between them and apply it to the third shape.

is to　　　as　　　is to

A　　B　　C　　D

14 Look at the two shapes on the left immediately below. Find the connection between them and apply it to the third shape.

is to　　　as　　　is to

A　　B　　C　　D

15 Look at the two shapes on the left immediately below. Find the connection between them and apply it to the third shape.

is to　　　as　　　is to

A　　B　　C　　D

STOP AND WAIT FOR FURTHER INSTRUCTIONS ⊗

Antonyms

INSTRUCTIONS

 YOU HAVE 6 MINUTES TO COMPLETE THE FOLLOWING SECTION.

YOU HAVE 18 QUESTIONS TO COMPLETE WITHIN THE TIME GIVEN.

EXAMPLES

Example 1

Which word is most opposite in meaning to the following word?

hot

A	B	C	D	E
follow	cold	freeze	ice	jelly

The correct answer is B. This has already been marked in Example 1 in the Antonyms section of your answer sheet.

Practice Question 1

Which word is most opposite in meaning to the following word?

below

A	B	C	D	E
attack	deep	lower	above	before

The correct answer is D. Please mark the answer D in Practice Question 1 in the Antonyms section of your answer sheet.

STOP AND WAIT FOR FURTHER INSTRUCTIONS

For each row, select the word from the table that is most opposite in meaning to the word above the table.

(1) major

A	B	C	D	E
level	manner	oblige	grow	minor

(2) minimum

A	B	C	D	E
malady	maximum	eaten	miniature	suppose

(3) freeze

A	B	C	D	E
sigh	stink	joke	melt	drop

(4) niece

A	B	C	D	E
mother	daughter	son	neighbour	nephew

(5) front

A	B	C	D	E
follow	neither	rear	heart	soul

(6) sharp

A	B	C	D	E
kind	blunt	driven	former	shallow

CONTINUE WORKING ➡

(7) stop

A	B	C	D	E
tiger	sign	meander	hapless	start

(8) teach

A	B	C	D	E
frighten	hold	learn	broken	thing

(9) compulsory

A	B	C	D	E
blind	voluntary	force	free	safety

(10) succeed

A	B	C	D	E
fail	yell	gain	seed	win

(11) smooth

A	B	C	D	E
hang	cover	open	rough	soft

(12) lose

A	B	C	D	E
life	artery	find	cunning	hide

CONTINUE WORKING ⟹

13 defend

A	B	C	D	E
deepen	block	cry	summer	attack

14 elementary

A	B	C	D	E
easy	merciless	advanced	beginner	gold

15 import

A	B	C	D	E
important	export	domicile	verify	excellent

16 horrify

A	B	C	D	E
horror	delight	pleased	skeleton	forgive

17 create

A	B	C	D	E
culture	bulldozer	build	deny	demolish

18 assist

A	B	C	D	E
age	system	obstruct	aid	former

STOP AND WAIT FOR FURTHER INSTRUCTIONS ⊗

Numeracy

INSTRUCTIONS

 YOU HAVE 9 MINUTES TO COMPLETE THE FOLLOWING SECTION.

YOU HAVE 18 QUESTIONS TO COMPLETE WITHIN THE TIME GIVEN.

EXAMPLES

The questions within this section are not multiple choice. Write the answer to each question on the answer sheet by selecting the correct digits from the columns provided.

Example 1

Calculate the answer to the following:

$12 + 42$

The correct answer is 54. This has already been marked in Example 1 in the Numeracy section of your answer sheet.

Practice Question 1

Calculate the answer to the following:

$55 - 47$

The correct answer is 8. Please mark this in Practice Question 1 in the Numeracy section of your answer sheet. Note that a single-digit answer should be marked with a 0 in the left-hand column, so mark 08 on your answer sheet.

STOP AND WAIT FOR FURTHER INSTRUCTIONS

1 Calculate the answer to the following:

123 − 24

2 Calculate the value of X in the following equation:

$4X - 3 = 45$

3 Calculate the next term in the following sequence:

45, 37, 29, 21, ?

4 What number is 6 less than double 36?

5 What is the area of this rectangle in cm²?

3 cm

7 cm   *Not drawn to scale*

6 What is the total number of days in the last 2 months of the year?

7 Calculate the mean of the following numbers:

8, 4, 7, 9, 2

8 Calculate the answer to the following:

−10 + 20

9 The cost of renting a car is £210 per day. Emily and 2 friends rent the car for 1 day.

They split the cost equally between them.

How much do they each pay in pounds?

CONTINUE WORKING ⇨

(10) The ratio 3:9 is equal to the ratio D:45

What is the value of D?

(11) How many different factors does the number 24 have?

(12) A bookseller decides to raise the price of a £5 book by 40%.

What is the new price of the book in pounds?

(13) The perimeter of an octagon is 46·3 cm.

All but one of its sides each have a length of 5.9 cm.

What is the length in centimetres of the remaining side of the octagon?

(14) What is the smallest number of coins from which I could make £0·78 exactly?

(15) How many sevenths of an orange are there in four whole oranges?

(16) 5 children each receive 3 pencils and 4 books.

How many books do they receive in total?

(17) Tom is third from the front of a queue and third from the back.

How many people are there in the queue?

(18) Calculate the answer to the following:

$\frac{1}{4}$ of $\frac{1}{2}$ of 88

END OF PAPER

Key abbreviations: *cm: centimetre, g: gram, kg: kilogram, km: kilometre, kph: kilometres per hour, m: metre, ml: millilitre, mm: millimetre*

Answers to Get Started Test A Paper 1

Comprehension (pages 7-9)

Q1 *D*
On the arrival of puberty

Q2 *C*
Because they sold mainly sweets rather than chocolate (the passage says 'There were very few delicious chocolate bars to tempt us. That's why sweet shops were called sweet shops and not chocolate shops.')

Q3 *C*
Bounty Bar

Q4 *C*
Options 1, 2 and 4 only (gobstoppers, sherbet-suckers and aniseed balls)

Q5 *C*
Rats' blood

Q6 *B*
Seven years (the passage says 'Then came the revolution and the entire world of chocolate was suddenly turned upside down in the space of seven glorious years.')

Q7 *B*
To make drinks

Q8 *A*
Switzerland

Q9 *C*
Amazing

Q10 *B*
1928

Shuffled Sentences (pages 11-12)

Q1 *D*
eaten *The boy ate the apple.*

Q2 *A*
ate *Sarah was eight years old.*

Q3 *C*
flight *The car sped along the road.*

Q4 *B*
animals *The farmer grew his crops.*

Q5 *D*
timing *We had lots of homework.*

Q6 *B*
lifted *The desk was made of wood.*

Q7 *D*
dislike *Most of the students enjoyed the course.*

Q8 *B*
to *She made too many mistakes.*

Q9 *E*
gaze *The wind blew through the forest.*

Q10 *D*
open *Noah loved his friends and family. OR Noah loved his family and friends.*

Q11 *E*
into *The young boy ran quickly.*

Q12 *B*
capability *The city's inhabitants were upset.*

Q13 *D*
figure *Frequent exercise can help prevent illness.*

Q14 *A*
four *The lawyer summarised the case for the jury.*

Q15 *D*
suffer *The prisoner attacked his fellow inmates.*

Numeracy (pages 13-14)

Q1 *73*
17 + 56 = 73

Q2 *60*
120 ÷ 2 = 60

Q3 *56*
54 − 7 + 9 = 47 + 9 = 56

Q4 *5*
The 'mode' is the value that appears most frequently. The value 5 appears 3 times, which is the most common, so it is the mode.

Q5 *44*
The sequence is +7 +8 +7 +8 +7
So next term is +8; 36 + 8 = 44

Q6 *70*
There are 60 minutes in an hour and so $\frac{1}{6}$ of an hour = 10 minutes; $1\frac{1}{6}$ hours = 60 minutes + 10 minutes = 70 minutes

Q7 *4*

$15 + X = 31 - 12$
$X = 31 - 12 - 15$
$X = 4$

Q8 *3*

$75 \div 8 = 9$ Remainder 3

Q9 *60*

1 decade = 10 years; half a decade = 5 years
There are 12 months in a year.
Half a decade = 5×12 months = 60 months

Q10 *65*

$8 \times 5 = 40; 8 \times 11 = 88; 8 \times 3 = 24;$
$8 \times 7 = 56$
So the answer is 65

Q11 *9*

Factors of 36: 1, 36, 2, 18, 3, 12, 4, 9, 6

Q12 *12*

Calculate in reverse: $8 \times 3 = 24$
$24 \div 2 = 12$

Q13 *11*

Mean: $(12 + 18 + 10 + 4) \div 4$
$= 44 \div 4 = 11$

Problem Solving (pages 16-17)

Q1 *E*

10 a.m. to 12:30 p.m. is 2 hours and
30 minutes; there are 60 minutes in 1 hour
So 60 minutes + 60 minutes + 30 minutes
= 150 minutes

Q2 *C*

48 kilometres $\times 3 = 144$ km

Q3 *B*

$45 + 66 + 34 = 145$

Q4 *E*

One quarter of 44 = $44 \div 4 = 11$
So $44 - 11 = 33$

Q5 *D*

Cost of 2 packets of crisps = $22p \times 2 = 44p$
Change received = £1 - 44p = £1 - £0·44
= £0·56

Q6 *C*

A regular hexagon has 6 equal sides.
Length of one side = Perimeter $\div 6$
= 54 cm $\div 6 = 9$ cm

Q7 *A*

Let X equal the number of sweets Tim
receives.
Tim:Robert = 3:2 = X:12
12 is 6 times bigger than 2
So 6 times bigger than 3 is 18, so $X = 18$

Q8 *B*

1

Q9 *E*

564 is the largest number that rounds to
560, to the nearest 10

Q10 *D*

20% of £40 = £8
Sale price = £40 - £8 = £32

Synonyms (pages 19-21)

Q1 *C* permit

Q2 *E* empty

Q3 *B* clever

Q4 *D* untrue

Q5 *A* happy

Q6 *E* enormous

Q7 *C* faithful

Q8 *D* noisy

Q9 *E* courteous

Q10 *E* rapid

Q11 *B* scarce

Q12 *D* genuine

Q13 *D* leave

Q14 *C* wealthy

Q15 *B* impolite

Q16 *E* secure

Q17 *E* drowsy

Q18 *D* feeble

Q19 *D* reply

Q20 *B* act

Q21 *C* categorise

Q22 *D* criticise

Q23 *B* doubtful

Q24 *C* clash

Non-Verbal Reasoning (pages 24-26)

Q1 *C*

The figure in the top right is the same as the
figure in the top left except it is shaded black
instead of white.
Therefore, the figure in the bottom right
should be the same as the figure in the
bottom left except it should be shaded black.
Therefore, the answer is C.

Q2 *A*

The figure in the top right is a reflection of the
figure in the top left in a vertical mirror line.
Therefore, the figure in the bottom right
should be a reflection of the figure in the
bottom left in a vertical mirror line.
Therefore, the answer is A.

Q3 *C*

The figure in the top right has one more side
than the figure in the top left. Both figures
are shaded white.
Therefore, the figure in the bottom right
should have one more side than the figure
in the bottom left. Both figures should be
shaded white.
Therefore, the answer is C.

Q4 *C*

The figure in the top right is the same as the figure in the top left except the line shading is in the opposite direction.

Therefore, the figure in the bottom right should be the same as the figure in the bottom left except the line shading should be in the opposite direction.

Therefore, the answer is C.

Q5 *C*

Q6 *A*

Q7 *B*

Q8 *D*

Q9 *A*

Q10 *D*

Q11 *B*

Q12 *A*

Q13 *C*

Answers to *Get Started* Test A Paper 2

Problem Solving (pages 29-30)

Q1 H
10 p.m. to 7 a.m. is 9 hours

Q2 E
4 out of 12 eggs $= \frac{4}{12} = \frac{1}{3}$

Q3 A
It takes 30 minutes for James to drive 12 km
60 minutes is double 30 minutes
Double 12 km is 24 km
So it would take him 60 minutes to drive
24 km; 60 minutes in 1 hour
So his speed is 24 kph

Q4 F
$97 - 23 = 74$

Q5 B
12×10 minutes $= 120$ minutes $= 2$ hours

Q6 J
Total spent $= £2·50 + £1·20 = £3·70$
Change received $= £5 - £3·70 = £1·30$

Q7 E
1 hour = 60 minutes;
$\frac{20 \text{ minutes}}{60 \text{ minutes}} = \frac{20}{60} = \frac{1}{3}$

Q8 C
$£7·50 ÷ 2 = £3·75$

Q9 I
It takes 20 minutes for James to drive 9 km
60 minutes is triple 20 minutes
Triple 9 km is 27 km
So it would take him 60 minutes to drive
27 km; 1 hour = 60 minutes
So his speed is 27 kph

Q10 D
James brushes his teeth twice per day.
There are 31 days in August.
$31 \times 2 = 62$

Cloze (pages 32-33)

Q1 F essential
Q2 C strong
Q3 E absorbed
Q4 I directly
Q5 D adequate
Q6 A minutes
Q7 G deficiency
Q8 J brittle
Q9 B found
Q10 H pills
Q11 C fought
Q12 I army
Q13 A estimate
Q14 G forces
Q15 E morning
Q16 F flee
Q17 D crowned
Q18 B death
Q19 H significant
Q20 J attempts

Non-Verbal Reasoning (pages 36-38)

Q1 E
The figures on the left are all shaded black.
Therefore, the answer is E.

Q2 B
The figures on the left each have four sides.
Therefore, the answer is B.

Q3 A
The figures on the left are all stars with an
even number of points.
Therefore, the answer is A.

Q4 A
The figures on the left each consist of an
outer shape with a white heart shape inside.
Therefore, the answer is A.

Q5 E
The figures on the left each consist of two
shapes. The external shape has one more
side than the internal shape.
Therefore, the answer is E.

Q6 B
Q7 A
Q8 C
Q9 D
Q10 A
Q11 A
The boxes alternate between grey and black
circular shapes.
Therefore, the answer is A.

Q12 B
From left to right, each box has one less
black shape in it.
Therefore, the correct answer box should
have two black shapes in it.
Therefore, the answer is B.

Q13 B
From left to right, the heart shape rotates
90° clockwise from one box to the next.
Therefore, the answer is B.

Q14 B
From left to right, the pentagon moves in a
clockwise direction from one corner to the
next.
From left to right, the circle moves in a
clockwise direction from one corner to the
next.
Therefore, the answer is B.

Q15 *C*

From left to right, each shape has one more side than the shape in the preceding box. Therefore, the correct answer box contains a shape with seven sides.

Therefore, the answer is C.

Grammar & Spelling (page 40)

Q1 *B feint*
Q2 *D adverb*
Q3 *B disagreeable*
Q4 *D phrozen (should be frozen)*
Q5 *B resauceful (should be resourceful)*
Q6 *C calender (should be calendar)*
Q7 *B greatful (should be grateful)*
Q8 *B seperate (should be separate)*

Antonyms (pages 42-43)

Q1 *D before*　　　　　**Q9** *B broad*
Q2 *C ugly*　　　　　　**Q10** *C never*
Q3 *B loser*　　　　　　**Q11** *B complicated*
Q4 *D compliment*　　　**Q12** *D careless*
Q5 *E forbid*　　　　　**Q13** *C particular*
Q6 *D abundance*　　　**Q14** *E war*
Q7 *E senior*　　　　　**Q15** *C natural*
Q8 *A cruel*

Numeracy (pages 45-47)

Q1 *15*
　　　74 − 59 = 15
Q2 *42*
　　　Sequence is +7 +6 +5 +4
　　　So next term is +3; 39 + 3 = 42
Q3 *55*
　　　55 ÷ 3 = 18 Remainder 1
Q4 *35*
　　　1 whole has 4 quarters
　　　So there are (8 × 4) quarters in 8
　　　So total number of quarters = 32 + 3 = 35
Q5 *16*
　　　$0·5 = \dfrac{5}{10} = \dfrac{1}{2}$ *so* $\dfrac{1}{2} = \dfrac{8}{X}$
　　　So X = 16
Q6 *0*
　　　55 ÷ 11 = 5 (no remainder)
Q7 *48*
　　　1 cm = 10 mm
　　　So 4·8 cm = 48 mm

Q8 *1*
　　　$\dfrac{1}{4}$ *of 60 = 15;* $\dfrac{1}{5}$ *of 70 = 14*
　　　15 − 14 = 1
Q9 *B*
　　　Total number of balls = 7 + 6 + 5 + 2 = 20
　　　Total number of non-green balls = 20 − 6
　　　$= 14; \dfrac{14}{20} = \dfrac{7}{10}$
Q10 *D*
　　　Diameter = 2 × radius = 2 × 32 cm
　　　= 64 cm
Q11 *E*
　　　Arrange numbers in order:
　　　1, 12, 23, 32, 34, 43, 45, 74, 98
　　　Middle number is 34
Q12 *B*
　　　A fair die has 6 possible outcomes:
　　　1, 2, 3, 4, 5, 6
　　　3 out of 6 of these outcomes are even:
　　　2, 4, 6
　　　So probability of rolling an even number
　　　$= \dfrac{3}{6} = \dfrac{1}{2}$
Q13 *A*
　　　The distance between the vertices is 4 units.
　　　4th vertex must be 4 units above (6, 2)
　　　So y-coordinate increases by 4
　　　So 4th vertex is (6, 6)
Q14 *D*
　　　$\dfrac{1}{2} + \dfrac{1}{3} = \dfrac{3}{6} + \dfrac{2}{6} = \dfrac{5}{6}$
Q15 *C*
　　　$\dfrac{2}{3} \times \dfrac{1}{4} = \dfrac{2}{12} = \dfrac{1}{6}$
Q16 *E*
　　　$\dfrac{1}{2} \div 3 = \dfrac{1}{2} \times \dfrac{1}{3} = \dfrac{1}{6}$
Q17 *E*
　　　D = 3P; F = 2D
　　　So F = 2(3P) = 2 × 3P = 6P
Q18 *E*
　　　Length = 7 cm so width = 7 cm ÷ 2
　　　= 3·5 cm
　　　Perimeter = 7 cm + 7 cm + 3·5 cm
　　　+ 3·5 cm = 21 cm

Answers to *Get Started* Test B Paper 1

Comprehension (pages 51-52)

Q1 A
Botswana

Q2 C
'Did you sleep well?'

Q3 C
Using sprays or nets

Q4 D
To remind us to be remorseful for our mistakes (the passage says 'Bad consciences, it would appear, are there for a purpose: to make us feel regret over our failings.')

Q5 A
10 p.m.

Q6 B
Because they are tired from a hard day's work (the passage says 'Mechanics in general sleep well, as do many others whose day is taken up with physically demanding labour.')

Q7 B
Options 2 and 4 only (Mma Makutsi sitting at her desk and driving her vehicle)

Q8 B
How to tend to cows (the passage says 'explaining to her about the ways of cattle, a subject that he knew so well.')

Q9 D
Quench

Q10 D
They were close (the passage says 'so many memories and sayings and observations, that she, his daughter, could now call up and cherish')

Shuffled Sentences (pages 54-55)

Q1 E
on *There were many mistakes in the book.*

Q2 A
with *I can rely on my friends.*

Q3 B
allowed *The butcher sliced through the piece of meat.*

Q4 C
watches *The train was delayed by half an hour.*

Q5 B
punch *You should always carry an umbrella here.*
OR Here you should always carry an umbrella.

Q6 B
attacked *The bird searched for worms in the bush.*
OR The bird searched in the bush for worms.

Q7 D
players *The football match was unexpectedly cancelled.*
OR The football match was cancelled unexpectedly.

Q8 A
assume *The chef cooked the sausage on the grill.*

Q9 C
able *You must eat fruit and vegetables every day.*
OR You must eat vegetables and fruit every day.

Q10 A
permit *The doctor was unable to save the woman's life.*

Q11 A
fly *Hyenas tend to hunt in packs.*

Q12 E
farm *Rome is my favourite city in Europe.*

Q13 B
robe *My new shoes are very fashionable.*

Q14 D
persuade *The glass window shattered instantly.*
OR The window glass shattered instantly.

Q15 C
froze *The sun shone over the mountains.*

Numeracy (pages 56-57)

Q1 *26*
1 year = 52 weeks so $\frac{1}{2}$ a year = 26 weeks

Q2 *15*
It takes Omar 1 hour to run 10 km
2·5 km is $\frac{1}{4}$ of 10 km
$\frac{1}{4}$ of 1 hour is 15 minutes

Q3 *58*
$7 + (6 \times 9) - 3 = 7 + 54 - 3 = 58$

Q4 *64*

$\frac{1}{4}$ *of 256 = 256 ÷ 4 = 64*

Q5 *13*

Sequence is +2 −3 +2 −3
So next term is +2; 11 + 2 = 13

Q6 *33*

All sides of an equilateral triangle are the same length.
11 cm × 3 = 33 cm

Q7 *11*

Last year Bob was 7 so he is now 8
In 3 years, Bob will be 11 years old
(8 + 3 = 11)

Q8 *56*

Kags in 1 Kig = 7 × 8 = 56

Q9 *6*

Cube has 12 edges and 6 faces
12 − 6 = 6

Q10 *88*

579 − 491 = 88

Q11 *42*

Fortnight = 14 days
14 × 3 = 42

Q12 *10*

$\frac{3}{4}$ *of a litre = 750 ml*
750 ml ÷ 75 ml = 10

Q13 *6*

27th Sep to 30th Sep is 4 days
1st Oct to 2nd Oct is 2 days
4 + 2 = 6

Q14 *20*

0·8 kg = 800 g
800 g ÷ 40 g = 20

Q15 *0*

$\frac{1}{4}$ *of 44 = 11;* $\frac{1}{3}$ *of 33 = 11*
11 − 11 = 0

Problem Solving (pages 58–59)

Q1 *E*

3 smallest positive prime numbers are 2, 3 and 5
2 + 3 + 5 = 10

Q2 *D*

35 minutes before 12:22 p.m. is 11:47 a.m.

Q3 *D*

4X + 3X = 54 − 2X
4X + 3X + 2X = 54
9X = 54
X = 6

Q4 *E*

£1 worth is equal to 10 ten-pence coins
Total weight = 10 × 7 g = 70 g

Q5 *D*

1 litre lasts 3 days
So 18 litres lasts (18 × 3) days
18 × 3 = 54 days

Q6 *C*

Ken gets $\frac{4}{5}$ *of the questions correct*
Percentage = $\left(\frac{4}{5} \times 100\right)$ *% =* $\left(\frac{400}{5}\right)$ *% = 80%*

Q7 *E*

1·5 m = 150 cm
Length of 1 part = 150 cm ÷ 10 = 15 cm
Length of 3 parts = 15 cm × 3 = 45 cm

Q8 *D*

180° is half a turn so she will face the opposite of her current direction.
Southeast is opposite northwest.

Q9 *D*

1 interval on the timeline is equivalent to 1 unit
B is 3 intervals after −4
−4 + 3 = −1

Q10 *D*

10 men take 3 hours
20 is double 10 so 20 men should take half as long
3 hours ÷ 2 = 1·5 hours

Synonyms (pages 61–63)

Q1 **A** *nearly*	**Q13** **D** *final*
Q2 **D** *annoy*	**Q14** **C** *deadly*
Q3 **B** *commence*	**Q15** **E** *maintain*
Q4 **C** *beneficial*	**Q16** **C** *mild*
Q5 **B** *sprint*	**Q17** **C** *mirror*
Q6 **E** *protest*	**Q18** **E** *bare*
Q7 **C** *disagreeable*	**Q19** **E** *numerous*
Q8 **D** *eager*	**Q20** **C** *function*
Q9 **B** *fundamental*	**Q21** **A** *overlook*
Q10 **D** *disregard*	**Q22** **D** *praise*
Q11 **C** *examine*	**Q23** **B** *pressing*
Q12 **B** *envious*	**Q24** **E** *provide*

Non-Verbal Reasoning (pages 65-67)

Q1 *C*

Q2 *D*

Q3 *D*

Q4 *A*

Q5 *D*

Q6 *B*

Q7 *D*

All the other shapes have four sides.

Q8 *E*

All the other shapes are shaded black.

Q9 *C*

All the other arrows point to the right.

Q10 *A*

In all the other figures, the black circle is on top of the white circle.

Q11 *C*

All the other figures consist of rotations of the same shape.

Q12 *B*

All the other figures have a line of symmetry.

Answers to *Get Started* Test B Paper 2

Problem Solving (pages 70-71)

Q1 E
40% of 500 = 200

Q2 K
Number of students with brown hair $= \dfrac{1}{5}$
of 500 = 100
So number of students without brown hair
= 500 − 100 = 400

Q3 O
8:30 a.m. to 4:30 p.m. is 8 hours

Q4 I
Maria's spend per week = £2·50 × 5 days
= £12·50

Q5 M
Probability that students are 8, 9, 10 or 11
$= \dfrac{1}{2} + \dfrac{1}{4} = \dfrac{3}{4}$
Therefore, probability that students are **not**
8, 9, 10 or 11 $= 1 - \dfrac{3}{4} = \dfrac{1}{4}$

Q6 D
Total time spent in gym class =
4 × 45 minutes = 180 minutes = 3 hours

Q7 J
Perimeter = length + length + width + width
Let width = W
68 m = 20 m + 20 m + W + W
2W = 68 m − 40 m
2W = 28 m
W = 14 m

Q8 A
Total number of students = 500
500 × £1 = £500

Q9 C
1 day = 24 hours; time spent doing
homework = 2 hours
$\dfrac{2}{24} = \dfrac{1}{12}$

Q10 H
Car park garage is 7 m long
Annexe building is twice car park garage
2 × 7 m = 14 m
Main building is three times annexe building
3 × 14 m = 42 m

Q11 G
Total sales = (42 × £2) + (31 × £1)
= £84 + £31 = £115

Q12 N
Difference in distance = 1·567 km −
1·487 km = 1,567 m − 1,487 m = 80 m

Q13 L
12:10 to 13:40 is $1\dfrac{1}{2}$ hours

Q14 B
Fraction who walk to school $= 1 - \dfrac{1}{4} - \dfrac{1}{3}$
$= 1 - \dfrac{3}{12} - \dfrac{4}{12} = \dfrac{5}{12}$

Q15 F
Increase in students next year = 5% of
500 = 25
Number of students next year = 500 + 25
= 525

Cloze (pages 73-74)

Q1 C *cities*
Q2 A *banks*
Q3 E *parks*
Q4 I *culture*
Q5 F *fascinating*
Q6 D *divided*
Q7 B *built*
Q8 J *travelling*
Q9 G *families*
Q10 H *torn*

Q11 F *writing*
Q12 J *unacceptable*
Q13 D *husband*
Q14 H *forward*
Q15 B *reservation*
Q16 E *finally*
Q17 A *thirty*
Q18 I *hungry*
Q19 C *dish*
Q20 G *evening*

Non-Verbal Reasoning (pages 77-79)

Q1 A
The figures on the left each have an odd
number of sides.
Therefore, the answer is A.

Q2 E
The figures on the left are each rotations of
the same shape.
Therefore, the answer is E.

Q3 B
The figures on the left each contain the same
two overlapping shapes. The black shape is
always on top of the white shape.
Therefore, the answer is B.

Q4 C
The figures on the left each consist of two
smaller shapes within a larger shape. The two
smaller shapes are different to each other
and one is always a circle.
Therefore, the answer is C.

Q5 C

The figures on the left all have line shading in the same direction.

Therefore, the answer is C.

Q6 B

Q7 A

Q8 B

Q9 C

Q10 A

Q11 A

The shading of the figure changes from black to white.

Therefore, the answer is A.

Q12 C

The figure is reflected in a vertical mirror line.

Therefore, the answer is C.

Q13 A

The outline of the figure changes from dashed to solid.

Therefore, the answer is A.

Q14 D

The figure rotates 90° anticlockwise and its shading changes from white to black.

Therefore, the answer is D.

Q15 C

The line shading of the figure changes to the opposite direction.

Therefore, the answer is C.

Antonyms (pages 81–83)

Q1 E minor

Q2 B maximum

Q3 D melt

Q4 E nephew

Q5 C rear

Q6 B blunt

Q7 E start

Q8 C learn

Q9 B voluntary

Q10 A fail

Q11 D rough

Q12 C find

Q13 E attack

Q14 C advanced

Q15 B export

Q16 B delight

Q17 E demolish

Q18 C obstruct

Numeracy (pages 85–86)

Q1 99

$123 - 24 = 99$

Q2 12

$4X - 3 = 45$

$4X = 48$

$X = 12$

Q3 13

Sequence is −8 −8 −8 −8

So next term is −8; $21 - 8 = 13$

Q4 66

Double $36 = 72$

$72 - 6 = 66$

Q5 21

Area = width × length = 7 cm × 3 cm

$= 21$ cm²

Q6 61

Last two months of the year are November (30 days) and December (31 days)

$30 + 31 = 61$

Q7 6

Mean = (Sum) ÷ (Number of terms)

$= (8 + 4 + 7 + 9 + 2) \div 5$

$= 30 \div 5 = 6$

Q8 10

$-10 + 20 = 10$

Q9 70

Cost of rental = £210

Cost per person = £210 ÷ 3 = £70

Q10 15

45 is five times bigger than 9 so D must be five times bigger than 3

$D = 5 \times 3 = 15$

Q11 8

Factors of 24: 1, 24, 2, 12, 3, 8, 4, 6

Q12 7

10% of £5 = £0·50 so 40% of £5 = £2

New price = £5 + £2 = £7

Q13 5

5·9 cm × 7 = 41·3 cm

46·3 cm − 41·3 cm = 5 cm

Q14 5

50 p + 20 p + 5 p + 2 p + 1 p = 78 p

Q15 28

Total number of sevenths = 4 × 7 = 28

Q16 20

5 × 4 books = 20

Q17 5

2 people in front of him and 2 people behind him so 5 in the queue.

Q18 11

$\frac{1}{2}$ of 88 = 44

$\frac{1}{4}$ of 44 = 11

Pupil's Full Name:

Instructions:
Mark the boxes correctly like this ▰

Please sign your name here:

Comprehension (pages 6-9)

Example 1

A	B	C	D

Practice Question 1

A	B	C	D

	A	B	C	D
1	A	B	C	D
2	A	B	C	D
3	A	B	C	D
4	A	B	C	D
5	A	B	C	D
6	A	B	C	D
7	A	B	C	D
8	A	B	C	D
9	A	B	C	D
10	A	B	C	D

Shuffled Sentences (pages 10-12)

Example 1

A	B	C	D	E

Practice Question 1

A	B	C	D	E

	A	B	C	D	E
1	A	B	C	D	E
2	A	B	C	D	E
3	A	B	C	D	E
4	A	B	C	D	E
5	A	B	C	D	E
6	A	B	C	D	E
7	A	B	C	D	E
8	A	B	C	D	E
9	A	B	C	D	E
10	A	B	C	D	E
11	A	B	C	D	E
12	A	B	C	D	E
13	A	B	C	D	E
14	A	B	C	D	E
15	A	B	C	D	E

Numeracy (pages 13-14)

Example 1   Practice
5 4   Question 1   1   2

Numeracy bubble grids for Practice Question 1 and questions 1–13, each with two columns of digits 0–9.

3   4   5   6

7   8   9   10

11   12   13

Problem Solving (pages 15-17)

Example 1

     A   B   ~~C~~   D   E

Practice Question 1

     A   B   C   D   E

	A	B	C	D	E
1	A	B	C	D	E
2	A	B	C	D	E
3	A	B	C	D	E
4	A	B	C	D	E
5	A	B	C	D	E
6	A	B	C	D	E
7	A	B	C	D	E
8	A	B	C	D	E
9	A	B	C	D	E
10	A	B	C	D	E

Synonyms (pages 18-21)

Example 1

     A   ~~B~~   C   D   E

Practice Question 1

     A   B   C   D   E

	A	B	C	D	E
1	A	B	C	D	E
2	A	B	C	D	E
3	A	B	C	D	E
4	A	B	C	D	E
5	A	B	C	D	E
6	A	B	C	D	E
7	A	B	C	D	E
8	A	B	C	D	E
9	A	B	C	D	E
10	A	B	C	D	E
11	A	B	C	D	E
12	A	B	C	D	E
13	A	B	C	D	E
14	A	B	C	D	E
15	A	B	C	D	E
16	A	B	C	D	E
17	A	B	C	D	E
18	A	B	C	D	E
19	A	B	C	D	E
20	A	B	C	D	E
21	A	B	C	D	E
22	A	B	C	D	E

	A	B	C	D	E
23	A	B	C	D	E
24	A	B	C	D	E

Non-Verbal Reasoning (pages 22-26)

COMPLETE THE SQUARE Example 1

     A   B   C   ~~D~~   E

COMPLETE THE SQUARE Practice Question 1

     A   B   C   D   E

REFLECTION Example 2

     A   B   ~~C~~   D

REFLECTION Practice Question 2

     A   B   C   D

DIMENSION Example 3

     A   B   ~~C~~   D

DIMENSION Practice Question 3

     A   B   C   D

	A	B	C	D	E
1	A	B	C	D	E
2	A	B	C	D	E
3	A	B	C	D	E
4	A	B	C	D	E
5	A	B	C	D	
6	A	B	C	D	
7	A	B	C	D	
8	A	B	C	D	
9	A	B	C	D	
10	A	B	C	D	
11	A	B	C	D	
12	A	B	C	D	
13	A	B	C	D	

Pupil's Full Name:

Instructions:
Mark the boxes correctly like this ✦

Please sign your name here:

Problem Solving (pages 28-30)

Example 1

A B ⊂ D E F G H I J

Practice Question 1

A B C D E F G H I J

1   A B C D E F G H I J
2   A B C D E F G H I J
3   A B C D E F G H I J
4   A B C D E F G H I J
5   A B C D E F G H I J
6   A B C D E F G H I J
7   A B C D E F G H I J
8   A B C D E F G H I J
9   A B C D E F G H I J
10 A B C D E F G H I J

15 A B C D E F G H I J
16 A B C D E F G H I J
17 A B C D E F G H I J
18 A B C D E F G H I J
19 A B C D E F G H I J
20 A B C D E F G H I J

Non-Verbal Reasoning (pages 34-38)

SIMILARITY Example 1

A   B   C   D   E

SIMILARITY Practice Question 1

A   B   C   D   E

CUBE NET Example 2

A   B   C   D

CUBE NET Practice Question 2

A   B   C   D

COMPLETE THE SEQUENCE Example 3

A   B   C   D   E

COMPLETE THE SEQUENCE Practice Question 3

A   B   C   D   E

Cloze (pages 31-33)

Example 1

A B C D E

Practice Question 1

A B C D E

1   A B C D E F G H I J
2   A B C D E F G H I J
3   A B C D E F G H I J
4   A B C D E F G H I J
5   A B C D E F G H I J
6   A B C D E F G H I J
7   A B C D E F G H I J
8   A B C D E F G H I J
9   A B C D E F G H I J
10 A B C D E F G H I J
11 A B C D E F G H I J
12 A B C D E F G H I J
13 A B C D E F G H I J
14 A B C D E F G H I J

1   A B C D E
2   A B C D E
3   A B C D E
4   A B C D E
5   A B C D E
6   A B C D
7   A B C D
8   A B C D
9   A B C D
10 A B C D
11 A B C D E
12 A B C D E
13 A B C D E
14 A B C D E
15 A B C D E

Grammar & Spelling (page 39-40)

Example 1

A	B	C	D	E
✗	B	C	D	E

Practice Question 1

A	B	C	D	E
A	B	C	D	E

	A	B	C	D	E
1	A	B	C	D	E
2	A	B	C	D	E
3	A	B	C	D	E
4	A	B	C	D	E
5	A	B	C	D	E
6	A	B	C	D	E
7	A	B	C	D	E
8	A	B	C	D	E

Antonyms (pages 41-43)

Example 1

A	B	C	D	E
A	✗	C	D	E

Practice Question 1

A	B	C	D	E
A	B	C	D	E

	A	B	C	D	E
1	A	B	C	D	E
2	A	B	C	D	E
3	A	B	C	D	E
4	A	B	C	D	E
5	A	B	C	D	E
6	A	B	C	D	E
7	A	B	C	D	E
8	A	B	C	D	E
9	A	B	C	D	E
10	A	B	C	D	E
11	A	B	C	D	E
12	A	B	C	D	E
13	A	B	C	D	E
14	A	B	C	D	E
15	A	B	C	D	E

Numeracy (pages 44-47)

Example 1

5 4

Practice Question 1

(grid of digits 0–9 in two columns, with 4 and 5 marked)

1

(grid of digits 0–9 in two columns)

2

(grid of digits 0–9 in two columns)

3

(grid of digits 0–9 in two columns)

4

(grid of digits 0–9 in two columns)

5

(grid of digits 0–9 in two columns)

6

(grid of digits 0–9 in two columns)

7

(grid of digits 0–9 in two columns)

8

(grid of digits 0–9 in two columns)

	A	B	C	D	E
9	A	B	C	D	E
10	A	B	C	D	E
11	A	B	C	D	E
12	A	B	C	D	E
13	A	B	C	D	E
14	A	B	C	D	E
15	A	B	C	D	E
16	A	B	C	D	E
17	A	B	C	D	E
18	A	B	C	D	E

Pupil's Full Name:

Instructions:
Mark the boxes correctly like this

Please sign your name here:

Comprehension (pages 49–52)

Example 1

   A   B   C   D

Practice Question 1

   A   B   C   D

1   A B C D
2   A B C D
3   A B C D
4   A B C D
5   A B C D
6   A B C D
7   A B C D
8   A B C D
9   A B C D
10   A B C D

Shuffled Sentences (pages 53–55)

Example 1

   A   B   C   D   E

Practice Question 1

   A   B   C   D   E

1   A B C D E
2   A B C D E
3   A B C D E
4   A B C D E
5   A B C D E
6   A B C D E
7   A B C D E
8   A B C D E
9   A B C D E
10   A B C D E
11   A B C D E
12   A B C D E
13   A B C D E
14   A B C D E
15   A B C D E

Numeracy (pages 56–57)

Example 1   Practice Question 1   1

5 4

2   3   4

5   6   7

8   9   10

(Each numeracy answer grid contains two columns of digits 0–9.)

Continued over page

11 **12** **13**

0 0	0 0	0 0
1 1	1 1	1 1
2 2	2 2	2 2
3 3	3 3	3 3
4 4	4 4	4 4
5 5	5 5	5 5
6 6	6 6	6 6
7 7	7 7	7 7
8 8	8 8	8 8
9 9	9 9	9 9

14 **15**

0 0	0 0
1 1	1 1
2 2	2 2
3 3	3 3
4 4	4 4
5 5	5 5
6 6	6 6
7 7	7 7
8 8	8 8
9 9	9 9

Problem Solving (pages 58–59)

Example 1

A B ~~C~~ D E

Practice Question 1

A B C D E

1   A B C D E
2   A B C D E
3   A B C D E
4   A B C D E
5   A B C D E
6   A B C D E
7   A B C D E
8   A B C D E
9   A B C D E
10 A B C D E

Synonyms (pages 60–63)

Example 1

A ~~B~~ C D E

Practice Question 1

A B C D E

1   A B C D E
2   A B C D E
3   A B C D E
4   A B C D E
5   A B C D E

6   A B C D E
7   A B C D E
8   A B C D E
9   A B C D E
10 A B C D E
11 A B C D E
12 A B C D E
13 A B C D E
14 A B C D E
15 A B C D E
16 A B C D E
17 A B C D E
18 A B C D E
19 A B C D E
20 A B C D E
21 A B C D E
22 A B C D E
23 A B C D E
24 A B C D E

Non-Verbal Reasoning (pages 64–67)

REFLECTION Example 1

A B ~~C~~ D

REFLECTION Practice Question 1

A B C D

LEAST SIMILAR Example 2

A ~~B~~ C D E

LEAST SIMILAR Practice Question 2

A B C D E

1   A B C D
2   A B C D
3   A B C D
4   A B C D
5   A B C D
6   A B C D
7   A B C D E
8   A B C D E
9   A B C D E
10 A B C D E
11 A B C D E
12 A B C D E

Pupil's Full Name:

Instructions:
Mark the boxes correctly like this ▬

Please sign your name here:

Problem Solving (pages 69-71)

Example 1

Ⓐ Ⓑ ⊜ Ⓓ Ⓔ Ⓕ Ⓖ Ⓗ ⊞ ⊟

Practice Question 1

Ⓐ Ⓑ Ⓒ Ⓓ Ⓔ Ⓕ Ⓖ Ⓗ ⊞ ⊟

1 Ⓐ Ⓑ Ⓒ Ⓓ Ⓔ Ⓕ Ⓖ Ⓗ ⊞ ⊟
Ⓚ Ⓛ Ⓜ Ⓝ Ⓞ

2 Ⓐ Ⓑ Ⓒ Ⓓ Ⓔ Ⓕ Ⓖ Ⓗ ⊞ ⊟
Ⓚ Ⓛ Ⓜ Ⓝ Ⓞ

3 Ⓐ Ⓑ Ⓒ Ⓓ Ⓔ Ⓕ Ⓖ Ⓗ ⊞ ⊟
Ⓚ Ⓛ Ⓜ Ⓝ Ⓞ

4 Ⓐ Ⓑ Ⓒ Ⓓ Ⓔ Ⓕ Ⓖ Ⓗ ⊞ ⊟
Ⓚ Ⓛ Ⓜ Ⓝ Ⓞ

5 Ⓐ Ⓑ Ⓒ Ⓓ Ⓔ Ⓕ Ⓖ Ⓗ ⊞ ⊟
Ⓚ Ⓛ Ⓜ Ⓝ Ⓞ

6 Ⓐ Ⓑ Ⓒ Ⓓ Ⓔ Ⓕ Ⓖ Ⓗ ⊞ ⊟
Ⓚ Ⓛ Ⓜ Ⓝ Ⓞ

7 Ⓐ Ⓑ Ⓒ Ⓓ Ⓔ Ⓕ Ⓖ Ⓗ ⊞ ⊟
Ⓚ Ⓛ Ⓜ Ⓝ Ⓞ

8 Ⓐ Ⓑ Ⓒ Ⓓ Ⓔ Ⓕ Ⓖ Ⓗ ⊞ ⊟
Ⓚ Ⓛ Ⓜ Ⓝ Ⓞ

9 Ⓐ Ⓑ Ⓒ Ⓓ Ⓔ Ⓕ Ⓖ Ⓗ ⊞ ⊟
Ⓚ Ⓛ Ⓜ Ⓝ Ⓞ

10 Ⓐ Ⓑ Ⓒ Ⓓ Ⓔ Ⓕ Ⓖ Ⓗ ⊞ ⊟
Ⓚ Ⓛ Ⓜ Ⓝ Ⓞ

11 Ⓐ Ⓑ Ⓒ Ⓓ Ⓔ Ⓕ Ⓖ Ⓗ ⊞ ⊟
Ⓚ Ⓛ Ⓜ Ⓝ Ⓞ

12 Ⓐ Ⓑ Ⓒ Ⓓ Ⓔ Ⓕ Ⓖ Ⓗ ⊞ ⊟
Ⓚ Ⓛ Ⓜ Ⓝ Ⓞ

13 Ⓐ Ⓑ Ⓒ Ⓓ Ⓔ Ⓕ Ⓖ Ⓗ ⊞ ⊟
Ⓚ Ⓛ Ⓜ Ⓝ Ⓞ

14 Ⓐ Ⓑ Ⓒ Ⓓ Ⓔ Ⓕ Ⓖ Ⓗ ⊞ ⊟
Ⓚ Ⓛ Ⓜ Ⓝ Ⓞ

15 Ⓐ Ⓑ Ⓒ Ⓓ Ⓔ Ⓕ Ⓖ Ⓗ ⊞ ⊟
Ⓚ Ⓛ Ⓜ Ⓝ Ⓞ

Cloze (pages 72-74)

Example 1

▬ Ⓑ Ⓒ Ⓓ Ⓔ

Practice Question 1

Ⓐ Ⓑ Ⓒ Ⓓ Ⓔ

1 Ⓐ Ⓑ Ⓒ Ⓓ Ⓔ Ⓕ Ⓖ Ⓗ ⊞ ⊟

---

2 Ⓐ Ⓑ Ⓒ Ⓓ Ⓔ Ⓕ Ⓖ Ⓗ ⊞ ⊟
3 Ⓐ Ⓑ Ⓒ Ⓓ Ⓔ Ⓕ Ⓖ Ⓗ ⊞ ⊟
4 Ⓐ Ⓑ Ⓒ Ⓓ Ⓔ Ⓕ Ⓖ Ⓗ ⊞ ⊟
5 Ⓐ Ⓑ Ⓒ Ⓓ Ⓔ Ⓕ Ⓖ Ⓗ ⊞ ⊟
6 Ⓐ Ⓑ Ⓒ Ⓓ Ⓔ Ⓕ Ⓖ Ⓗ ⊞ ⊟
7 Ⓐ Ⓑ Ⓒ Ⓓ Ⓔ Ⓕ Ⓖ Ⓗ ⊞ ⊟
8 Ⓐ Ⓑ Ⓒ Ⓓ Ⓔ Ⓕ Ⓖ Ⓗ ⊞ ⊟
9 Ⓐ Ⓑ Ⓒ Ⓓ Ⓔ Ⓕ Ⓖ Ⓗ ⊞ ⊟
10 Ⓐ Ⓑ Ⓒ Ⓓ Ⓔ Ⓕ Ⓖ Ⓗ ⊞ ⊟
11 Ⓐ Ⓑ Ⓒ Ⓓ Ⓔ Ⓕ Ⓖ Ⓗ ⊞ ⊟
12 Ⓐ Ⓑ Ⓒ Ⓓ Ⓔ Ⓕ Ⓖ Ⓗ ⊞ ⊟
13 Ⓐ Ⓑ Ⓒ Ⓓ Ⓔ Ⓕ Ⓖ Ⓗ ⊞ ⊟
14 Ⓐ Ⓑ Ⓒ Ⓓ Ⓔ Ⓕ Ⓖ Ⓗ ⊞ ⊟
15 Ⓐ Ⓑ Ⓒ Ⓓ Ⓔ Ⓕ Ⓖ Ⓗ ⊞ ⊟
16 Ⓐ Ⓑ Ⓒ Ⓓ Ⓔ Ⓕ Ⓖ Ⓗ ⊞ ⊟
17 Ⓐ Ⓑ Ⓒ Ⓓ Ⓔ Ⓕ Ⓖ Ⓗ ⊞ ⊟
18 Ⓐ Ⓑ Ⓒ Ⓓ Ⓔ Ⓕ Ⓖ Ⓗ ⊞ ⊟
19 Ⓐ Ⓑ Ⓒ Ⓓ Ⓔ Ⓕ Ⓖ Ⓗ ⊞ ⊟
20 Ⓐ Ⓑ Ⓒ Ⓓ Ⓔ Ⓕ Ⓖ Ⓗ ⊞ ⊟

Non-Verbal Reasoning (pages 75-79)

SIMILARITY Example 1

Ⓐ Ⓑ Ⓒ ⊖ Ⓔ

SIMILARITY Practice Question 1

Ⓐ Ⓑ Ⓒ Ⓓ Ⓔ

CUBE NET Example 2

Ⓐ ⊟ Ⓒ Ⓓ

CUBE NET Practice Question 2

Ⓐ Ⓑ Ⓒ Ⓓ

CONNECTION Example 3

Ⓐ Ⓑ ⊜ Ⓓ

CONNECTION Practice Question 3

Ⓐ Ⓑ Ⓒ Ⓓ

1 Ⓐ Ⓑ Ⓒ Ⓓ Ⓔ
2 Ⓐ Ⓑ Ⓒ Ⓓ Ⓔ

Continued over page

3	A	B	C	D	E
4	A	B	C	D	E
5	A	B	C	D	E
6	A	B	C	D	
7	A	B	C	D	
8	A	B	C	D	
9	A	B	C	D	
10	A	B	C	D	
11	A	B	C	D	
12	A	B	C	D	
13	A	B	C	D	
14	A	B	C	D	
15	A	B	C	D	

Antonyms (pages 80-83)

Example 1

	A	B	C	D	E

Practice Question 1

	A	B	C	D	E
1	A	B	C	D	E
2	A	B	C	D	E
3	A	B	C	D	E
4	A	B	C	D	E
5	A	B	C	D	E
6	A	B	C	D	E
7	A	B	C	D	E
8	A	B	C	D	E
9	A	B	C	D	E
10	A	B	C	D	E
11	A	B	C	D	E
12	A	B	C	D	E
13	A	B	C	D	E
14	A	B	C	D	E
15	A	B	C	D	E
16	A	B	C	D	E
17	A	B	C	D	E
18	A	B	C	D	E

Numeracy (pages 84-86)

Example 1

5 4

Practice Question 1

Questions 1–18: numeric grid answer boxes, each with two columns of digits 0–9.

11+ Success for CEM

Practice Test Papers

4 test papers

- Comprehension
- Verbal Reasoning
- Maths
- Non-Verbal Reasoning

Get ahead

Audio

Faisal Nasim

Contents

Guidance notes for parents

What your child will need to sit these papers

- A quiet place to sit the exam
- A clearly visible clock
- A way to play the audio download
- A pencil and an eraser
- A piece of paper

Your child should not use a calculator for any of these papers.

How to invigilate the test papers

It is recommended that your child sits Test A (with a 15-minute break between Papers 1 and 2) and then sits Test B in the same way at a later date. Don't help your child or allow any talking. Review the answers with your child and help improve their weaker areas.

Step 1: Cut out the answers and keep them hidden from your child.

Step 2: Cut out the answer sheet section. Your child should write their full name on top of the first answer sheet. Give them the question paper booklet. They must not open the paper until they are told to do so by the audio instructions.

Step 3: Start the audio.

Step 4: Ask your child to work through the practice questions before the time starts for each section. An example is already marked on each section of the answer sheet. Your child should mark the answer sheet clearly and check that the practice questions are correctly marked.

Step 5: Mark the answer sheet. Then, together with your child, work through the questions that were answered incorrectly. When working through the Non-Verbal Reasoning sections, ensure you have the question papers open to help explain the answers to your child.

How your child should complete the answer sheet

Your child MUST NOT write their answers on the question paper; they must use the answer sheet. They should put a horizontal line through the boxes on the answer sheet. To change an answer, your child should fully erase the incorrect answer and then clearly select a new answer. Any rough workings should be done on a separate piece of paper.

The audio instructions

Both papers have audio instructions in order to prepare your child to listen and act upon them. Audio instructions are at the start, during and at the end of the sections. Audio warnings on the time remaining will be given at varying intervals. Your child should listen out for these warnings.

The symbols at the foot of the page

Written instructions are at the foot of the page. Your child MUST follow these instructions:

Continue working

Stop and wait for instructions

Your child can review questions within the allocated time, but must not move on to the next section until they are allowed to do so.

The instructions and examples at the beginning of the section

In the instructions, your child should look for: the time allowed; how many questions there are; and how to complete the answers.

Examples are at the beginning of every section to show the type of question included in a particular section. The example questions will be worked through as part of the audio instructions.

How to work out your child's overall score for each Test

Each question is worth one mark. For the purpose of marking, each test is split into two subject areas:

1) Maths (which includes Numeracy and Problem Solving) & Non-Verbal Reasoning

2) English (which includes the remaining sections).

For each test follow these steps to calculate your child's overall score:

1) Add up your child's scores for each of the two subject areas in both papers and note them in the blue boxes on the next page.

   For example, Test A Paper 1: 33 for English and 28 for Maths & Non-Verbal Reasoning and in Test A Paper 2: 29 for English and 30 for Maths & Non-Verbal Reasoning.

2) Add together both your child's total scores in English and then add together both your child's total scores in Maths & Non-Verbal Reasoning. Fill in each total in the blue boxes on the next page.

   For example: For English $33 + 29 = 62$ and for Maths & Non-Verbal Reasoning $28 + 30 = 58$.

3) Take your child's total English score and divide it by the maximum total English score (as shown in the table on the next page) and then multiply that figure by 100 to give you a percentage. Repeat this process for Maths & Non-Verbal reasoning.

   For example: English: $62 \div 92 \times 100 = 67\%$

   Maths & Non-Verbal Reasoning: $58 \div 79 \times 100 = 73\%$

4) Now add both percentages together and divide by 2 to give you your child's overall score for one test.

   For example $67 + 73 = 140 \div 2 = 70\%$

5) Repeat the steps above to calculate your child's overall score for Test B.

Test A	Subject	Your child's score	Maximum score
Test A Paper 1	English		49
Test A Paper 1	Maths & Non-Verbal Reasoning		36
Test A Paper 2	English		43
Test A Paper 2	Maths & Non-Verbal Reasoning		43
		Your child's total English score	Maximum total English score
			92
		Your child's total Maths & Non-Verbal Reasoning score	Maximum total Maths & Non-Verbal Reasoning score
			79

Your child's English percentage score	Your child's Maths & Non-Verbal Reasoning percentage score	Your child's overall score

Test B	Subject	Your child's score	Maximum score
Test B Paper 1	English		49
Test B Paper 1	Maths & Non-Verbal Reasoning		37
Test B Paper 2	English		38
Test B Paper 2	Maths & Non-Verbal Reasoning		48
		Your child's total English score	Maximum total English score
			87
		Your child's total Maths & Non-Verbal Reasoning score	Maximum total Maths & Non-Verbal Reasoning score
			85

Your child's English percentage score	Your child's Maths & Non-Verbal Reasoning percentage score	Your child's overall score

Please note: Your child should be aiming for an overall score of at least 70-75% in each Test. If your child does not score a good mark, focus on the areas where your child did not perform well and continue practising under timed conditions.

Once your child feels confident with these papers, move on to the Letts 11+ *Get test-ready practice test papers.*

Get Ahead
Test A Paper 1

Instructions

1. Ensure you have pencils and an eraser with you.

2. Make sure you are able to see a clock or watch.

3. Write your name on the answer sheet.

4. Do not open the question booklet until you are told to do so by the audio instructions.

5. Listen carefully to the audio instructions given.

6. Mark your answers on the answer sheet only.

7. All workings must be completed on a separate piece of paper.

8. You should not use a calculator, dictionary or thesaurus at any point in this paper.

9. Move through the papers as quickly as possible and with care.

10. Follow the instructions at the foot of each page.

11. You should mark your answers with a horizontal line, as shown on the answer sheet.

12. If you want to change your answer, ensure that you rub out your first answer and that your second answer is clearly more visible.

13. You can go back and review any questions that are within the section you are working on only. You must await further instructions before moving on to another section.

Symbols and Phrases used in the Tests

 Instructions    Time allowed for this section   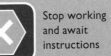 Stop working and await instructions   Continue working

Comprehension

 YOU HAVE 9 MINUTES TO COMPLETE THE FOLLOWING SECTION.

YOU HAVE 10 QUESTIONS TO COMPLETE WITHIN THE TIME GIVEN.

EXAMPLES

Comprehension Example

South Africa is becoming an increasingly popular holiday destination. People from all over the world are being attracted by its natural beauty, cosmopolitan cities and diverse wildlife. Cape Town, the capital of South Africa, is especially popular. The city is dynamic and exciting and has a rich history and culture. It is also home to the stunning Table Mountain, which you can ascend on foot or by cable car.

Example 1

Which of the following is not mentioned as a reason why people are attracted to South Africa?

A   Natural beauty
B   Excellent food
C   Cosmopolitan cities
D   Diverse wildlife

The correct answer is B. This has already been marked in Example 1 in the Comprehension section of your answer sheet.

Practice Question 1

What is the name of the mountain in Cape Town?

A   Cape Mountain
B   Africa Mountain
C   Table Mountain
D   Leopard Mountain

The correct answer is C. Please mark this in Practice Question 1 in the Comprehension section of your answer sheet.

STOP AND WAIT FOR FURTHER INSTRUCTIONS ⊗

Read the passage below and then answer the questions that follow.

An extract from: **Loki's Wolves**

by Kelley Armstrong & Melissa Marr

Matt walked through the centre of Blackwell, gym bag in hand, jacket thrown over his shoulder. It was dark now, with an icy wind from the north, but the cold felt good blowing back his sweat-soaked hair. After two hours of boxing practice, he'd been tempted to take a detour and jump in the Norrström River, even if he had noticed ice on it that morning. Ice in September. Weird. Even in South Dakota, winter never came this early.

A muscle spasmed in his leg, and he winced as he stopped to rub it. The upcoming tournament might be for charity – raising money to help tsunami victims in Hawaii – but Coach Forde still made Matt work as hard as he would before a title match.

Matt started walking again, limping slightly. As much as he wished he could call for a ride, he knew better. He'd made that mistake last winter, when Coach had said a blizzard was coming. He'd gotten his ride – and a lecture on how his brothers had never needed one, even when it was storming. He couldn't catch a lift with his friends, either – that was worse because it set a bad example. If Sheriff Thorsen's boys weren't safe walking through Blackwell at night, who was?

Matt was reaching down to rub his leg again when something moved in the town square. His head shot up, eyes narrowing. Outside the rec centre, two kids climbed onto the weathered Viking longship. Shields lined both sides as if invisible warriors rowed the old wooden boat, protection always within reach. A carved dragon arched from the hull.

The kids were probably setting up a prank, trying to beat the one Matt had done with his friend Cody at Sigrblot, the spring festival. The parade had arrived at the longship to find it covered in a tarp... and making honking noises. Underneath the tarp, they'd discovered a flock of geese wearing little Viking helmets.

Best prank ever, that's what everyone said. Unfortunately, Matt had to pretend he didn't have anything to do with it. If his parents had found out... well, they wouldn't ground him or anything. He'd just get 'the talk'. How disappointed they were. How embarrassed they were. How much more responsible his brothers were. Personally, he'd rather be grounded.

In a few more steps, he saw that one of the kids was a guy with shaggy brown hair that needed cutting and clothes that needed washing. With him was a girl. Her clothes weren't in such rough shape, but her blonde hair needed a trim just as badly.

Fen and Laurie Brekke. Great. The cousins were always getting into trouble. Still, Matt told himself they really might just be pulling a prank... until he saw Fen wrench at one of the shields.

There were a lot of things Fen could do and Matt would just look away, tell himself it was none of his business. That wasn't always easy. Being the sheriff's kid meant he'd had lectures about vandalism since he was old enough to carve his name into a park bench. But this wasn't a park bench. It was an actual longship – something the people in Blackwell were really proud of. And there was Fen, yanking on it and kicking at it.

CONTINUE WORKING

As Matt's temper flared, his amulet flared with it. He reached for the silver pendant. It was in the shape of an upside-down hammer and almost as old as the longship. Thor's Hammer. Everyone in Matt's family had one. Thorsen wasn't just their name. They really were descendants of the Norse god.

As Matt looked at Fen and Laurie again, his amulet burned hotter. He was about to yell at them, then he stopped and took deep breaths, sucking in cold air.

He could hear his mother's voice. You need to learn to control it, Matty. I don't know why you have so much trouble with that. No other Thorsen has this problem. Your brothers could handle theirs even when they were younger than you.

Controlling his temper – and Thor's Hammer – seemed especially hard around the Brekkes. It was like the Hammer knew they were related to the trickster god Loki. The cousins didn't know that, but Matt did, and he could feel it when he looked at them.

Matt took another deep breath. Yes, he needed to stop Fen and Laurie, but he had to be cool about it. Maybe he could just walk past, pretend he didn't notice them, and they'd see him and take off before they were caught.

Fen spotted him. Matt continued walking, giving them a chance to sneak off. Being fair. His dad would be proud –

Fen turned back to the longship and yanked on the shield again.

(1) What had Matt been doing before the passage begins?

A   He had been doing his homework
B   He had been attending boxing practice
C   He had been working in the town centre
D   He had been visiting a friend

(2) What was unusual about the Norrström River?

A   It was covered in ice in September
B   It was unusually warm for this time of year
C   The river was flowing faster than usual
D   It was full of sharp rocks and objects

(3) Why did Matt not call for a ride?

A   He could not afford it
B   His phone's battery was dead
C   He preferred to walk
D   His parents would disapprove

CONTINUE WORKING ⟹

④ Which word best describes the Viking longship?

A   Worn
B   Hideous
C   Glistening
D   Modern

⑤ In which month might 'Sigrblot' have taken place?

A   December
B   August
C   March
D   October

⑥ What did everyone in Matt's family have?

A   A necklace
B   A potion
C   A wooden weapon
D   A sense of humour

⑦ Which of the following statements are true?

Statement 1: Fen and Laurie were cousins.
Statement 2: Matt was descended from a
            Norse god.
Statement 3: Matt struggled to control his
            temper.
Statement 4: The Brekkes were
            renovating the longship.

A   Options 1 and 3 only
B   Options 2 and 4 only
C   Options 1, 2 and 3 only
D   All of the above

⑧ What does the word 'pretend' mean?

A   Prevent
B   Blow
C   Feign
D   Depart

⑨ Which word is an antonym of 'yanking'?

A   Burning
B   Pulling
C   Yelling
D   Shoving

⑩ What type of word is 'unfortunately'?

A   Noun
B   Adjective
C   Adverb
D   Verb

STOP AND WAIT FOR FURTHER INSTRUCTIONS ⊗

Shuffled Sentences

 INSTRUCTIONS

 YOU HAVE 8 MINUTES TO COMPLETE THE FOLLOWING SECTION.

YOU HAVE 15 QUESTIONS TO COMPLETE WITHIN THE TIME GIVEN.

EXAMPLES

Example 1

The following sentence is shuffled and also contains one unnecessary word. Rearrange the sentence correctly in order to identify the unnecessary word.

wake under before must sunrise up we.

A	B	C	D	E
up	before	under	wake	sunrise

The correct answer is C. This has already been marked in Example 1 in the Shuffled Sentences section of your answer sheet.

Practice Question 1

The following sentence is shuffled and also contains one unnecessary word. Rearrange the sentence correctly in order to identify the unnecessary word.

very girl quickly the ran throw.

A	B	C	D	E
quickly	girl	the	ran	throw

The correct answer is E. Please mark this in Practice Question 1 in the Shuffled Sentences section of your answer sheet.

STOP AND WAIT FOR FURTHER INSTRUCTIONS

Each sentence below is shuffled and also contains one unnecessary word.
Rearrange each sentence correctly in order to identify the unnecessary word.

(1) burning fireman the building equal into the dashed.

A	B	C	D	E
fireman	building	into	dashed	equal

(2) loved summer the to read fiction boy historical.

A	B	C	D	E
summer	fiction	read	boy	to

(3) legs giraffes and have tongue long necks.

A	B	C	D	E
necks	have	giraffes	tongue	legs

(4) many space the trained for astronaut years determined.

A	B	C	D	E
many	space	trained	astronaut	years

(5) many shocked observers hers were his by behaviour.

A	B	C	D	E
shocked	behaviour	his	hers	were

(6) fell throughout the day rain light falling.

A	B	C	D	E
falling	the	rain	fell	day

(7) the are rare temperatures Arctic in common freezing.

A	B	C	D	E
in	are	Arctic	freezing	rare

CONTINUE WORKING ⇨

8 the to returning dreaded to accountant work.

A	B	C	D	E
work	dreaded	the	to	accountant

9 healthy vital of exercise lifestyle a a is part two.

A	B	C	D	E
two	exercise	vital	part	lifestyle

10 he to pretended her passed understand question.

A	B	C	D	E
to	pretended	understand	passed	question

11 lawyer arguments skilful attempt the summarised the.

A	B	C	D	E
the	lawyer	summarised	skilful	attempt

12 girl three spoke young the different languages talk.

A	B	C	D	E
girl	talk	languages	different	spoke

13 be sentence the the criminal to decided judge with lenient.

A	B	C	D	E
sentence	decided	judge	with	lenient

14 and desert unusual plants of animals heating the full is.

A	B	C	D	E
full	desert	is	heating	plants

15 must toothpaste at to teeth your brush night you not forget.

A	B	C	D	E
toothpaste	at	brush	teeth	forget

STOP AND WAIT FOR FURTHER INSTRUCTIONS ⊗

Numeracy

 YOU HAVE 6 MINUTES TO COMPLETE THE FOLLOWING SECTION.

YOU HAVE 13 QUESTIONS TO COMPLETE WITHIN THE TIME GIVEN.

EXAMPLES

The questions within this section are not multiple choice. Write the answer to each question on the answer sheet by selecting the correct digits from the columns provided.

Example 1

Calculate the answer to the following:

12 + 42

The correct answer is 54. This has already been marked in Example 1 in the Numeracy section of your answer sheet.

Practice Question 1

Calculate the answer to the following:

55 – 47

The correct answer is 8. Please mark this in Practice Question 1 in the Numeracy section of your answer sheet. Note that a single-digit answer should be marked with a 0 in the left-hand column, so mark 08 on your answer sheet.

STOP AND WAIT FOR FURTHER INSTRUCTIONS

(1) Calculate the answer to the following:

123 + 456

CONTINUE WORKING

(2) Calculate the answer to the following:

$477 \div 3$

(3) Calculate the answer to the following:

$32 + 64 + 19 - 12$

(4) Which number should replace the '?' in the following sequence?

74, 71, 66, 63, ?, 55

(5) Calculate the mean of the following numbers:

14, 12, 5, 6, 18

(6) How many hours are there in 3 whole days?

(7) What is the value of Y in this equation?

$11 + 2Y = 44 - 13$

(8) David watches television from 8:30 a.m. until 11:15 a.m.

For how many minutes does David watch television?

(9) How many more factors does the number 48 have than the number 10?

(10) A van can hold 40 boxes. Each box can hold 24 bananas.

How many bananas can the van hold?

(11) How many squares with a side length of 4 cm can fit on a rectangular board that measures 8 cm by 12 cm?

(12) $\frac{1}{3}$ of X is 32.

What is $\frac{1}{2}$ of X?

(13) There were 30 birds in a tree on Tuesday. On Wednesday, the number of birds in the tree increased by 30%. How many birds were in the tree on Wednesday?

STOP AND WAIT FOR FURTHER INSTRUCTIONS ⊗

Problem Solving

INSTRUCTIONS

 YOU HAVE 8 MINUTES TO COMPLETE THE FOLLOWING SECTION.

YOU HAVE 10 QUESTIONS TO COMPLETE WITHIN THE TIME GIVEN.

EXAMPLES

Example 1

Calculate the answer to the following:

Tom buys a chocolate bar for £1·50. He pays with a £5 note.
How much change does he receive?

A £1·50	**B** £3	**C** £3·50
D £4	**E** £5	

The correct answer is C. This has already been marked in Example 1 in the Problem Solving section of your answer sheet.

Practice Question 1

Sarah eats $\frac{1}{4}$ of a pizza.

What fraction of the pizza remains?

A $\frac{1}{2}$	**B** $\frac{1}{3}$	**C** $\frac{2}{5}$
D $\frac{3}{4}$	**E** $\frac{5}{6}$	

The correct answer is D. Please mark this in Practice Question 1 in the Problem Solving section of your answer sheet.

STOP AND WAIT FOR FURTHER INSTRUCTIONS ⊗

Calculate the answers to the following.

(1) Zac and his friends watch a film. The film is 1 hour 35 minutes long.
If they start watching the film at 7:50 p.m., what will the time be when the film ends?

A 7:35 p.m.   **B** 9:25 p.m.   **C** 8:50 p.m.
D 7:50 a.m.   **E** 9:15 p.m.

(2) What is this shape called?

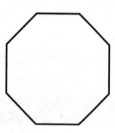

A decagon   **B** pentagon   **C** octagon
D hexagon   **E** quadrilateral

(3) What is 20^2?

A 20   **B** 40   **C** 400
D 800   **E** 80

(4) Ella orders a pizza and eats $\frac{1}{3}$ of it. She then gives $\frac{1}{2}$ of the remainder to her brother.
What fraction of the pizza does Ella give to her brother?

A $\frac{1}{2}$ **B** $\frac{1}{3}$ **C** $\frac{1}{4}$

D $\frac{2}{3}$ **E** $\frac{5}{6}$

(5) Ben, Harry and Mia win a lottery prize of £30,000. They share it in the ratio 3:1:2.
How much money does Mia receive?

A £1,000   **B** £5,000   **C** £10,000
D £20,000   **E** £30,000

(6) A white triangle has a base of 18 cm and a height of 10 cm. Lora shades $\frac{1}{3}$ of the triangle
black. What area of the triangle is now shaded black?

A 180 cm²   **B** 30 cm²   **C** 10 cm²
D 60 cm²   **E** 90 cm²

CONTINUE WORKING ⇨

(7) 1 out of every 8 attendees at a conference has ginger hair.
3 out of every 4 attendees at the conference have black hair.
What fraction of the conference attendees has neither ginger nor black hair?

A $\frac{1}{8}$ **B** $\frac{1}{4}$ **C** $\frac{3}{8}$

D $\frac{1}{2}$ **E** $\frac{5}{8}$

(8) The coordinates of 3 vertices of a square are (−1, 4), (3, 4) and (3, 0).
What are the coordinates of the 4th vertex of the square?

A (3, −4) **B** (−1, 0) **C** (−3, 4)
D (−1, −1) **E** (0, 3)

(9) In his pocket, Fred has £1·20 made up of an equal number of five-pence and one-pence coins.
How many five-pence coins does Fred have in his pocket?

A 1 **B** 24 **C** 20
D 30 **E** 15

(10) 20 people attend a party and eat 50 muffins there.
What is the mean number of muffins eaten per person at the party?

A $\frac{2}{5}$ **B** $\frac{1}{2}$ **C** 5

D $\frac{1}{5}$ **E** $2\frac{1}{2}$

STOP AND WAIT FOR FURTHER INSTRUCTIONS ⊗

Synonyms

 INSTRUCTIONS

 YOU HAVE 7 MINUTES TO COMPLETE THE FOLLOWING SECTION.

YOU HAVE 24 QUESTIONS TO COMPLETE WITHIN THE TIME GIVEN.

EXAMPLES

Example 1

Select the word that is most similar in meaning to the following word:

push

A	B	C	D	E
shallow	shove	tug	hollow	cry

The correct answer is B. This has already been marked in Example 1 in the Synonyms section of your answer sheet.

Practice Question 1

Select the word that is most similar in meaning to the following word:

imitate

A	B	C	D	E
cover	copy	grow	live	irritate

The correct answer is B. Please mark this in Practice Question 1 in the Synonyms section of your answer sheet.

STOP AND WAIT FOR FURTHER INSTRUCTIONS

For each row, select the word from the table that is most similar in meaning to the word above the table.

(1) admit

A	B	C	D	E
assure	harbour	confess	perceive	attempt

(2) obvious

A	B	C	D	E
soldier	apparent	frustrated	sold	hidden

(3) seem

A	B	C	D	E
hold	seam	know	shoulder	appear

(4) assure

A	B	C	D	E
sure	beneath	guarantee	deceive	frozen

(5) delicate

A	B	C	D	E
destroy	flower	fascinated	pattern	fragile

(6) conflict

A	B	C	D	E
contain	country	address	conserve	clash

(7) cope

A	B	C	D	E
cape	strengthen	manage	collapse	support

(8) opposite

A	B	C	D	E
less	equal	oppose	haven	contrary

CONTINUE WORKING ⏩

(9) act

A	B	C	D	E
play	fly	sing	behave	theatre

(10) class

A	B	C	D	E
classify	perform	lesson	case	gender

(11) attractive

A	B	C	D	E
attract	repel	assert	potential	appealing

(12) restrict

A	B	C	D	E
confine	appeal	free	liberate	tight

(13) discount

A	B	C	D	E
sum	allow	reduction	addition	count

(14) vanish

A	B	C	D	E
varnish	project	disappear	pollute	grow

(15) eager

A	B	C	D	E
sick	beaver	hover	keen	reluctant

(16) disclose

A	B	C	D	E
dismiss	perceive	closed	hunt	reveal

CONTINUE WORKING ⇨

17 exactly

A	B	C	D	E
measured	frostily	easily	calm	precisely

18 dubious

A	B	C	D	E
double	sure	design	certain	doubtful

19 fortunate

A	B	C	D	E
forgetful	notorious	lucky	wretched	fortune

20 overlook

A	B	C	D	E
sea	underneath	horizon	offer	miss

21 honest

A	B	C	D	E
truth	coward	sincere	crafty	statement

22 compliment

A	B	C	D	E
complement	attack	cover	signal	praise

23 mad

A	B	C	D	E
driven	disastrous	insane	damaged	dog

24 transparent

A	B	C	D	E
obvious	difficult	target	glass	opaque

STOP AND WAIT FOR FURTHER INSTRUCTIONS ⬡✖

Non-Verbal Reasoning

 INSTRUCTIONS

 YOU HAVE 7 MINUTES TO COMPLETE THE FOLLOWING SECTION.

YOU HAVE 13 QUESTIONS TO COMPLETE WITHIN THE TIME GIVEN.

EXAMPLES

COMPLETE THE SQUARE Example 1

Which figure on the right should replace the blank square in the pattern?

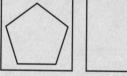
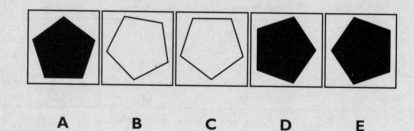

The correct answer is D. This has already been marked in Example 1 in the Non-Verbal Reasoning section of your answer sheet.

COMPLETE THE SQUARE Practice Question 1

Which figure on the right should replace the blank square in the pattern?

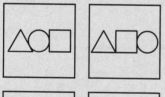

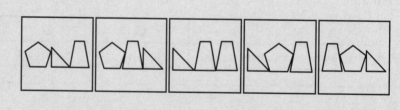

The correct answer is A. Please mark this in Practice Question 1 in the Non-Verbal Reasoning section of your answer sheet.

CONTINUE WORKING

REFLECTION Example 2

Select how the following shape or pattern would appear when reflected in the dashed line.

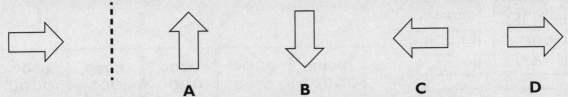

The correct answer is C. This has already been marked in Example 2 in the Non-Verbal Reasoning section of your answer sheet.

REFLECTION Practice Question 2

Select how the following shape or pattern would appear when reflected in the dashed line.

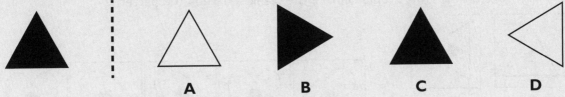

The correct answer is C. Please mark this in Practice Question 2 in the Non-Verbal Reasoning section of your answer sheet.

DIMENSION Example 3

Select how the following 3D figure would appear in a top-down, plan view.

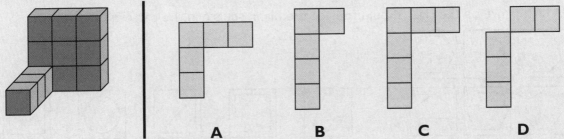

The correct answer is C. This has already been marked in Example 3 in the Non-Verbal Reasoning section of your answer sheet.

DIMENSION Practice Question 3

Select how the following 3D figure would appear in a top-down, plan view.

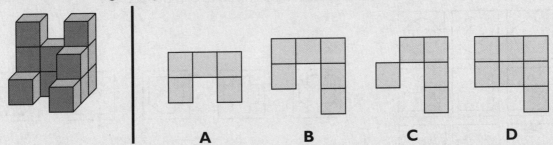

The correct answer is B. Please mark this in Practice Question 3 in the Non-Verbal Reasoning section of your answer sheet.

STOP AND WAIT FOR FURTHER INSTRUCTIONS

1 Which figure on the right should replace the blank square in the pattern?

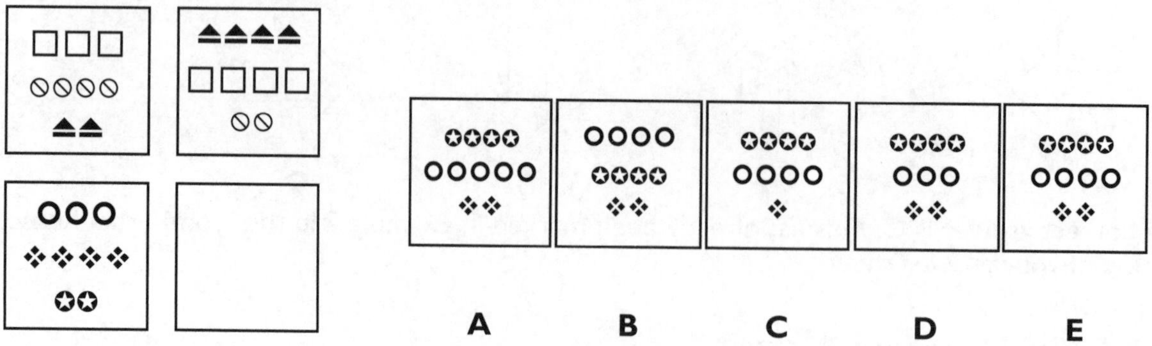

2 Which figure on the right should replace the blank square in the pattern?

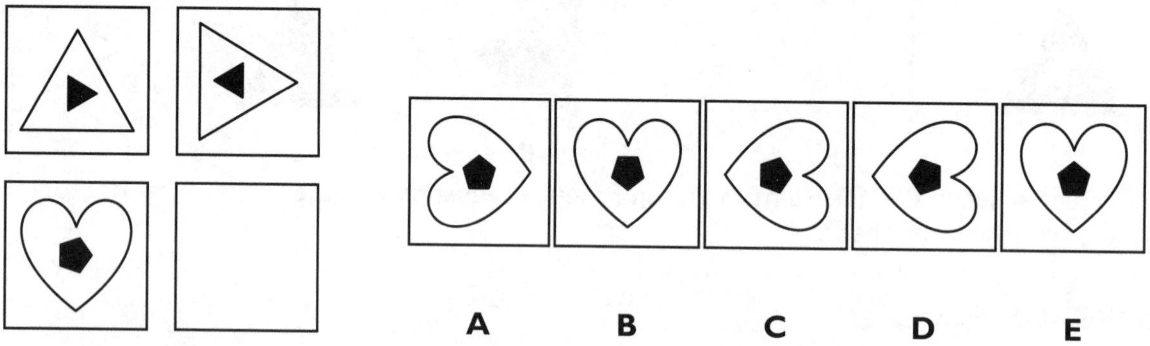

3 Which figure on the right should replace the blank square in the pattern?

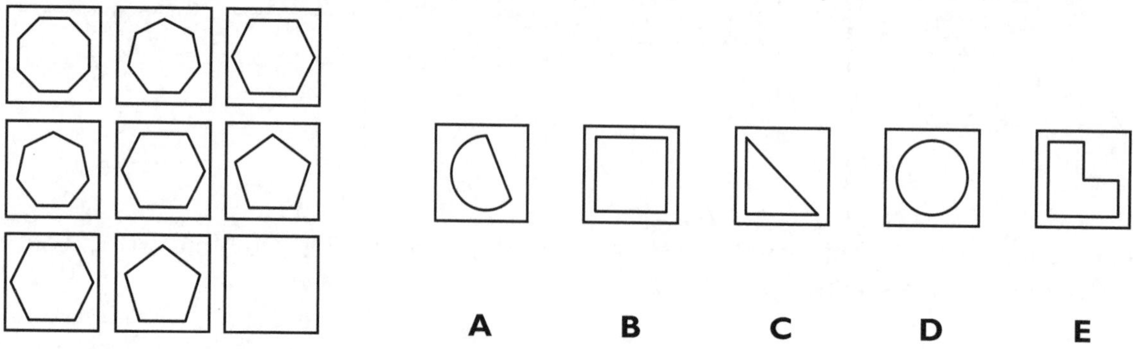

4 Which figure on the right should replace the blank square in the pattern?

A   B   C   D   E

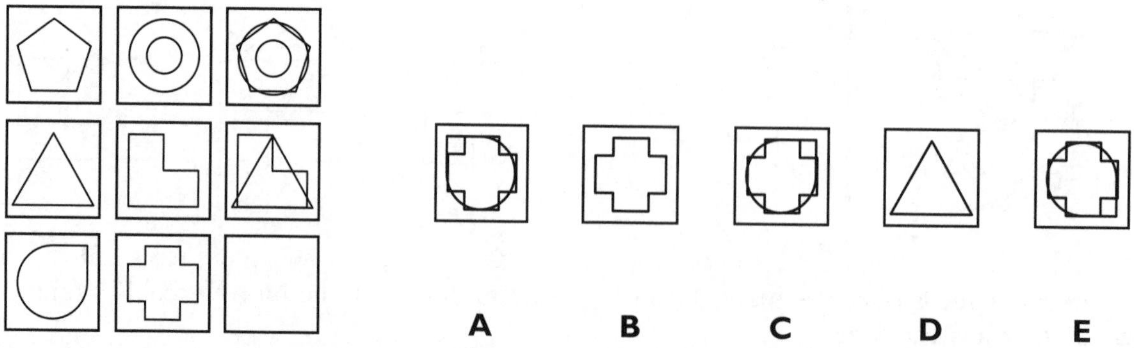

CONTINUE WORKING

5 Select how the following shape or pattern would appear when reflected in the dashed line.

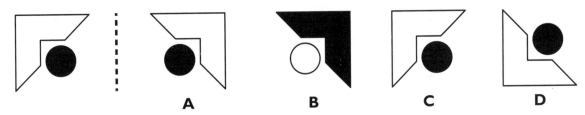

A   **B**   **C**   **D**

6 Select how the following shape or pattern would appear when reflected in the dashed line.

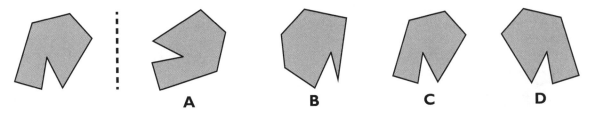

A   **B**   **C**   **D**

7 Select how the following shape or pattern would appear when reflected in the dashed line.

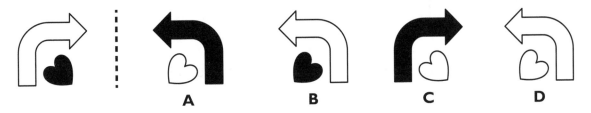

A   **B**   **C**   **D**

8 Select how the following shape or pattern would appear when reflected in the dashed line.

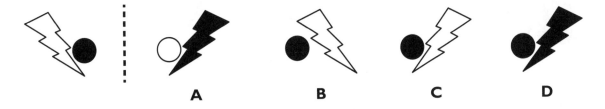

A   **B**   **C**   **D**

9 Select how the following 3D figure would appear in a top-down, plan view.

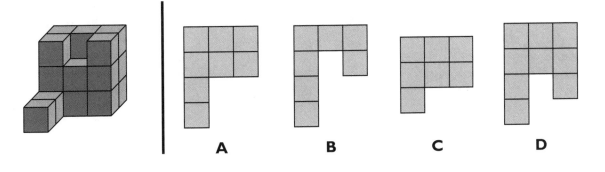

A   **B**   **C**   **D**

CONTINUE WORKING ⇨

(10) Select how the following 3D figure would appear in a top-down, plan view.

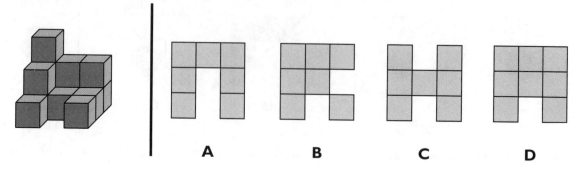

A   B   C   D

(11) Select how the following 3D figure would appear in a top-down, plan view.

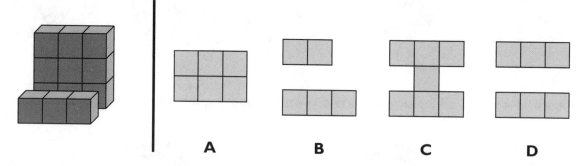

A   B   C   D

(12) Select how the following 3D figure would appear in a top-down, plan view.

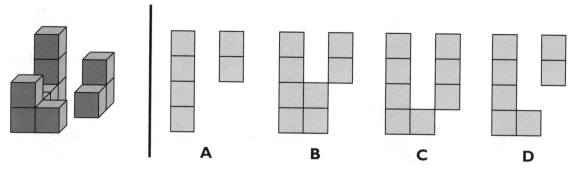

A   B   C   D

(13) Select how the following 3D figure would appear in a top-down, plan view.

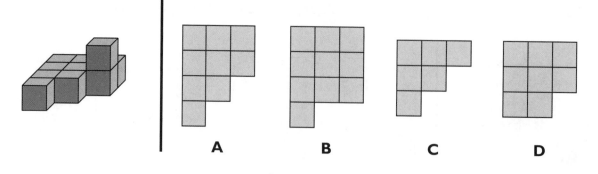

A   B   C   D

END OF PAPER

Get Ahead
Test A Paper 2

Instructions

1. Ensure you have pencils and an eraser with you.

2. Make sure you are able to see a clock or watch.

3. Write your name on the answer sheet.

4. Do not open the question booklet until you are told to do so by the audio instructions.

5. Listen carefully to the audio instructions given.

6. Mark your answers on the answer sheet only.

7. All workings must be completed on a separate piece of paper.

8. You should not use a calculator, dictionary or thesaurus at any point in this paper.

9. Move through the papers as quickly as possible and with care.

10. Follow the instructions at the foot of each page.

11. You should mark your answers with a horizontal line, as shown on the answer sheet.

12. If you want to change your answer, ensure that you rub out your first answer and that your second answer is clearly more visible.

13. You can go back and review any questions that are within the section you are working on only. You must await further instructions before moving on to another section.

Symbols and Phrases used in the Tests

 Instructions

 Time allowed for this section

 Stop working and await instructions

 Continue working

Problem Solving

 INSTRUCTIONS

 YOU HAVE 8 MINUTES TO COMPLETE THE FOLLOWING SECTION.

YOU HAVE 10 QUESTIONS TO COMPLETE WITHIN THE TIME GIVEN.

EXAMPLES

A $\dfrac{1}{2}$	B £3	C £3·50	D $\dfrac{3}{4}$	E $\dfrac{1}{3}$
F £1·50	G £5	H $\dfrac{2}{5}$	I £4	J $\dfrac{5}{6}$

Example 1

Select an answer to the question from the 10 different possible answers in the table above.

Tom buys a chocolate bar for £1·50. He pays with a £5 note.
How much change does he receive?

The correct answer is C. This has already been marked in Example 1 in the Problem Solving section of your answer sheet.

Practice Question 1

Sarah eats $\dfrac{1}{4}$ of a pizza.

What fraction of the pizza remains?

The correct answer is D. Please mark this in Practice Question 1 in the Problem Solving section of your answer sheet.

STOP AND WAIT FOR FURTHER INSTRUCTIONS

A $\frac{1}{26}$	**B** 22:37	**C** $\frac{1}{10}$	**D** £660	**E** 25%
F 18:45	**G** 1·75 litres	**H** £37·50	**I** 3·46 litres	**J** 50%

Several questions will follow for you to answer. Select an answer to each question from the 10 different possible answers in the table above. You may use an answer for more than one question.

The Smith family consists of two adults and two children. The two adults are called John and Sarah. The two children are called Amy and James. They live in London.

1. Last year, the Smiths went on holiday to Spain. The cost of an adult return flight ticket was £220 and the cost of a child return flight ticket was half as much as an adult one.

   How much did the Smith family spend on flights?

2. The flight lasted for 3 hours. Amy spent 90 minutes of the flight watching films.

   For what percentage of the flight did Amy watch films?

3. The time at their holiday destination was 2 hours ahead of the time in London.

   If the plane took off at 13:45 London time, what was the time at their holiday destination when it landed?

4. Whilst on holiday, James drank 250 ml of orange juice every morning.

   How much orange juice did James drink in 1 week?

5. John bought a new pair of sandals that were on sale for £30. This represented a 20% discount from their original price.

   What was the original price of the sandals?

6. Sarah brought £450 in cash to spend on the holiday. After the first day, £405 remained.

   What fraction of the cash did Sarah spend on the first day?

7. On the second day, Amy woke up at 07:17 and went to bed 15 hours and 20 minutes later.

   At what time did Amy go to bed on the second day?

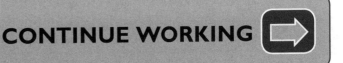

CONTINUE WORKING

(8) 9 out of every 16 guests at their hotel were from France and 3 out of every 16 guests were from Germany.

What percentage of guests at their hotel were from neither France nor Germany?

(9) 1% of the water in the hotel pool evaporated every hour.

If there were 346 litres of water in the pool, how many litres would evaporate after 1 hour?

(10) The Smith family's holiday lasted 2 weeks.

For what fraction of a year were they on holiday?

STOP AND WAIT FOR FURTHER INSTRUCTIONS ⊗

Cloze

 YOU HAVE 10 MINUTES TO COMPLETE THE FOLLOWING SECTION.

YOU HAVE 20 QUESTIONS TO COMPLETE WITHIN THE TIME GIVEN.

EXAMPLES

Example 1

Read the sentence below and select the most appropriate word from the table.

A	B	C	D	E
defeated	heaved	master	flow	politely

The skilful chess player easily (Q1) _____ his opponent.

Please select your answer to go in the place of (Q1) in the above sentence.

The correct answer is A. This has already been marked in Example 1 in the Cloze section of your answer sheet.

Practice Question 1

Read the sentence below and select the most appropriate word from the table.

A	B	C	D	E
crunching	eating	dreading	reading	shining

The sun was (Q2) _____ and there was not a single cloud in the sky.

Please select your answer to go in the place of (Q2) in the above sentence.

The correct answer is E. Please mark the answer E in Practice Question 1 in the Cloze section of your answer sheet.

STOP AND WAIT FOR FURTHER INSTRUCTIONS

Read the passage and select the most appropriate word from the table below by choosing the letter above the word. There are 10 questions. For example, Q1 is where you should put your answer to Question 1 on your answer sheet.

A	B	C	D	E
role	effectively	extremely	aid	responsible

F	G	H	I	J
creatures	types	related	consumed	collect

Bees

Bees are flying insects that are closely (Q1) _____ to wasps and ants. Bees are known for their (Q2) _____ in pollination and are some of the hardest working (Q3) _____ on the planet. Worldwide, bees are (Q4) _____ for pollinating about one sixth of plant species and approximately 400 different types of agricultural plant. If bees did not exist, it would be (Q5) _____ difficult for humans to survive on earth.

There are around 25,000 different (Q6) _____ of bee species and they have all evolved to become very efficient pollinators. For example, all bees have stiff hairs and pockets on their legs, allowing them to (Q7) _____ as much pollen as possible and transport it (Q8) _____ to other plants. Not only do bees (Q9) _____ in the production of various crops, they also produce honey, a sweet delicacy that is (Q10) _____ all over the world.

CONTINUE WORKING ⟹

Read the passage and select the most appropriate word from the table below by choosing the letter above the word. There are 10 questions. For example, Q11 is where you should put your answer to Question 11 on your answer sheet.

A	B	C	D	E
overwhelming	creating	expanding	slowly	consider

F	G	H	I	J
harder	communicate	offers	satisfying	owners

Business

Launching and running a successful business is a lot (Q11) ＿＿＿＿＿＿＿＿ than it seems. There are so many things that one needs to (Q12) ＿＿＿＿＿＿＿＿ before even getting started. These include coming up with an idea, (Q13) ＿＿＿＿＿＿＿＿ a business plan, saving some money to get started and working out how to advertise so people can learn about the business and the services that it (Q14) ＿＿＿＿＿＿＿＿. The process can quickly become (Q15) ＿＿＿＿＿＿＿＿!

For this reason, it's good to start (Q16) ＿＿＿＿＿＿＿＿ and locally. In this way, one has the time to (Q17) ＿＿＿＿＿＿＿＿ directly with customers and gain valuable feedback. All aspects of the business can thus be gradually improved before (Q18) ＿＿＿＿＿＿＿＿ and taking on increased responsibility. Though many business (Q19) ＿＿＿＿＿＿＿＿ find their work to be challenging, they also find it to be extremely rewarding and (Q20) ＿＿＿＿＿＿＿＿.

STOP AND WAIT FOR FURTHER INSTRUCTIONS ⊗

Non-Verbal Reasoning

 YOU HAVE 8 MINUTES TO COMPLETE THE FOLLOWING SECTION.

YOU HAVE 15 QUESTIONS TO COMPLETE WITHIN THE TIME GIVEN.

EXAMPLES

SIMILARITY Example 1

The three figures given are similar in some way.

Work out how they are similar and select the figure that goes with them.

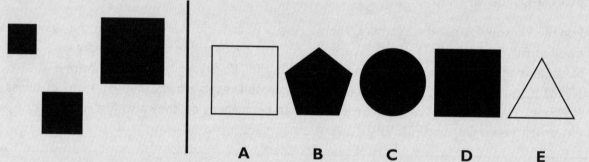

The correct answer is D. This has already been marked in Example 1 in the Non-Verbal Reasoning section of your answer sheet.

SIMILARITY Practice Question 1

The three figures given are similar in some way.

Work out how they are similar and select the figure that goes with them.

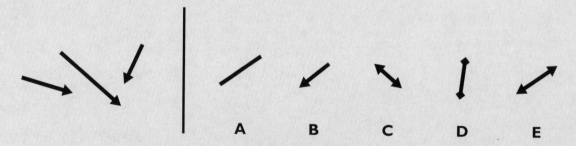

The correct answer is B. Please mark this in Practice Question 1 in the Non-Verbal Reasoning section of your answer sheet.

CONTINUE WORKING

CUBE NET Example 2

Look at the cube net below. Select the only cube that could be formed from the net.

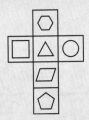

A   B   C   D

The correct answer is B. This has already been marked in Example 2 in the Non-Verbal Reasoning section of your answer sheet.

CUBE NET Practice Question 2

Look at the cube net below. Select the only cube that could be formed from the net.

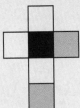

A   B   C   D

The correct answer is C. Please mark this in Practice Question 2 in the Non-Verbal Reasoning section of your answer sheet.

COMPLETE THE SEQUENCE Example 3

Select the correct picture from the row on the right in order to finish the incomplete sequence on the left.

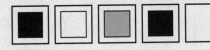

A   B   C   D   E

The correct answer is A. This has already been marked in Example 3 in the Non-Verbal Reasoning section of your answer sheet.

COMPLETE THE SEQUENCE Practice Question 3

Select the correct picture from the row on the right in order to finish the incomplete sequence on the left.

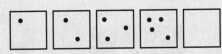

A   B   C   D   E

The correct answer is D. Please mark this in Practice Question 3 in the Non-Verbal Reasoning section of your answer sheet.

STOP AND WAIT FOR FURTHER INSTRUCTIONS

1 The three figures given are similar in some way. Work out how they are similar and select the figure that goes with them.

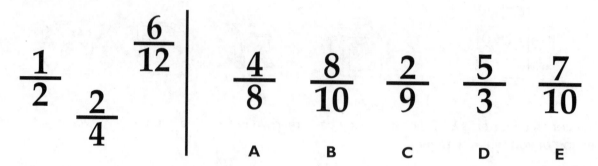

$$\frac{1}{2} \qquad \frac{6}{12} \qquad \frac{2}{4}$$

$$\frac{4}{8} \qquad \frac{8}{10} \qquad \frac{2}{9} \qquad \frac{5}{3} \qquad \frac{7}{10}$$

     A   B   C   D   E

2 The three figures given are similar in some way. Work out how they are similar and select the figure that goes with them.

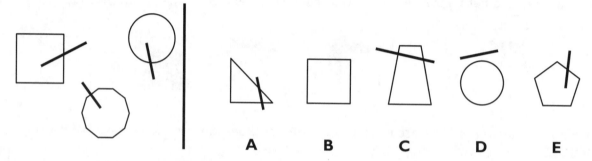

     A   B   C   D   E

3 The three figures given are similar in some way. Work out how they are similar and select the figure that goes with them.

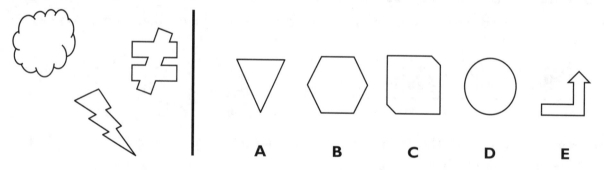

     A   B   C   D   E

4 The three figures given are similar in some way. Work out how they are similar and select the figure that goes with them.

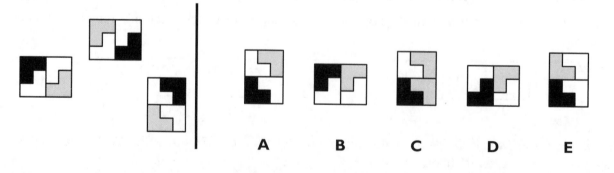

     A   B   C   D   E

CONTINUE WORKING ➡

5 The three figures given are similar in some way. Work out how they are similar and select the figure that goes with them.

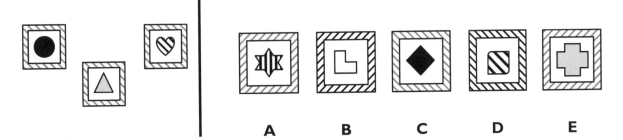

A   B   C   D   E

6 Look at the cube net below. Select the only cube that could be formed from the net.

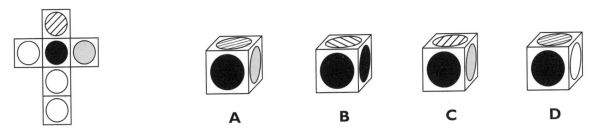

A   B   C   D

7 Look at the cube net below. Select the only cube that could be formed from the net.

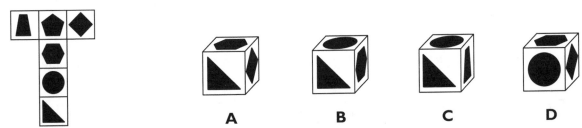

A   B   C   D

8 Look at the cube net below. Select the only cube that could be formed from the net.

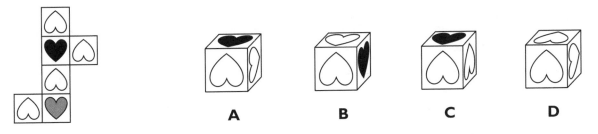

A   B   C   D

9 Look at the cube net below. Select the only cube that could be formed from the net.

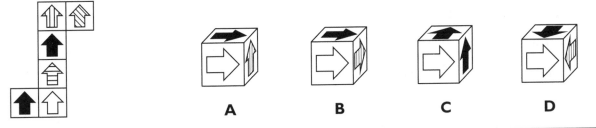

A   B   C   D

CONTINUE WORKING ➡

10 Look at the cube net below. Select the only cube that could be formed from the net.

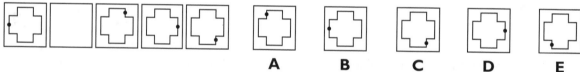

11 Select the correct picture from the row on the right in order to finish the incomplete sequence on the left.

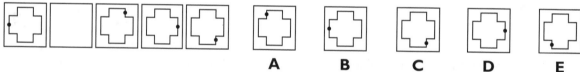

12 Select the correct picture from the row on the right in order to finish the incomplete sequence on the left.

13 Select the correct picture from the row on the right in order to finish the incomplete sequence on the left.

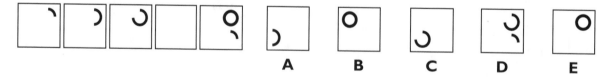

14 Select the correct picture from the row on the right in order to finish the incomplete sequence on the left.

15 Select the correct picture from the row on the right in order to finish the incomplete sequence on the left.

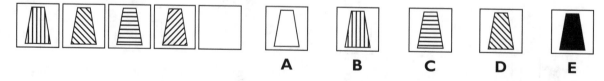

STOP AND WAIT FOR FURTHER INSTRUCTIONS

Grammar & Spelling

INSTRUCTIONS

 YOU HAVE 5 MINUTES TO COMPLETE THE FOLLOWING SECTION.

YOU HAVE 8 QUESTIONS TO COMPLETE WITHIN THE TIME GIVEN.

EXAMPLES

Example 1

Identify a homophone of the word 'night' from the words below.

A	B	C	D	E
knight	dark	bright	summer	light

The correct answer is A. This has already been marked in Example 1 in the Grammar & Spelling section of your answer sheet.

Practice Question 1

Select the correct prefix to give the opposite of the word 'believable'.

A	B	C	D	E
in	un	on	mis	pro

The correct answer is B. Please mark the answer B in Practice Question 1 in the Grammar & Spelling section of your answer sheet.

STOP AND WAIT FOR FURTHER INSTRUCTIONS

1 Identify a homophone of the word 'sleigh' from the words below.

A	B	C	D	E
slight	slime	slay	swoon	slain

2 Identify the plural of the word 'fish' from the words below.

A	B	C	D	E
fishe	fish	fisher	fishies	fished

3 Select the correct prefix to give the opposite of the word 'understand'.

A	B	C	D	E
for	dis	un	in	mis

4 Select the word below that is misspelt.

A	B	C	D	E
severe	pertain	judgemant	smoke	pollute

5 Select the word below that is misspelt.

A	B	C	D	E
nervous	proceed	sullen	follow	arguement

6 Select the word below that is misspelt.

A	B	C	D	E
embarass	summary	earnest	withhold	labourer

7 Select the word below that is misspelt.

A	B	C	D	E
example	emerging	existance	elephant	energetic

8 Select the word below that is misspelt.

A	B	C	D	E
velvet	covering	ocassion	pining	abreast

STOP AND WAIT FOR FURTHER INSTRUCTIONS ⊗

Antonyms

 INSTRUCTIONS

 YOU HAVE 5 MINUTES TO COMPLETE THE FOLLOWING SECTION.

YOU HAVE 15 QUESTIONS TO COMPLETE WITHIN THE TIME GIVEN.

EXAMPLES

Example 1

Which word is most opposite in meaning to the following word?

hot

A	B	C	D	E
follow	cold	freeze	ice	jelly

The correct answer is B. This has already been marked in Example 1 in the Antonyms section of your answer sheet.

Practice Question 1

Which word is most opposite in meaning to the following word?

below

A	B	C	D	E
attack	deep	lower	above	before

The correct answer is D. Please mark the answer D in Practice Question 1 in the Antonyms section of your answer sheet.

STOP AND WAIT FOR FURTHER INSTRUCTIONS

For each row, select the word from the table that is most opposite in meaning to the word above the table.

1 descendant

A	B	C	D	E
descent	man	delivered	family	ancestor

2 artificial

A	B	C	D	E
leaf	natural	plastic	fake	artistic

3 awful

A	B	C	D	E
imagined	atrocious	delicious	forgetful	fearsome

4 tragedy

A	B	C	D	E
comedy	story	play	message	tragic

5 destroy

A	B	C	D	E
blow	gather	believe	construct	needless

6 distant

A	B	C	D	E
disabled	caravan	near	horizon	killer

7 hidden

A	B	C	D	E
plan	concealed	secret	furtive	exposed

CONTINUE WORKING ▶

8 generous

A	B	C	D	E
expensive	mean	flavour	general	powerful

9 violent

A	B	C	D	E
violet	crab	gentle	cuddle	war

10 notice

A	B	C	D	E
better	ignore	remark	board	noted

11 accidental

A	B	C	D	E
apparent	fluke	signal	intentional	bearded

12 mend

A	B	C	D	E
malicious	fix	martyr	hurry	break

13 occupied

A	B	C	D	E
full	sold	vacant	rental	toilet

14 seldom

A	B	C	D	E
summer	selfish	sold	often	dome

15 poverty

A	B	C	D	E
wealth	coin	poor	bread	rich

STOP AND WAIT FOR FURTHER INSTRUCTIONS ⊗

Numeracy

INSTRUCTIONS

 YOU HAVE 9 MINUTES TO COMPLETE THE FOLLOWING SECTION.

YOU HAVE 18 QUESTIONS TO COMPLETE WITHIN THE TIME GIVEN.

EXAMPLES

Some questions within this section are not multiple choice. For these write the answer to each question on the answer sheet by selecting the correct digits from the columns provided.

Example 1

Calculate the answer to the following:

12 + 42

The correct answer is 54. This has already been marked in Example 1 in the Numeracy section of your answer sheet.

Practice Question 1

Calculate the answer to the following:

55 − 47

The correct answer is 8. Please mark this in Practice Question 1 in the Numeracy section of your answer sheet. Note that a single-digit answer should be marked with a 0 in the left-hand column, so mark 08 on your answer sheet.

STOP AND WAIT FOR FURTHER INSTRUCTIONS ⬡

(1) Calculate the answer to the following:

$(642 \div 2) \div 3$

(2) Which number comes next in the following sequence?

1, 4, 9, 16, 25, ?

(3) What is the numerator when $\frac{1}{2}$ is added to $\frac{1}{6}$ and expressed in its lowest terms?

(4) Calculate the value of X in the following equation:

$0 \cdot 4 = \dfrac{X}{20}$

(5) How many tenths greater is $4 \cdot 567$ rounded to 1 decimal place than $4 \cdot 291$ rounded to 1 decimal place?

(6) Calculate the value of X in the following equation:

$7X - 7 = 2X + 28$

(7) I think of a number, divide it by 3, multiply it by 4 and then add 1. My answer is 49.

What number did I think of?

(8) Calculate $\dfrac{7}{5}$ of 80

(9) A regular hexagon has a perimeter of $36 \cdot 6$ cm.

What is the total length of 4 sides of the hexagon?

A	B	C	D	E
36·6 cm	6·6 cm	18·3 cm	30·6 cm	24·4 cm

(10) Which of the following is most likely to be the measurement of a woman's height?

A	B	C	D	E
3 km	3·2 m	154 cm	200 mm	1·6 cm

CONTINUE WORKING ⟶

(11) This circle has been split into equal parts.

What fraction of the circle is not shaded?

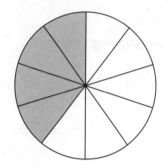

A	B	C	D	E
$\dfrac{1}{10}$	$\dfrac{1}{2}$	$\dfrac{4}{10}$	$\dfrac{3}{4}$	$\dfrac{3}{5}$

(12) Lucy, Jane, Rahul and Tim run a race. Lucy finishes the race in 54 seconds. Jane finishes 7 seconds faster than Lucy and Rahul finishes 5 seconds slower than Jane. Tim finishes 8 seconds faster than Rahul.

What is Tim's finishing time?

A	B	C	D	E
53 seconds	63 seconds	56 seconds	44 seconds	48 seconds

(13) George cuts a 4·5 kg block of marble into 9 pieces.

What is the average weight of each of the 9 pieces?

A	B	C	D	E
300 g	0·5 kg	900 g	450 g	2 kg

(14) What is the measurement of the largest angle in this triangle?

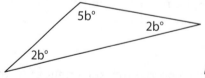

Not drawn to scale

A	B	C	D	E
40°	90°	50°	70°	100°

CONTINUE WORKING ▶

15 Tara swims 750 m per day from 27ᵗʰ September to 3ʳᵈ October, inclusively.

What is the total distance that Tara swims in this period?

A	B	C	D	E
4·5 km	3·75 km	1·5 km	5·25 km	6 km

16 250 people were asked to choose their favourite colour. 40% of them chose red and $\frac{1}{5}$ of them chose blue. $\frac{1}{2}$ of the remainder chose green.

How many people in the group chose green?

A	B	C	D	E
75	125	100	60	50

17 This diagram consists of 4 identical shaded circles inside a square.

The area of 1 shaded circle is 3·5 cm². The square has a side length of 7 cm.

What area of the square is not covered by shaded circles?

Not drawn to scale

A	B	C	D	E
3·5 cm²	63 cm²	49 cm²	35 cm²	14 cm²

18 Amanda bought £6·50 of groceries and paid with a £10 note.

What percentage of £10 did she receive in change?

A	B	C	D	E
65%	90%	35%	100%	350%

END OF PAPER

Get Ahead
Test B Paper 1

Instructions

1. Ensure you have pencils and an eraser with you.
2. Make sure you are able to see a clock or watch.
3. Write your name on the answer sheet.
4. Do not open the question booklet until you are told to do so by the audio instructions.
5. Listen carefully to the audio instructions given.
6. Mark your answers on the answer sheet only.
7. All workings must be completed on a separate piece of paper.
8. You should not use a calculator, dictionary or thesaurus at any point in this paper.
9. Move through the papers as quickly as possible and with care.
10. Follow the instructions at the foot of each page.
11. You should mark your answers with a horizontal line, as shown on the answer sheet.
12. If you want to change your answer, ensure that you rub out your first answer and that your second answer is clearly more visible.
13. You can go back and review any questions that are within the section you are working on only. You must await further instructions before moving on to another section.

Symbols and Phrases used in the Tests

 Instructions

 Time allowed for this section

 Stop working and await instructions

 Continue working

Comprehension

INSTRUCTIONS

 YOU HAVE 9 MINUTES TO COMPLETE THE FOLLOWING SECTION.

YOU HAVE 10 QUESTIONS TO COMPLETE WITHIN THE TIME GIVEN.

EXAMPLES

Comprehension Example

South Africa is becoming an increasingly popular holiday destination. People from all over the world are being attracted by its natural beauty, cosmopolitan cities and diverse wildlife. Cape Town, the capital of South Africa, is especially popular. The city is dynamic and exciting and has a rich history and culture. It is also home to the stunning Table Mountain, which you can ascend on foot or by cable car.

Example 1

Which of the following is not mentioned as a reason why people are attracted to South Africa?

A Natural beauty
B Excellent food
C Cosmopolitan cities
D Diverse wildlife

The correct answer is B. This has already been marked in Example 1 in the Comprehension section of your answer sheet.

Practice Question 1

What is the name of the mountain in Cape Town?

A Cape Mountain
B Africa Mountain
C Table Mountain
D Leopard Mountain

The correct answer is C. Please mark this in Practice Question 1 in the Comprehension section of your answer sheet.

STOP AND WAIT FOR FURTHER INSTRUCTIONS

Read the passage below and then answer the questions that follow.

An extract from: **Wicked**

by Gregory Maguire

"Storm on the horizon," said the Scarecrow. Miles off, thunder echoed. "There-is-a-Witch on the horizon," said the Tin Woodman, tickling the Lion. The Lion got spooked and rolled on top of the Scarecrow, whimpering, and the Tin Woodman collapsed on top of them both.

"Good friends, should we be wary of that storm?" said the girl. The rising winds moved the curtain of greenery at last, and the Witch caught sight of the girl. She was sitting with her feet tucked underneath her and her arms wrapped around her knees. She was not a dainty thing but a good-size farm girl, dressed in blue-and-white checks and a pinafore. In her lap, a vile little dog cowered and whined.

"The storm makes you skittish. It's natural after what you've been through," said the Tin Woodman. "Relax."

The Witch's fingers dug into the bark of the tree. She still could not see the girl's face, just her strong forearms and the crown of her head where her dark hair was pulled back into pigtails. Was she to be taken seriously, or was she merely a blow-away dandelion seed, caught on the wrong side of the wind? If she could see the girl's face, the Witch felt she might know. But as the Witch craned outward from the trunk, the girl at the same time twisted her face, turning away.

"That storm is coming closer, and in a hurry." The feeling in her voice rose as the wind rose. She had a throaty vehemence, like someone arguing through the threat of impending tears. "I know storms, I know how they come upon you!"

"We're safer here," said the Tin Woodman.

"Certainly we are not," answered the girl, "because this tree is the highest point around, and if lightning is to strike, it will strike here." She clutched her dog. "Didn't we see a shed farther up the road? Come, come; Scarecrow, if there's lightning, you'll burn the fastest! Come on!"

She was up and running in an ungainly way, and her companions followed in a mounting panic. As the first hard drops of rain fell, the Witch caught sight, not of the girl's face, but of the shoes. Her sister's shoes. They sparkled even in the darkening afternoon. They sparkled like yellow diamonds, and embers of blood, and thorny stars.

If she had seen the shoes first, the Witch would never have been able to listen to the girl or her friends. But the girl's legs had been tucked beneath her skirt. Now the Witch was reminded of her need. The shoes should be hers! Hadn't she endured enough, hadn't she earned them? The Witch would fall on the girl from the sky, and wrestle those shoes off her impertinent feet, if only she could.

CONTINUE WORKING

But the storm from which the companions raced, farther and faster along the Yellow Brick Road, troubled the Witch more than it did the girl who had gone through rain and the Scarecrow whom lightning could burn. The Witch could not venture out in such a vicious, insinuating wetness. Instead, she had to tuck herself between some exposed roots of the black willow tree, where no water could endanger her, and wait for the storm to pass.

She would emerge. She always had before. The punishing political climate of Oz had beat her down, dried her up, tossed her away – like a seedling she had drifted, apparently too desiccated ever to take root. But surely the curse was on the land of Oz, not on her. Though Oz had given her a twisted life, hadn't it also made her capable? No matter that the companions had hurried away. The Witch could wait. They would meet again.

1 What was the girl doing when first seen by the Witch?

    A   The girl was running
    B   The girl was eating
    C   The girl was crying
    D   The girl was sitting

2 Which word best describes the girl's physical appearance?

    A   Skinny
    B   Obese
    C   Slim
    D   Robust

3 According to the Tin Woodman, how did the girl feel about the storm?

    A   Nervous
    B   Prepared
    C   Indifferent
    D   Relaxed

4 Why did the Witch want to see the girl's face?

    A   The Witch wanted to see if she could recognise the girl
    B   The Witch thought it would help her get the measure of the girl
    C   The Witch had heard that the girl was very beautiful
    D   The Witch wanted to take a picture of the girl's face

CONTINUE WORKING

(5) Which word best describes how the girl ran?

    A   Clumsily
    B   Powerfully
    C   Correctly
    D   Elegantly

(6) Which literary technique is used in this phrase: 'They sparkled like yellow diamonds…' ?

    A   Metaphor
    B   Alliteration
    C   Simile
    D   Personification

(7) Why did the Witch not chase the girl immediately?

    A   She was tired from her earlier exertions
    B   The girl was running too fast
    C   She could not venture out in the rain
    D   She had no interest in chasing the girl

(8) How had the Witch fared in the land of Oz?

    A   She had thrived and prospered
    B   She had faced many obstacles and setbacks
    C   She had avoided any difficulties
    D   She had been treated well by all

(9) What does the word 'impending' mean?

    A   Pendulum
    B   Imminent
    C   Impatient
    D   Imploring

(10) Which of the following is the best antonym of 'mounting'?

    A   Riding
    B   Decreasing
    C   Melting
    D   Rising

STOP AND WAIT FOR FURTHER INSTRUCTIONS ⊗

Shuffled Sentences

 YOU HAVE 8 MINUTES TO COMPLETE THE FOLLOWING SECTION.

YOU HAVE 15 QUESTIONS TO COMPLETE WITHIN THE TIME GIVEN.

EXAMPLES

Example 1

The following sentence is shuffled and also contains one unnecessary word. Rearrange the sentence correctly in order to identify the unnecessary word.

wake under before must sunrise up we.

A	B	C	D	E
up	before	under	wake	sunrise

The correct answer is C. This has already been marked in Example 1 in the Shuffled Sentences section of your answer sheet.

Practice Question 1

The following sentence is shuffled and also contains one unnecessary word. Rearrange the sentence correctly in order to identify the unnecessary word.

very girl quickly the ran throw.

A	B	C	D	E
quickly	girl	the	ran	throw

The correct answer is E. Please mark this in Practice Question 1 in the Shuffled Sentences section of your answer sheet.

STOP AND WAIT FOR FURTHER INSTRUCTIONS

Each sentence below is shuffled and also contains one unnecessary word.
Rearrange each sentence correctly in order to identify the unnecessary word.

1. the student left unanswered questions sing many.

A	B	C	D	E
left	sing	questions	the	many

2. the of enjoyed many the participants describe experience.

A	B	C	D	E
describe	the	of	participants	experience

3. ecosystem a forests in play role tree our vital.

A	B	C	D	E
role	our	in	vital	tree

4. the on was undeniably talented and doctor intelligent.

A	B	C	D	E
was	on	doctor	intelligent	talented

5. by to is way the plane travel to Rome on quickest.

A	B	C	D	E
plane	travel	by	on	quickest

6. discussed of traveller destinations the holiday potential group friends.

A	B	C	D	E
traveller	holiday	destinations	potential	group

7. decided several to quit gym exercised members of the.

A	B	C	D	E
quit	gym	exercised	several	members

8. importance quality of ingredients cookery highlighted chef the the.

A	B	C	D	E
cookery	highlighted	ingredients	chef	quality

CONTINUE WORKING ⟹

9 all occur world phase disasters the natural over.

A	B	C	D	E
occur	disasters	world	over	phase

10 happy couple the to apartment with the agreed purchase.

A	B	C	D	E
with	couple	agreed	to	apartment

11 billion China the population of grows one exceeds.

A	B	C	D	E
billion	population	one	exceeds	grows

12 bravery heroic rewarded was stifle soldier's the the by politician.

A	B	C	D	E
stifle	rewarded	was	politician	bravery

13 businessman volume up to determined give the refused.

A	B	C	D	E
give	determined	up	refused	volume

14 flowers the against on grow variety mountain a of.

A	B	C	D	E
a	against	variety	of	flowers

15 and the rose fees rapidly company's legal costs money.

A	B	C	D	E
rose	legal	money	fees	rapidly

STOP AND WAIT FOR FURTHER INSTRUCTIONS ⊗

Numeracy

 INSTRUCTIONS

 YOU HAVE 7 MINUTES TO COMPLETE THE FOLLOWING SECTION.

YOU HAVE 15 QUESTIONS TO COMPLETE WITHIN THE TIME GIVEN.

EXAMPLES

The questions within this section are not multiple choice. Write the answer to each question on the answer sheet by selecting the correct digits from the columns provided.

Example 1

Calculate the answer to the following: $12 + 42$

The correct answer is 54. This has already been marked in Example 1 in the Numeracy section of your answer sheet.

Practice Question 1

Calculate the answer to the following: $55 - 47$

The correct answer is 8. Please mark this in Practice Question 1 in the Numeracy section of your answer sheet. Note that a single-digit answer should be marked with a 0 in the left-hand column, so mark 08 on your answer sheet.

STOP AND WAIT FOR FURTHER INSTRUCTIONS

(1) What is $\frac{1}{4}$ of $\frac{1}{2}$ of 96?

(2) How many weeks are there in 2 years?

CONTINUE WORKING

(3) A square plate has sides of 4 cm.

How many square plates can fit side by side on a square piece of paper which has sides of 16 cm?

(4) How many vertices does a cube have?

(5) A water tank can hold a maximum of 65 litres of water.

If the water tank is $\frac{3}{5}$ full, how many more litres of water could it hold?

(6) A plant grows 3 cm per day. If the plant measures 12 cm at the beginning of 30th July, what will its height be in centimetres at the end of 3rd August?

(7) What number should come next in the following sequence?

43, 45, 49, 57, ?

(8) How many lines of symmetry does this isosceles triangle have?

(9) Calculate the answer to the following:

6,850 − 5,874

(10) How many more fifths are there in 10 than thirds in 8?

(11) Calculate the answer to the following:

74 − (8 + 16)

(12) A car travels at 120 kph (kilometres per hour).

How many kilometres will the car have covered in $\frac{1}{6}$ of an hour?

(13) How many mm are there in 1 m?

(14) Subtract eighty-nine from three thousand and twenty-seven.

(15) Gina walks her dog twice per day. Each walk is 2·5 km.

What distance, in km, does Gina walk with her dog in the month of November?

STOP AND WAIT FOR FURTHER INSTRUCTIONS

Problem Solving

INSTRUCTIONS

 YOU HAVE 8 MINUTES TO COMPLETE THE FOLLOWING SECTION.

YOU HAVE 10 QUESTIONS TO COMPLETE WITHIN THE TIME GIVEN.

EXAMPLES

Example 1

Calculate the answer to the following:

Tom buys a chocolate bar for £1·50. He pays with a £5 note.
How much change does he receive?

   A £1·50   **B** £3   **C** £3·50   **D** £4   **E** £5

The correct answer is C. This has already been marked in Example 1 in the Problem Solving section of your answer sheet.

Practice Question 1

Sarah eats $\frac{1}{4}$ of a pizza.

What fraction of the pizza remains?

   A $\frac{1}{2}$ **B** $\frac{1}{3}$ **C** $\frac{2}{5}$ **D** $\frac{3}{4}$ **E** $\frac{5}{6}$

The correct answer is D. Please mark this in Practice Question 1 in the Problem Solving section of your answer sheet.

STOP AND WAIT FOR FURTHER INSTRUCTIONS

Calculate the answers to the following.

(1) How many oranges that cost 45 pence can be bought for £2·50?

   A 2   **B** 3   **C** 4   **D** 5   **E** 6

CONTINUE WORKING

(2) The temperature in London is 14°C and the temperature in Oslo is −6°C.

What is the difference in temperature between London and Oslo?

A 14°C   **B** 0°C   **C** 20°C   **D** 6°C   **E** 12°C

(3) Round 100,045 to the nearest 20.

A 100,060   **B** 100,025   **C** 100,050   **D** 100,040   **E** 100,020

(4) Hannah eats 4 grapes per day and Reena eats 7 grapes per day.

How many grapes do they eat in total in a fortnight?

A 11   **B** 77   **C** 56   **D** 80   **E** 154

(5) Point A has the coordinates (4, 4). Point B is a reflection of Point A in the y-axis.

What are the coordinates of Point B?

A (4, 0)   **B** (4, 4)   **C** (4, −4)   **D** (−4, 4)   **E** (0, 4)

(6) Baking a cake for 12 people requires 8 eggs.

How many eggs are required to bake a cake for 3 people?

A 0   **B** 2   **C** 3   **D** 8   **E** 12

(7) 60 peaches are divided into 3 piles with a ratio of 8:1:6.

How many peaches are there in the largest pile?

A 32   **B** 30   **C** 24   **D** 4   **E** 15

(8) There are 40 rats in a sewer. $\frac{1}{5}$ of the rats have brown fur and the rest have black fur. $\frac{1}{4}$ of the rats have long tails and the rest have short tails.

What is the largest number of rats that could have black fur and long tails?

A 5   **B** 10   **C** 15   **D** 32   **E** 40

(9) Rectangle A has a width of 5 cm and an area of 40 cm². The width and length of Rectangle B are double that of Rectangle A.

What is the area of Rectangle B?

A 10 cm²   **B** 80 cm²   **C** 200 cm²   **D** 400 cm²   **E** 160 cm²

(10) 120 students were asked to choose their favourite soup. 20% of them chose chicken and 35% chose tomato.

How many students chose neither chicken nor tomato?

A 24   **B** 60   **C** 80   **D** 54   **E** 60

STOP AND WAIT FOR FURTHER INSTRUCTIONS

Synonyms

INSTRUCTIONS

 YOU HAVE 7 MINUTES TO COMPLETE THE FOLLOWING SECTION.

YOU HAVE 24 QUESTIONS TO COMPLETE WITHIN THE TIME GIVEN.

EXAMPLES

Example 1

Select the word that is most similar in meaning to the following word:

push

A	B	C	D	E
shallow	shove	tug	hollow	cry

The correct answer is B. This has already been marked in Example 1 in the Synonyms section of your answer sheet.

Practice Question 1

Select the word that is most similar in meaning to the following word:

imitate

A	B	C	D	E
cover	copy	grow	live	irritate

The correct answer is B. Please mark this in Practice Question 1 in the Synonyms section of your answer sheet.

STOP AND WAIT FOR FURTHER INSTRUCTIONS

For each row, select the word from the table that is most similar in meaning to the word above the table.

(1) maintain

A	B	C	D	E
destroy	bring	develop	hang	preserve

(2) distress

A	B	C	D	E
stressed	envelope	appetite	misery	dress

(3) reasonably

A	B	C	D	E
happily	holy	moderately	openly	sometimes

(4) inform

A	B	C	D	E
hide	injure	information	restrict	notify

(5) abroad

A	B	C	D	E
home	overseas	wide	open	narrow

(6) dependable

A	B	C	D	E
reliable	deepening	huge	unsure	scattered

(7) choice

A	B	C	D	E
choose	forced	flatter	selection	place

(8) outlive

A	B	C	D	E
suffer	survive	propose	live	die

CONTINUE WORKING ⇨

9 stable

A	B	C	D	E
standard	storm	steady	steep	shaky

10 symbolise

A	B	C	D	E
flag	operate	mutter	meaningless	represent

11 ultimate

A	B	C	D	E
cover	final	signal	commence	untimely

12 propose

A	B	C	D	E
populate	hustle	engage	deepen	suggest

13 seize

A	B	C	D	E
fiercely	loosen	grab	flow	sold

14 lonely

A	B	C	D	E
harshly	quickly	maturely	lively	isolated

15 faulty

A	B	C	D	E
fault	omission	defective	heave	summon

16 embrace

A	B	C	D	E
cut	hug	brace	tug	embarrass

CONTINUE WORKING ⟶

(17) destiny

A	B	C	D	E
fate	grammar	denial	fatal	stone

(18) divide

A	B	C	D	E
destroy	armour	separate	hold	gather

(19) everlasting

A	B	C	D	E
natural	master	grip	eternal	powder

(20) peril

A	B	C	D	E
danger	period	violent	juicy	peace

(21) linger

A	B	C	D	E
remain	shape	forward	love	forgive

(22) roam

A	B	C	D	E
pardon	roll	cower	reveal	wander

(23) pledge

A	B	C	D	E
pine	ledge	promise	prosper	dramatic

(24) cry

A	B	C	D	E
shiver	velocity	exclaim	deny	tears

STOP AND WAIT FOR FURTHER INSTRUCTIONS ⊗

Non-Verbal Reasoning

 INSTRUCTIONS

 YOU HAVE 6 MINUTES TO COMPLETE THE FOLLOWING SECTION.

YOU HAVE 12 QUESTIONS TO COMPLETE WITHIN THE TIME GIVEN.

EXAMPLES

REFLECTION Example 1

Select how the following shape or pattern would appear when reflected in the dashed line.

A   B   C   D

The correct answer is C. This has already been marked in Example 1 in the Non-Verbal Reasoning section of your answer sheet.

REFLECTION Practice Question 1

Select how the following shape or pattern would appear when reflected in the dashed line.

A   B   C   D

The correct answer is C. Please mark this in Practice Question 1 in the Non-Verbal Reasoning section of your answer sheet.

CONTINUE WORKING ⇨

LEAST SIMILAR Example 2

Select the figure that is least similar to other figures.

  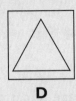 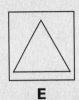

A   B   C   D   E

The correct answer is B. This has already been marked in Example 2 in the Non-Verbal Reasoning section of your answer sheet.

LEAST SIMILAR Practice Question 2

Select the figure that is least similar to other figures.

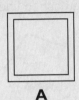 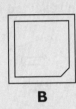 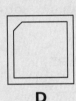 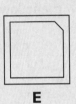

A   B   C   D   E

The correct answer is A. Please mark this in Practice Question 2 in the Non-Verbal Reasoning section of your answer sheet.

STOP AND WAIT FOR FURTHER INSTRUCTIONS

① Select how the following shape or pattern would appear when reflected in the dashed line.

A   B   C   D

② Select how the following shape or pattern would appear when reflected in the dashed line.

   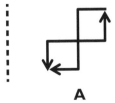   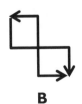

A   B   C   D

CONTINUE WORKING

3. Select how the following shape or pattern would appear when reflected in the dashed line.

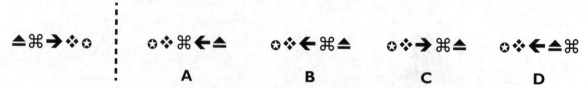

A   B   C   D

4. Select how the following shape or pattern would appear when reflected in the dashed line.

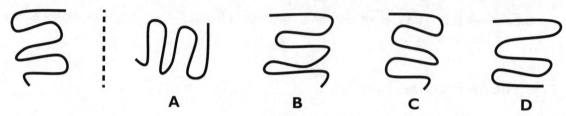

A   B   C   D

5. Select how the following shape or pattern would appear when reflected in the dashed line.

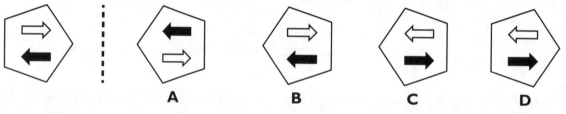

A   B   C   D

6. Select how the following shape or pattern would appear when reflected in the dashed line.

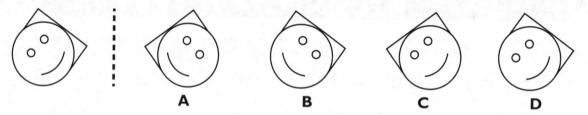

A   B   C   D

7. Select the figure that is least similar to other figures.

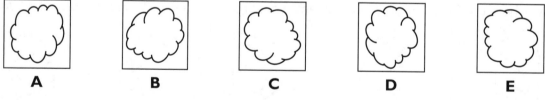

A   B   C   D   E

8. Select the figure that is least similar to other figures.

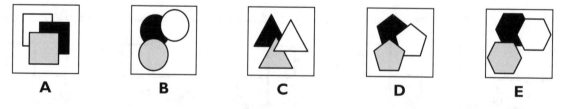

A   B   C   D   E

CONTINUE WORKING

9) Select the figure that is least similar to other figures.

10) Select the figure that is least similar to other figures.

11) Select the figure that is least similar to other figures.

12) Select the figure that is least similar to other figures.

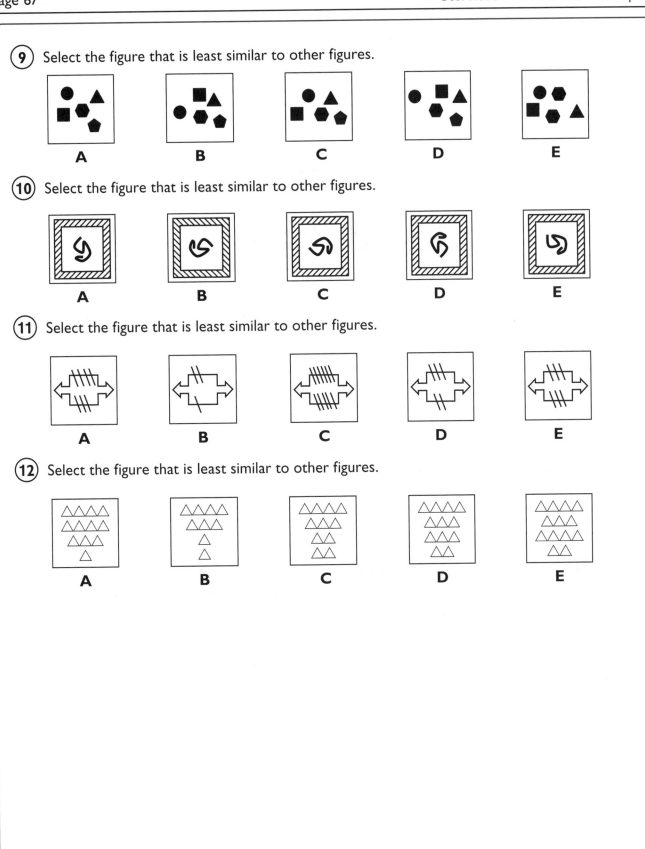

END OF PAPER

Get Ahead
Test B Paper 2

Instructions

1. Ensure you have pencils and an eraser with you.

2. Make sure you are able to see a clock or watch.

3. Write your name on the answer sheet.

4. Do not open the question booklet until you are told to do so by the audio instructions.

5. Listen carefully to the audio instructions given.

6. Mark your answers on the answer sheet only.

7. All workings must be completed on a separate piece of paper.

8. You should not use a calculator, dictionary or thesaurus at any point in this paper.

9. Move through the papers as quickly as possible and with care.

10. Follow the instructions at the foot of each page.

11. You should mark your answers with a horizontal line, as shown on the answer sheet.

12. If you want to change your answer, ensure that you rub out your first answer and that your second answer is clearly more visible.

13. You can go back and review any questions that are within the section you are working on only. You must await further instructions before moving on to another section.

Symbols and Phrases used in the Tests

 Instructions   Time allowed for this section   Stop working and await instructions   Continue working

Problem Solving

 INSTRUCTIONS

 YOU HAVE 12 MINUTES TO COMPLETE THE FOLLOWING SECTION.

YOU HAVE 15 QUESTIONS TO COMPLETE WITHIN THE TIME GIVEN.

EXAMPLES

A	$\frac{1}{2}$	B	£3	C	£3·50	D	$\frac{3}{4}$	E	$\frac{1}{3}$
F	£1·50	G	£5	H	$\frac{2}{5}$	I	£4	J	$\frac{5}{6}$

Example 1

Select an answer to the question from the 10 different possible answers in the table above.

Tom buys a chocolate bar for £1·50. He pays with a £5 note.
How much change does he receive?

The correct answer is C. This has already been marked in Example 1 in the Problem Solving section of your answer sheet.

Practice Question 1

Sarah eats $\frac{1}{4}$ of a pizza.

What fraction of the pizza remains?

The correct answer is D. Please mark this in Practice Question 1 in the Problem Solving section of your answer sheet.

STOP AND WAIT FOR FURTHER INSTRUCTIONS

A	110 kg	B	£1,625	C	104 kg	D	80 kph	E	60%
F	60 kph	G	1,728	H	£1,500	I	1,820	J	£1,584
K	24 kph	L	125%	M	1,200	N	103 kg	O	55%

Several questions will follow for you to answer. Select an answer to each question from the 15 different possible answers in the table above. You may use an answer for more than one question.

(1) 7,000 students began an online course but only 2,800 of them completed it.

What percentage of the students did not complete the online course?

(2) Each male sheep produces 12 kg of wool per year. Each female sheep produces 10 kg of wool per year.

If there are 30 male sheep and 25 female sheep on a farm, how many more kilograms of wool do the male sheep produce than the females per year?

(3) The cost of installing a new window is £150. Company A needs to have 15 windows installed. They agree a deal to pay the full installation price for the first 5 windows and $\frac{1}{2}$ the installation price for the rest.

What is the total amount Company A must pay?

(4) A train departs from Station A at 16:40 and arrives at Station B at 18:10.

The distance from Station A to Station B is 90 km.

What is the train's average speed in kph (kilometres per hour) on this journey?

(5) Every day, a factory produces twice as many garments as the day before.

If the factory produced 75 garments on Day 1, how many garments did it produce on Day 5?

(6) A box contains 2 green balls, 4 red balls, 3 yellow balls and the remainder are black balls.

If there are 20 balls in the box in total, what percentage of them are black?

(7) Lucas weighs 120 kg. Simon and Edward both weigh 100 kg. Ian weighs 92 kg.

What is their average weight?

CONTINUE WORKING

(8) The ratio of black and white mice in a pet shop is 5:7.

If there are 1,300 black mice in the pet shop, how many white mice are there?

(9) The cost of an airline ticket is reduced by $\frac{1}{5}$.

If the reduced price is £1,300, what was the original price?

(10) Bus A travels a distance of 45 km in 30 minutes. Bus B travels a distance of 70 km in 60 minutes.

What is the average speed of Bus A and Bus B in kph (kilometres per hour)?

(11) The Smith family gas bill was 10% less than their gas bill last year.

If the gas bill last year was £1,760, what was the Smith family's gas bill this year?

(12) Sam runs 400 m in 60 seconds.

What is Sam's speed in kph (kilometres per hour)?

(13) The number of flowers in a garden increased by 20% from Year 1 to Year 2. The number of flowers in the garden increased by 20% from Year 2 to Year 3.

If there were 1,200 flowers in the garden in Year 1, how many were there in Year 3?

(14) What percentage is 15 of 12?

(15) Round 103,500 g to the nearest kg.

STOP AND WAIT FOR FURTHER INSTRUCTIONS ⊗

Cloze

 INSTRUCTIONS

 YOU HAVE 10 MINUTES TO COMPLETE THE FOLLOWING SECTION.

YOU HAVE 20 QUESTIONS TO COMPLETE WITHIN THE TIME GIVEN.

EXAMPLES

Example 1

Read the sentence below and select the most appropriate word from the table.

A	B	C	D	E
defeated	heaved	master	flow	politely

The skilful chess player easily (Q1) _____ his opponent.

Please select your answer to go in the place of (Q1) in the above sentence.

The correct answer is A. This has already been marked in Example 1 in the Cloze section of your answer sheet.

Practice Question 1

Read the sentence below and select the most appropriate word from the table.

A	B	C	D	E
crunching	eating	dreading	reading	shining

The sun was (Q2) _____ and there was not a single cloud in the sky.

Please select your answer to go in the place of (Q2) in the above sentence.

The correct answer is E. Please mark the answer E in Practice Question 1 in the Cloze section of your answer sheet.

STOP AND WAIT FOR FURTHER INSTRUCTIONS ⊗

Read the passage and select the most appropriate word from the table below by choosing the letter above the word. There are 10 questions. For example, Q1 is where you should put your answer to Question 1 on your answer sheet.

A	B	C	D	E
looking	neither	attention	juice	said

F	G	H	I	J
although	reminded	reading	presenting	suspicious

Breakfast

There was only orange (Q1) _____ in the fridge. Nothing else that you could put on cereal, unless you think that ketchup or mayonnaise or pickle juice would be nice on your Toastios, which I do not, and (Q2) _____ did my little sister, (Q3) _____ she has eaten some pretty weird things in her day, like mushrooms in chocolate.

"No milk," (Q4) _____ my sister.

"Nope," I said, (Q5) _____ behind the jam in the fridge, just in case. "None at all."

Our mum had gone off to a conference. She was (Q6) _____ a paper on lizards. Before she went, she (Q7) _____ us of the important things that had to happen while she was away.

My dad was (Q8) _____ the paper. I do not think he pays a lot of (Q9) _____ to the world while he is reading his paper.

"Did you hear me?" asked my mum, who is (Q10) _____. "What did I say?"

An extract from: **Fortunately, the Milk**
by Neil Gaiman

CONTINUE WORKING ⟶

Read the passage and select the most appropriate word from the table below by choosing the letter above the word. There are 10 questions. For example, Q11 is where you should put your answer to Question 11 on your answer sheet.

A	B	C	D	E
wished	planned	listened	danger	talk

F	G	H	I	J
opposite	family	different	understood	anything

Danger

This kind of (Q11) _____ made Carla feel queasy. She could not bear to hear that the (Q12) _____ was in danger. Life must go on as it always had. She (Q13) _____ she could sit in this kitchen for an eternity of mornings, with her parents at (Q14) _____ ends of the pine table, Ada at the counter, and her brother, Erik, thumping around upstairs, late again. Why should (Q15) _____ change?

She had (Q16) _____ to political talk every breakfast-time of her life and she thought she (Q17) _____ what her parents did, and how they (Q18) _____ to make Germany a better place for everyone. But lately they had begun to talk in a (Q19) _____ way. They seemed to think that a terrible (Q20) _____ loomed, but Carla could not quite imagine what it was.

An extract from: **The Winter of the World**
by Ken Follett

STOP AND WAIT FOR FURTHER INSTRUCTIONS ⊗

Non-Verbal Reasoning

INSTRUCTIONS

 YOU HAVE 8 MINUTES TO COMPLETE THE FOLLOWING SECTION.

YOU HAVE 15 QUESTIONS TO COMPLETE WITHIN THE TIME GIVEN.

EXAMPLES

SIMILARITY Example 1

The three figures given are similar in some way.

Work out how they are similar and select the figure that goes with them.

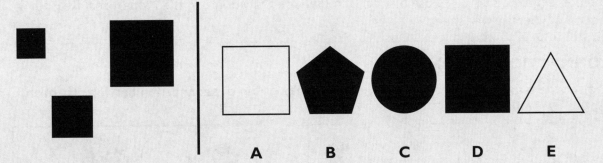

The correct answer is D. This has already been marked in Example 1 in the Non-Verbal Reasoning section of your answer sheet.

SIMILARITY Practice Question 1

The three figures given are similar in some way.

Work out how they are similar and select the figure that goes with them.

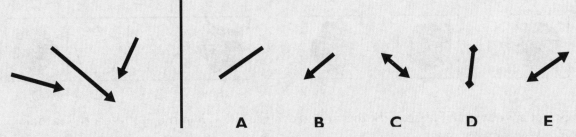

The correct answer is B. Please mark this in Practice Question 1 in the Non-Verbal Reasoning section of your answer sheet.

CONTINUE WORKING

CUBE NET Example 2

Look at the cube net below. Select the only cube that could be formed from the net.

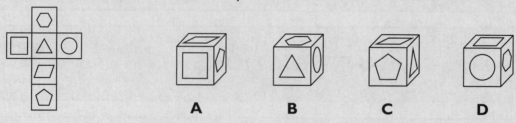

The correct answer is B. This has already been marked in Example 2 in the Non-Verbal Reasoning section of your answer sheet.

CUBE NET Practice Question 2

Look at the cube net below. Select the only cube that could be formed from the net.

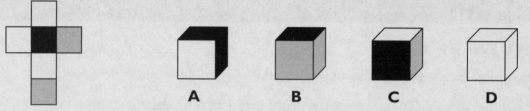

The correct answer is C. Please mark this in Practice Question 2 in the Non-Verbal Reasoning section of your answer sheet.

CONNECTION Example 3

Look at the two shapes on the left immediately below. Find the connection between them and apply it to the third shape.

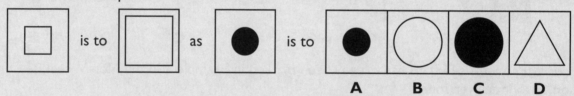

The correct answer is C. This has already been marked in Example 3 in the Non-Verbal Reasoning section of your answer sheet.

CONNECTION Practice Question 3

Look at the two shapes on the left immediately below. Find the connection between them and apply it to the third shape.

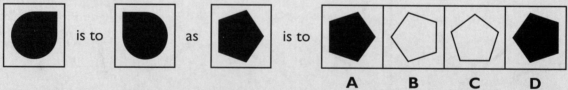

The correct answer is D. Please mark this in Practice Question 3 in the Non-Verbal Reasoning section of your answer sheet.

STOP AND WAIT FOR FURTHER INSTRUCTIONS

① The three figures given are similar in some way. Work out how they are similar and select the figure that goes with them.

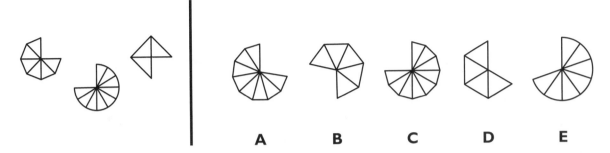

A   B   C   D   E

② The three figures given are similar in some way. Work out how they are similar and select the figure that goes with them.

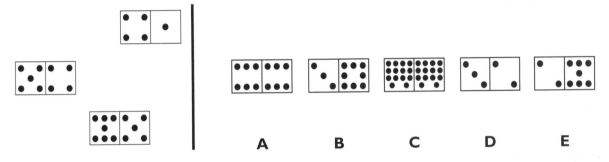

A   B   C   D   E

③ The three figures given are similar in some way. Work out how they are similar and select the figure that goes with them.

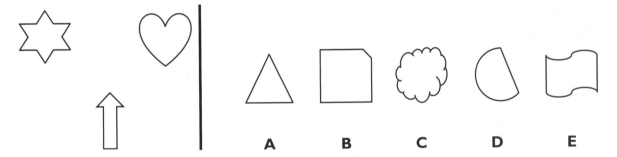

A   B   C   D   E

④ The three figures given are similar in some way. Work out how they are similar and select the figure that goes with them.

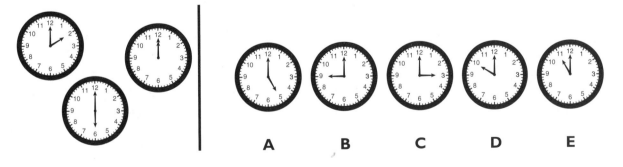

A   B   C   D   E

CONTINUE WORKING ⇨

5 The three figures given are similar in some way. Work out how they are similar and select the figure that goes with them.

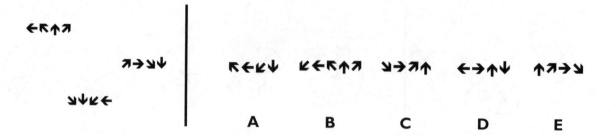

A	B	C	D	E

6 Look at the cube net below. Select the only cube that could be formed from the net.

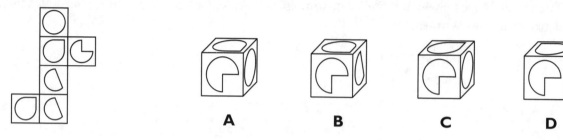

A	B	C	D

7 Look at the cube net below. Select the only cube that could be formed from the net.

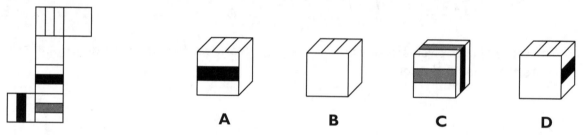

A	B	C	D

8 Look at the cube net below. Select the only cube that could be formed from the net.

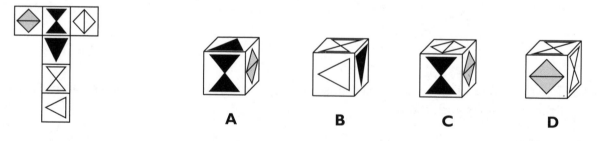

A	B	C	D

9 Look at the cube net below. Select the only cube that could be formed from the net.

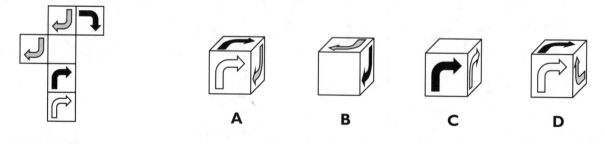

A	B	C	D

CONTINUE WORKING

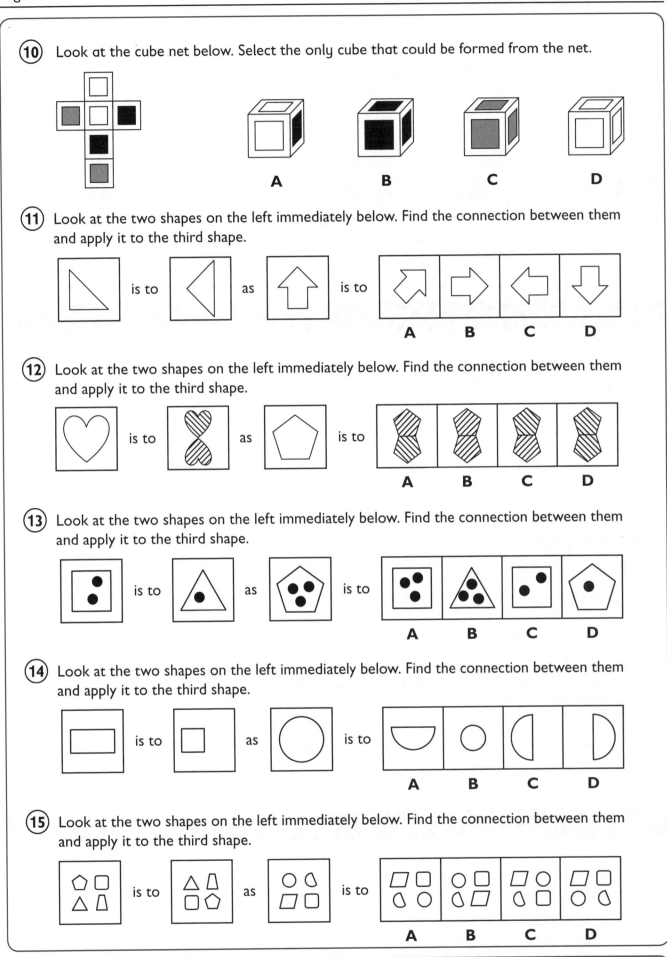

(10) Look at the cube net below. Select the only cube that could be formed from the net.

A   B   C   D

(11) Look at the two shapes on the left immediately below. Find the connection between them and apply it to the third shape.

is to   as   is to

A   B   C   D

(12) Look at the two shapes on the left immediately below. Find the connection between them and apply it to the third shape.

is to   as   is to

A   B   C   D

(13) Look at the two shapes on the left immediately below. Find the connection between them and apply it to the third shape.

is to   as   is to

A   B   C   D

(14) Look at the two shapes on the left immediately below. Find the connection between them and apply it to the third shape.

is to   as   is to

A   B   C   D

(15) Look at the two shapes on the left immediately below. Find the connection between them and apply it to the third shape.

is to   as   is to

A   B   C   D

STOP AND WAIT FOR FURTHER INSTRUCTIONS

Antonyms

INSTRUCTIONS

 YOU HAVE 6 MINUTES TO COMPLETE THE FOLLOWING SECTION.

YOU HAVE 18 QUESTIONS TO COMPLETE WITHIN THE TIME GIVEN.

EXAMPLES

Example 1

Which word is most opposite in meaning to the following word?

hot

A	B	C	D	E
follow	cold	freeze	ice	jelly

The correct answer is B. This has already been marked in Example 1 in the Antonyms section of your answer sheet.

Practice Question 1

Which word is most opposite in meaning to the following word?

below

A	B	C	D	E
attack	deep	lower	above	before

The correct answer is D. Please mark the answer D in Practice Question 1 in the Antonyms section of your answer sheet.

STOP AND WAIT FOR FURTHER INSTRUCTIONS

For each row, select the word from the table that is most opposite in meaning to the word above the table.

(1) answer

A	B	C	D	E
analyse	respond	support	question	restore

(2) below

A	B	C	D	E
lower	high	above	inner	beneath

(3) calm

A	B	C	D	E
comb	shower	stir	excited	peaceful

(4) halt

A	B	C	D	E
halo	thief	arrest	dream	start

(5) accept

A	B	C	D	E
deny	friendly	acquire	same	adapt

(6) humble

A	B	C	D	E
arrogant	smile	mild	slow	bumble

CONTINUE WORKING ➡

(7) credit

A	B	C	D	E
card	house	debit	suffer	lose

(8) inhabited

A	B	C	D	E
warm	island	light	animal	abandoned

(9) rowdy

A	B	C	D	E
humid	quiet	powder	heavy	crowded

(10) strict

A	B	C	D	E
row	powerful	asleep	lenient	harsh

(11) foe

A	B	C	D	E
rival	enemy	ally	hero	fry

(12) vacant

A	B	C	D	E
apartment	violent	empty	small	full

CONTINUE WORKING ⟶

(13) inhale

A	B	C	D	E
indeed	cry	air	exhale	summer

(14) weary

A	B	C	D	E
wary	frustrated	energetic	joking	exhausted

(15) whole

A	B	C	D	E
fragment	filled	complete	sky	hole

(16) imperfect

A	B	C	D	E
pale	factual	supported	flawless	human

(17) opaque

A	B	C	D	E
paste	opportunity	market	similar	transparent

(18) impartial

A	B	C	D	E
party	biased	improve	parity	equal

STOP AND WAIT FOR FURTHER INSTRUCTIONS ⊗

Numeracy

 INSTRUCTIONS

 YOU HAVE 9 MINUTES TO COMPLETE THE FOLLOWING SECTION.

YOU HAVE 18 QUESTIONS TO COMPLETE WITHIN THE TIME GIVEN.

EXAMPLES

The questions within this section are not multiple choice. Write the answer to each question on the answer sheet by selecting the correct digits from the columns provided.

Example 1

Calculate the answer to the following:

12 + 42

The correct answer is 54. This has already been marked in Example 1 in the Numeracy section of your answer sheet.

Practice Question 1

Calculate the answer to the following:

55 − 47

The correct answer is 8. Please mark this in Practice Question 1 in the Numeracy section of your answer sheet. Note that a single-digit answer should be marked with a 0 in the left-hand column, so mark 08 on your answer sheet.

STOP AND WAIT FOR FURTHER INSTRUCTIONS

(1) Calculate the answer to the following:

264 − 219

(2) Calculate the value of X in the following equation:

$3X + 7 = 2(X + 4)$

(3) Calculate the next number in the following sequence:

23, 19, 14, 10, 5, ?

(4) I think of a number, add 4 to it, divide by 2 and then multiply by 3. My answer is 30.

What number did I think of?

(5) How many more days are there in July and August combined than in October and November combined?

(6) What is the mode of the following numbers?

45, 69, 65, 23, 32, 87, 34, 54, 12, 87, 19, 95, 28, 49, 54

(7) Bruno, Monty and Joey are 3 different breeds of dog. Bruno is twice as tall as Monty. Monty is three times as tall as Joey. If Joey is 30 cm tall, how tall is Bruno in cm?

(8) A worker can complete 7 tasks per minute. How many tasks can 7 workers complete in 7 minutes?

(9) 2 years ago, I was 11 years old. How old will I be in 3 years' time?

(10) How many lines of symmetry does this shape have?

CONTINUE WORKING

(11) A dog's running speed is measured at 100 metres per minute. What is the dog's running speed in kph (kilometres per hour)?

(12) I eat $\frac{5}{7}$ of the sweets in a bag. 14 sweets remain in the bag. How many sweets did I eat?

(13) Tom and Bill take a test with 50 questions, each worth 1 mark. Tom scores 60% of the marks.

Bill scores 10% more marks than Tom. How many marks did Bill score?

(14) There are 52 cards in a deck. I remove $\frac{1}{4}$ of them and then select $\frac{2}{3}$ of the remainder. How many cards do I select?

(15) How many sevenths are there in $6\frac{2}{7}$?

(16) Caps cost £2·50 and belts cost £4·50. How many caps can I buy with £24·50?

(17) For the month of August, the sun shone for an average of $\frac{1}{3}$ of each day.

On average, for how many hours did the sun shine each day in August?

(18) Calculate the answer to the following:

9,898 − 8,989

END OF PAPER

Key abbreviations: *°C: degrees centigrade, cm: centimetre, d.p.: decimal place, kg: kilogram, km: kilometre, kph: kilometres per hour, m: metre, ml: millilitre, mm: millimetre, R: remainder*

Answers to *Get Ahead* Test A Paper 1

Comprehension (pages 8-9)

Q1 B
He had been attending boxing practice

Q2 A
It was covered in ice in September

Q3 D
His parents would disapprove (the passage says 'As much as he wished he could call for a ride, he knew better. He'd made that mistake last winter, when Coach had said a blizzard was coming. He'd gotten his ride and a lecture on how his brothers had never needed one, even when it was storming.')

Q4 A
Worn (the passage says 'the weathered Viking longship.')

Q5 C
March (the passage says 'at Sigrblot, the spring festival.')

Q6 A
A necklace (the passage says 'He reached for the silver pendant…Everyone in Matt's family had one.')

Q7 C
Options 1, 2 and 3 only (the passage says 1. 'Fen and Laurie Brekke. Great. The cousins were always…' 2. 'Thorsen wasn't just their name. They really were descendants of the Norse god.' 3. 'Controlling his temper and Thor's Hammer seemed especially hard around the Brekkes.')

Q8 C
Feign

Q9 D
Shoving

Q10 C
Adverb

Shuffled Sentences (pages 11-12)

Q1 E
equal *The fireman dashed into the burning building.*

Q2 A
summer *The boy loved to read historical fiction.*

Q3 D
tongue *Giraffes have long legs and necks. OR Giraffes have long necks and legs.*

Q4 B
space *The determined astronaut trained for many years.*

Q5 D
hers *Many observers were shocked by his behaviour.*

Q6 A
falling *Light rain fell throughout the day.*

Q7 E
rare *Freezing temperatures are common in the Arctic.*

Q8 D
to *The accountant dreaded returning to work.*

Q9 A
two *Exercise is a vital part of a healthy lifestyle.*

Q10 D
passed *He pretended to understand her question.*

Q11 E
attempt *The skilful lawyer summarised the arguments.*

Q12 B
talk *The young girl spoke three different languages.*

Q13 A
sentence *The judge decided to be lenient with the criminal.*

Q14 D
heating *The desert is full of unusual animals and plants. OR The desert is full of unusual plants and animals.*

Q15 A
toothpaste *You must not forget to brush your teeth at night. OR At night you must not forget to brush your teeth.*

Numeracy (pages 13-14)

Q1 579

123 + 456 = 579

Q2 159

477 ÷ 3 = 159

Q3 103

32 + 64 + 19 − 12 = 103

Q4 58

Sequence is −3, −5, −3, −5, −3

So missing term is −5; 63 − 5 = 58

Q5 11

Mean = (14 + 12 + 5 + 6 + 18) ÷ 5 =

55 ÷ 5 = 11

Q6 72

1 day = 24 hours

3 days = 3 × 24 hours = 72 hours

Q7 10

11 + 2Y = 44 − 13

2Y = 44 − 13 −11

2Y = 20; Y = 10

Q8 165

8:30 a.m. to 11:15 a.m. is 2 hours and
45 minutes

Time spent watching television in minutes =
(2 × 60) + 45 = 120 + 45 = 165

Q9 6

Factors of 48: 1, 48, 2, 24, 3, 16, 4, 12, 6, 8 =
10 factors

Factors of 10: 1, 10, 2, 5 = 4 factors

10 − 4 = 6

Q10 960

40 × 24 = 960

Q11 6

Area of board = 8 cm × 12 cm = 96 cm²

Area of 1 square = 4 cm × 4 cm = 16 cm²

Number of squares that fit on board =
96 cm² ÷ 16 cm² = 6

Q12 48

$\frac{1}{3}$ of X = 32; X = 3 × 32 = 96

$\frac{1}{2}$ of X = 96 ÷ 2 = 48

Q13 39

10% of 30 = 3 so 30% of 30 = 9

Number of birds in tree on Wednesday =
30 + 9 = 39

Problem Solving (pages 16-17)

Q1 B

1 hour 35 minutes after 7:50 p.m. is 9:25 p.m.

Q2 C

A shape with 8 sides is an octagon.

Q3 C

$20^2 = 20 \times 20 = 400$

Q4 B

She eats $\frac{1}{3}$ so $\frac{2}{3}$ remain

She gives $\frac{1}{2}$ of remainder to her brother

$\frac{1}{2} \times \frac{2}{3} = \frac{2}{6} = \frac{1}{3}$

Q5 C

Ben:Harry:Mia in the ratio 3:1:2

6 parts in total; Mia receives 2 out of
6 parts so she receives $\frac{1}{3}$

$\frac{1}{3}$ of £30,000 = £10,000

Q6 B

Area of triangle = $\frac{1}{2}$ × base × height =

$\frac{1}{2}$ × 18 cm × 10 cm = 90 cm²

Area shaded black = $\frac{1}{3}$ × 90 cm² = 30 cm²

Q7 A

Ginger hair = $\frac{1}{8}$; black hair = $\frac{3}{4}$

Neither black nor ginger hair = $1 - \frac{1}{8} - \frac{3}{4}$

$= 1 - \frac{1}{8} - \frac{6}{8} = \frac{1}{8}$

Q8 B

The square's sides are each 4 units long so
you can use this to calculate the missing
coordinate. **OR** Each x-coordinate and
y-coordinate must combine as the shape is a
square so the missing combination is (−1, 0)

Q9 C

1 one-pence coin and 1 five-pence coin
have a combined value of 6 pence
£1·20 ÷ 6 pence = 20 pence
So there are 20 one-pence coins and
20 five-pence coins

Q10 E

Mean = $50 ÷ 20 = 2\frac{1}{2}$

Synonyms (pages 19-21)

Q1 C confess

Q2 B apparent

Q3 E appear

Q4 C guarantee

Q5 E fragile

Q6 E clash

Q7 C manage

Q8 E contrary

Q9 D behave

Q10 C lesson

Q11 E appealing

Q12 A confine

Q13 C reduction   **Q19** C lucky
Q14 C disappear   **Q20** E miss
Q15 D keen   **Q21** C sincere
Q16 E reveal   **Q22** E praise
Q17 E precisely   **Q23** C insane
Q18 E doubtful   **Q24** A obvious

Non-Verbal Reasoning (pages 24-26)

Q1 E
The figure in the top right rearranges the order and number of symbols in the figure in the top left.
Therefore, the figure in the bottom right should rearrange the symbols in the figure in the bottom left in the same way.
Therefore, the answer is E.

Q2 D
The figure in the top left consists of two triangles. In the figure in the top right, the external triangle rotates 90° clockwise and the internal triangle rotates 180°.

Therefore, the figure in the bottom right should consist of the shapes in the figure in the bottom left rotated in the same way.
Therefore, the answer is D.

Q3 B
From left to right in each row, the number of sides of each shape decreases by one.
Therefore, the answer is B.

Q4 C
The third figure in each row consists of the first two figures laid one upon the other.
Therefore, the answer is C.

Q5 A
Q6 D
Q7 B
Q8 C
Q9 A
Q10 D
Q11 D
Q12 D
Q13 A

Answers to Get Ahead Test A Paper 2

Problem Solving (pages 29-30)

Q1 D
Cost of adult ticket = £220
Cost of child ticket = £220 ÷ 2 = £110
Total cost of flights = £220 + £220 + £110 + £110 = £660

Q2 J
3 hours = 3 × 60 mins = 180 mins
Percentage time spent watching films = $(\frac{90}{180}) \times 100 = 0.5 \times 100 = 50\%$

Q3 F
Flight time = 3 hours so flight lands at 16:45 London time
2 hours ahead of 16:45 is 18:45

Q4 G
1 week = 7 days; 250 ml × 7 = 1,750 ml = 1·75 litres

Q5 H
20% discount so £30 represents 80% of original price; 20% = £30 ÷ 4 = £7·50
So original price = 80% + 20% = £30 + £7·50 = £37·50

Q6 C
£450 − £405 = £45
Fraction spent on first day = $\frac{45}{450} = \frac{1}{10}$

Q7 B
15 hours and 20 minutes after 07:17 is 22:37

Q8 E
Fraction of German guests = $\frac{9}{16}$
Fraction of French guests = $\frac{3}{16}$
$\frac{9}{16} + \frac{3}{16} = \frac{12}{16} = \frac{3}{4} = 75\%$
So percentage neither French nor German = 100% − 75% = 25%

Q9 I
1% of 346 litres = 3·46 litres

Q10 A
1 year = 52 weeks; $\frac{2}{52} = \frac{1}{26}$

Cloze (pages 32-33)

Q1	**H** related	Q11	**F** harder
Q2	**A** role	Q12	**E** consider
Q3	**F** creatures	Q13	**B** creating
Q4	**E** responsible	Q14	**H** offers
Q5	**C** extremely	Q15	**A** overwhelming
Q6	**G** types	Q16	**D** slowly
Q7	**J** collect	Q17	**G** communicate
Q8	**B** effectively	Q18	**C** expanding
Q9	**D** aid	Q19	**J** owners
Q10	**I** consumed	Q20	**I** satisfying

Non-Verbal Reasoning (pages 36-38)

Q1 A

The three figures on the left are all fractions equivalent to one half.
Therefore, the answer is A.

Q2 E

The three figures on the left each consist of a black line that crosses over a shape at one point only.
Therefore, the answer is E.

Q3 E

The three figures on the left each have no lines of symmetry.
Therefore, the answer is E.

Q4 A

The three figures on the left are all rotations of the same shape.
Therefore, the answer is A.

Q5 C

The three figures on the left all contain a square border with grey line shading in the same direction.
Therefore, the answer is C.

Q6 A

Q7 D

Q8 A

Q9 B

Q10 C

Q11 C

From left to right, the shape in each box rotates 45° anticlockwise.
Therefore, the answer is C.

Q12 A

From left to right, each box contains a shape with one more side than in the preceding box.
Therefore, the answer is A.

Q13 A

From left to right, each box contains a black circle that moves two sides across on the shape in a clockwise direction.
Therefore, the answer is A.

Q14 E

From left to right, a quarter of a circle is added each time to the existing shape in each box.
Therefore, the missing box should contain a full circle in the top right.
Therefore, the answer is E.

Q15 B

From left to right, the line shading of the shape in each box rotates 45° anticlockwise.
Therefore, the correct answer is B.

Grammar & Spelling (page 40)

Q1 C slay

Q2 B fish

Q3 E mis (misunderstand)

Q4 C judgemant (should be judgment or judgement)

Q5 E arguement (should be argument)

Q6 A embarass (should be embarrass)

Q7 C existance (should be existence)

Q8 C ocassion (should be occasion)

Antonyms (pages 42-43)

Q1	**E** ancestor	Q9	**C** gentle
Q2	**B** natural	Q10	**B** ignore
Q3	**C** delicious	Q11	**D** intentional
Q4	**A** comedy	Q12	**E** break
Q5	**D** construct	Q13	**C** vacant
Q6	**C** near	Q14	**D** often
Q7	**E** exposed	Q15	**A** wealth
Q8	**B** mean		

Numeracy (pages 45-47)

Q1 107

$(642 \div 2) \div 3 = 321 \div 3 = 107$

Q2 36

Sequence is ascending square numbers so next square number is 36

Q3 2

$\frac{1}{2} + \frac{1}{6} = \frac{3}{6} + \frac{1}{6} = \frac{4}{6} = \frac{2}{3}$

Q4 8

$0\cdot4 = \frac{4}{10}$

$\frac{4}{10} = \frac{X}{20}$

$10X = 80$

$X = 8$

Q5 3

4·567 rounded to 1 d.p. is 4·6

4·291 rounded to 1 d.p. is 4·3

$4\cdot6 - 4\cdot3 = 0\cdot3$

$0\cdot3 = 3$ tenths

Q6 7

$7X - 7 = 2X + 28$

$7X - 2X = 28 + 7$

$5X = 35$

$X = 7$

Q7 36

Work backwards: $49 - 1 = 48; 48 \div 4 = 12;$

$12 \times 3 = 36$

Q8 112

$\frac{1}{5}$ of $80 = 80 \div 5 = 16$

So $\frac{7}{5}$ of $80 = 16 \times 7 = 112$

Q9 E

Length of 1 side = 36·6 cm ÷ 6 = 6·1 cm

Length of 4 sides = 6·1 cm × 4 = 24·4 cm

Q10 C

The other options are either too large or too small.

Q11 E

6 out of 10 equal parts are not shaded

$\frac{6}{10} = \frac{3}{5}$

Q12 D

Lucy's time is 54 seconds; Jane's time is 47 seconds; Rahul's time is 52 seconds

So Tim's time is 44 seconds

Q13 B

4·5 kg ÷ 9 = 0·5 kg

Q14 E

$2b° + 2b° + 5b° = 180°$

$9b° = 180°$

$b° = 20°$

$5b° = 100°$

Q15 D

27th September to 3rd October inclusively is 7 days

750 m × 7 = 5,250 m = 5·25 km

Q16 E

Number that chose red = 40% of 250 = 100

Number that chose blue = $\frac{1}{5}$ of 250 = 50

Remainder = 250 − 100 − 50 = 100

Number that chose green = $\frac{1}{2}$ of remainder = $\frac{1}{2}$ of 100 = 50

Q17 D

Total area of black circles = $4 \times 3\cdot5$ cm^2 = 14 cm^2

Total area of square = 7 cm × 7 cm = 49 cm^2

Unshaded area of square = 49 cm^2 − 14 cm^2 = 35 cm^2

Q18 C

Change received = £10 − £6·50 = £3·50

Percentage = $(\frac{£3\cdot50}{£10}) \times 100$ = $0\cdot35 \times 100 = 35\%$

Answers to *Get Ahead* Test B Paper 1

Comprehension (pages 51-52)

Q1 *D*
The girl was sitting

Q2 *D*
Robust (the passage says 'She was not a dainty thing but a good-size farm girl.')

Q3 *A*
Nervous (the passage says 'The storm makes you skittish.')

Q4 *B*
The Witch thought it would help her get the measure of the girl (the passage says 'Was she to be taken seriously, or was she merely a blow-away dandelion seed, caught on the wrong side of the wind? If she could see the girl's face, the Witch felt she might know.')

Q5 *A*
Clumsily (the passage says 'She was up and running in an ungainly way')

Q6 *C*
Simile

Q7 *C*
She could not venture out in the rain (the passage says 'The Witch could not venture out in such a vicious, insinuating wetness')

Q8 *B*
She had faced many obstacles and setbacks (the passage says 'The punishing political climate of Oz had beat her down, dried her up, tossed her away')

Q9 *B*
Imminent

Q10 *B*
Decreasing

Shuffled Sentences (pages 54-55)

Q1 *B*
sing *The student left many questions unanswered.*

Q2 *A*
describe *Many of the participants enjoyed the experience.*

Q3 *E*
tree *Forests play a vital role in our ecosystem.*

Q4 *B*
on *The doctor was undeniably intelligent and talented. OR The doctor was undeniably talented and intelligent.*

Q5 *D*
on *The quickest way to travel to Rome is by plane.*

Q6 *A*
traveller *The group of friends discussed potential holiday destinations.*

Q7 *C*
exercised *Several members of the gym decided to quit.*

Q8 *A*
cookery *The chef highlighted the importance of quality ingredients.*

Q9 *E*
phase *Natural disasters occur all over the world.*

Q10 *A*
with *The happy couple agreed to purchase the apartment. OR The happy couple agreed to the apartment purchase.*

Q11 *E*
grows *The population of China exceeds one billion.*

Q12 *A*
stifle *The soldier's heroic bravery was rewarded by the politician.*

Q13 *E*
volume *The determined businessman refused to give up.*

Q14 *B*
against *A variety of flowers grow on the mountain.*

Q15 *C*
money *The company's legal fees and costs rose rapidly. OR The company's legal costs and fees rose rapidly.*

Numeracy (pages 56-57)

Q1 *12*
$\frac{1}{2}$ of 96 = 48; $\frac{1}{4}$ of 48 = 12

Q2 *104*
52 weeks in 1 year; number of weeks in 2 years = 52 × 2 = 104

Q3 *16*

16 cm ÷ 4 cm = 4; 4 plates can fit in 1 row and there are 4 rows in total

4 × 4 = 16

Q4 *8*

Q5 *26*

Tank is $\frac{3}{5}$ full; $1 - \frac{3}{5} = \frac{2}{5}$

So it can hold a further $\frac{2}{5}$ of 65 litres

$\frac{2}{5}$ of 65 = 26

Q6 *27*

30th July to 3rd August is 5 days inclusive

Total growth = 3 cm × 5 = 15 cm

New height = 12 cm + 15 cm = 27 cm

Q7 *73*

Sequence is +2, +4, +8

So difference is doubling each time

So next term is +16; 57 + 16 = 73

Q8 *1*

Q9 *976*

6,850 − 5,874 = 976

Q10 *26*

Fifths in 10 = 5 × 10 = 50

Thirds in 8 = 3 × 8 = 24

50 − 24 = 26

Q11 *50*

74 − (8 + 16) = 74 − 24 = 50

Q12 *20*

120 km in 1 hour; $\frac{1}{6}$ of 120 km is 20 km

Q13 *1,000*

1 m = 100 cm = (100 × 10) mm = 1,000 mm

Q14 *2,938*

3,027 − 89 = 2,938

Q15 *150*

2·5 km × 2 = 5 km; there are 30 days in November; 30 × 5 km = 150 km

Problem Solving (pages 58-59)

Q1 **D**

£2·50 = 250 p; 250 ÷ 45 = 5 R 25

So 5 oranges is the most that can be bought for £2·50

Q2 **C**

−6°C to 14°C is 20°

Q3 **D**

Think in terms of multiples of 20:

100,000   100,020   100,040   100,060

100,045 is closest to 100,040

Q4 **E**

Total grapes eaten per day = 4 + 7 = 11

Total grapes eaten in a fortnight = 11 × 14

= 154

Q5 **D**

Reflecting (4, 4) in the y-axis means x-coordinate changes from positive to negative and y-coordinate stays the same so (−4, 4)

Q6 **B**

3 people is 4 times less than 12 people

4 times less than 8 eggs is 2 eggs

Q7 **A**

8 + 1 + 6 = 15 parts; 60 ÷ 15 = 4

So each part consists of 4 peaches

So largest pile is 8 × 4 = 32 peaches

Q8 **B**

$\frac{4}{5}$ have black fur; $\frac{4}{5}$ of 40 = 32

$\frac{1}{4}$ have long tails; $\frac{1}{4}$ of 40 = 10

So largest number that can have both is to assume all rats with long tails have black fur, which is a maximum of 10

Q9 **E**

Length of Rectangle A = 8 cm

Width of Rectangle B = 10 cm

Length of Rectangle B = 16 cm

Area of Rectangle B = 10 cm × 16 cm

= 160 cm²

Q10 **D**

Percentage who chose neither chicken nor tomato = 100% − 35% − 20% = 45%

45% of 120 = 54

Synonyms (pages 61-63)

Q1	**E** *preserve*	**Q13**	**C** *grab*
Q2	**D** *misery*	**Q14**	**E** *isolated*
Q3	**C** *moderately*	**Q15**	**C** *defective*
Q4	**E** *notify*	**Q16**	**B** *hug*
Q5	**B** *overseas*	**Q17**	**A** *fate*
Q6	**A** *reliable*	**Q18**	**C** *separate*
Q7	**D** *selection*	**Q19**	**D** *eternal*
Q8	**B** *survive*	**Q20**	**A** *danger*
Q9	**C** *steady*	**Q21**	**A** *remain*
Q10	**E** *represent*	**Q22**	**E** *wander*
Q11	**B** *final*	**Q23**	**C** *promise*
Q12	**E** *suggest*	**Q24**	**C** *exclaim*

Non-Verbal Reasoning (pages 65-67)

Q1 C

Q2 D

Q3 B

Q4 C

Q5 C

Q6 A

Q7 D

All the other figures are rotations of the same shape.

Q8 A

In all the other figures, the black shape is at the back.

Q9 E

All the other figures consist of the same five shapes.

Q10 B

In all other figures, the line shading of the frame is in the other direction.

Q11 E

All the other figures have more lines on the top than on the bottom and all the other figures have an odd number of lines.

Q12 E

In all the other figures, from the top row downwards, the number of triangles stays the same or decreases.

Answers to *Get Ahead* Test B Paper 2

Problem Solving (pages 70-71)

Q1 E

$\frac{2,800}{7,000} = \frac{2}{5}$; $\frac{2}{5}$ completed the course

$\frac{3}{5}$ did not complete it

$\frac{3}{5} = 60\%$

Q2 A

Total wool produced by male sheep =
12 kg × 30 = 360 kg
Total wool produced by female sheep =
10 kg × 25 = 250 kg
360 kg − 250 kg = 110 kg

Q3 H

Price per window = £150
5 windows at full price = £150 × 5 = £750
10 windows at half price = £150 × 10 × $\frac{1}{2}$
= £750
Total cost = £750 + £750 = £1,500

Q4 F

16:40 to 18:10 is 90 minutes
90 km in 90 minutes is equivalent to 60 km in 60 minutes
60 minutes = 1 hour so average speed =
60 kph

Q5 M

Day 1 = 75; Day 2 = 150; Day 3 = 300;
Day 4 = 600; Day 5 = 1,200

Q6 O

Number of black balls = 20 − 2 − 4 − 3
= 11
Percentage black = $(\frac{11}{20}) × 100 = 55\%$

Q7 N

Total weight = 120 kg + 100 kg + 100 kg +
92 kg = 412 kg
Average weight = 412 kg ÷ 4 = 103 kg

Q8 I

Let X be the number of white mice
5:7 = 1,300:X
So $X = (1,300 ÷ 5) × 7 = 1,820$

Q9 B

Reduced price is $\frac{4}{5}$ of original price

$\frac{4}{5} = £1,300$; $\frac{1}{5} = £1,300 ÷ 4 = £325$

$\frac{5}{5} = £325 × 5 = £1,625$

Q10 D

Bus A: 45 km in 30 minutes
90 km in 60 minutes so speed is 90 kph
Bus B: 70 km in 60 minutes so speed is
70 kph
Average speed = (90 kph + 70 kph) ÷ 2 =
80 kph

Q11 J

10% of £1,760 is £176
£1,760 − £176 = £1,584

Q12 K

60 seconds = 1 minute so his speed is
400 metres per minute
60 minutes = 1 hour so his speed is
(60 × 400) metres per hour
60 × 400 = 24,000 m; 24,000 m = 24 km
Speed = 24 kph

Q13 G

20% of 1,200 = 240; Number of flowers in
Year 2 = 1,200 + 240 = 1,440
20% of 1,440 = 288; Number of flowers in
Year 3 = 1,440 + 288 = 1,728

Q14 L

Percentage = $\frac{15}{12} \times 100 = \frac{1,500}{12} = 125\%$

Q15 C

103,500 g = 103·5 kg
103·5 kg rounded to the nearest kg is 104 kg

Cloze (pages 73-74)

Q1	**D** juice	**Q11**	**E** talk
Q2	**B** neither	**Q12**	**G** family
Q3	**F** although	**Q13**	**A** wished
Q4	**E** said	**Q14**	**F** opposite
Q5	**A** looking	**Q15**	**J** anything
Q6	**I** presenting	**Q16**	**C** listened
Q7	**G** reminded	**Q17**	**I** understood
Q8	**H** reading	**Q18**	**B** planned
Q9	**C** attention	**Q19**	**H** different
Q10	**J** suspicious	**Q20**	**D** danger

Non-Verbal Reasoning (pages 77-79)

Q1 C

The three figures on the left are all three
quarters of a whole shape.
Therefore, the answer is C.

Q2 D

In each figure on the left, the square on the
left contains more black circles than the
square on the right.
Therefore, the answer is D.

Q3 A

The three figures on the left all have a
vertical line of symmetry.
Therefore, the answer is A.

Q4 D

The three figures on the left all have an hour
hand pointing at an even number.
Therefore, the answer is D.

Q5 E

The three figures on the left each consist of
four arrows that rotate 45° from left to right
in a clockwise direction.
Therefore, the answer is E.

Q6 A

Q7 B

Q8 A

Q9 B

Q10 A

Q11 A

The second figure is a 45° clockwise rotation
of the first figure.
Therefore, the answer is a 45° rotation of
the third figure.
Therefore, the answer is A.

Q12 C

The second figure consists of two smaller
versions of the shape in the first figure with
opposite line shading.
Therefore, the answer must consist of two
smaller versions of the shape in the third
figure, with the same line shading pattern as
in the second figure.
Therefore, the answer is C.

Q13 C

The shape in the second figure has one less
side and contains one less circle than the
shape in the first figure.
The same changes must be made to the
third figure.
Therefore, the answer is C.

Q14 C

The right half of the shape in the first figure
is removed in the second figure.
Therefore, the right half of the shape in the
third figure must also be removed.
Therefore, the answer is C.

Q15 A

The shapes in the first figure are rearranged
to form the second figure.
The shapes in the third figure must be
rearranged in the same way.
Therefore, the answer is A.

Antonyms (pages 81-83)

Q1 D question
Q2 C above
Q3 D excited
Q4 E start
Q5 A deny
Q6 A arrogant
Q7 C debit
Q8 E abandoned
Q9 B quiet
Q10 D lenient
Q11 C ally
Q12 E full
Q13 D exhale
Q14 C energetic
Q15 A fragment
Q16 D flawless
Q17 E transparent
Q18 B biased

Numeracy (pages 85-86)

Q1 45
$264 - 219 = 45$

Q2 1
$3X + 7 = 2(X + 4)$
$3X + 7 = 2X + 8$
$3X - 2X = 8 - 7$
$X = 1$

Q3 1
Sequence is $-4, -5, -4, -5$
So next term is -4; $5 - 4 = 1$

Q4 16
Work backwards: $30 \div 3 = 10$; $10 \times 2 = 20$;
$20 - 4 = 16$

Q5 1
Days in July and August $= 31 + 31 = 62$
Days in October and November $= 31 + 30$
$= 61$
Difference $= 62 - 61 = 1$

Q6 54
Mode is the most common number, which is
54

Q7 180
Joey is 30 cm tall so Monty is 90 cm tall so
Bruno is 180 cm tall

Q8 343
Total tasks $= 7 \times 7 \times 7 = 343$

Q9 16
2 years ago I was 11; today I am 13 so in
3 years I will be 16

Q10 4

Q11 6
100 metres per minute; 60 minutes in an
hour so (60×100) metres per hour
$= 6,000$ metres per hour
6,000 metres $= 6$ km
So running speed is 6 kph

Q12 35
Let S be the number of sweets
Remaining sweets $= S - \frac{5}{7} S = \frac{2}{7} S$
$\frac{2}{7} S = 14$ so $\frac{1}{7} S = 7$
Sweets eaten $= \frac{5}{7} S = \frac{1}{7} S \times 5 = 7 \times 5 = 35$

Q13 33
Tom's score $= 60\%$
60% of 50 is 30
10% of 30 is 3
So Bill's score $= 30 + 3 = 33$

Q14 26
$\frac{1}{4}$ of 52 is 13
Number of cards remaining $= 52 - 13 = 39$
Cards selected $= \frac{2}{3} \times 39 = 26$

Q15 44
7 sevenths in 1 whole
So number of sevenths in $6 = 6 \times 7 = 42$
So number of sevenths in $6\frac{2}{7} = 42 + 2 = 44$

Q16 9
$9 \times £2 \cdot 50 = £22 \cdot 50$; $10 \times £2 \cdot 50 = £25$
So a maximum of 9 caps can be bought with
£24·50

Q17 8
1 day $= 24$ hours; $\frac{1}{3}$ of 24 hours is 8 hours

Q18 909
$9,898 - 8,989 = 909$

Pupil's Full Name:

Instructions:
Mark the boxes correctly like this ✎

Please sign your name here:

Comprehension (pages 6-9)

Example 1

| A | B̶ | C | D |

Practice Question 1

| A | B | C | D |

1. A B C D
2. A B C D
3. A B C D
4. A B C D
5. A B C D
6. A B C D
7. A B C D
8. A B C D
9. A B C D
10. A B C D

Shuffled Sentences (pages 10-12)

Example 1

| A | B | C̶ | D | E |

Practice Question 1

| A | B | C | D | E |

1. A B C D E
2. A B C D E
3. A B C D E
4. A B C D E
5. A B C D E
6. A B C D E
7. A B C D E
8. A B C D E
9. A B C D E
10. A B C D E
11. A B C D E
12. A B C D E
13. A B C D E
14. A B C D E
15. A B C D E

Numeracy (pages 13-14)

Example 1

5 4

Practice Question 1

1, 2, 3, 4, 5, 6, 7, 8, 9, 10, 11, 12, 13

(Numeracy answer grids with digits 0–9 for each question)

Problem Solving (pages 15-17)

Example 1

	A	B	C	D	E

Practice Question 1

	A	B	C	D	E

1	A	B	C	D	E
2	A	B	C	D	E
3	A	B	C	D	E
4	A	B	C	D	E
5	A	B	C	D	E
6	A	B	C	D	E
7	A	B	C	D	E
8	A	B	C	D	E
9	A	B	C	D	E
10	A	B	C	D	E

Synonyms (pages 18-21)

Example 1

	A	B	C	D	E

Practice Question 1

	A	B	C	D	E

1	A	B	C	D	E
2	A	B	C	D	E
3	A	B	C	D	E
4	A	B	C	D	E
5	A	B	C	D	E
6	A	B	C	D	E
7	A	B	C	D	E
8	A	B	C	D	E
9	A	B	C	D	E
10	A	B	C	D	E
11	A	B	C	D	E
12	A	B	C	D	E
13	A	B	C	D	E
14	A	B	C	D	E
15	A	B	C	D	E
16	A	B	C	D	E
17	A	B	C	D	E
18	A	B	C	D	E
19	A	B	C	D	E
20	A	B	C	D	E
21	A	B	C	D	E
22	A	B	C	D	E

23	A	B	C	D	E
24	A	B	C	D	E

Non-Verbal Reasoning (pages 22-26)

COMPLETE THE SQUARE Example 1

	A	B	C	D	E

COMPLETE THE SQUARE Practice Question 1

	A	B	C	D	E

REFLECTION Example 2

	A	B	C	D

REFLECTION Practice Question 2

	A	B	C	D

DIMENSION Example 3

	A	B	C	D

DIMENSION Practice Question 3

	A	B	C	D

1	A	B	C	D	E
2	A	B	C	D	E
3	A	B	C	D	E
4	A	B	C	D	E
5	A	B	C	D
6	A	B	C	D
7	A	B	C	D
8	A	B	C	D
9	A	B	C	D
10	A	B	C	D
11	A	B	C	D
12	A	B	C	D
13	A	B	C	D

Pupil's Full Name:

Instructions:
Mark the boxes correctly like this ▰

Please sign your name here:

Problem Solving (pages 28-30)

Example 1

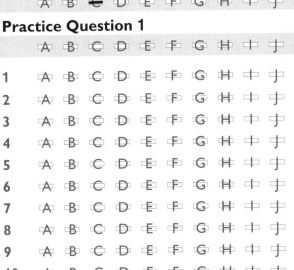

A B ⬤ D E F G H I J

Practice Question 1

A B C D E F G H I J

1   A B C D E F G H I J
2   A B C D E F G H I J
3   A B C D E F G H I J
4   A B C D E F G H I J
5   A B C D E F G H I J
6   A B C D E F G H I J
7   A B C D E F G H I J
8   A B C D E F G H I J
9   A B C D E F G H I J
10 A B C D E F G H I J

Cloze (pages 31-33)

Example 1

▰ B C D E

Practice Question 1

A B C D E

1   A B C D E F G H I J
2   A B C D E F G H I J
3   A B C D E F G H I J
4   A B C D E F G H I J
5   A B C D E F G H I J
6   A B C D E F G H I J
7   A B C D E F G H I J
8   A B C D E F G H I J
9   A B C D E F G H I J
10 A B C D E F G H I J
11 A B C D E F G H I J
12 A B C D E F G H I J
13 A B C D E F G H I J
14 A B C D E F G H I J

---

15 A B C D E F G H I J
16 A B C D E F G H I J
17 A B C D E F G H I J
18 A B C D E F G H I J
19 A B C D E F G H I J
20 A B C D E F G H I J

Non-Verbal Reasoning (pages 34-38)

SIMILARITY Example 1

A   B   C   ⬤   E

SIMILARITY Practice Question 1

A   B   C   D   E

CUBE NET Example 2

A   ⬤   C   D

CUBE NET Practice Question 2

A   B   C   D

COMPLETE THE SEQUENCE Example 3

⬤   B   C   D   E

COMPLETE THE SEQUENCE Practice Question 3

A   B   C   D   E

1   A   B   C   D   E
2   A   B   C   D   E
3   A   B   C   D   E
4   A   B   C   D   E
5   A   B   C   D   E
6   A   B   C   D
7   A   B   C   D
8   A   B   C   D
9   A   B   C   D
10   A   B   C   D
11   A   B   C   D   E
12   A   B   C   D   E
13   A   B   C   D   E
14   A   B   C   D   E
15   A   B   C   D   E

Grammar & Spelling (page 39-40)

Example 1

   A   B   C   D   E

Practice Question 1

   A   B   C   D   E

1   A   B   C   D   E
2   A   B   C   D   E
3   A   B   C   D   E
4   A   B   C   D   E
5   A   B   C   D   E
6   A   B   C   D   E
7   A   B   C   D   E
8   A   B   C   D   E

Antonyms (pages 41-43)

Example 1

   A   B   C   D   E

Practice Question 1

   A   B   C   D   E

1   A   B   C   D   E
2   A   B   C   D   E
3   A   B   C   D   E
4   A   B   C   D   E
5   A   B   C   D   E
6   A   B   C   D   E
7   A   B   C   D   E
8   A   B   C   D   E
9   A   B   C   D   E
10   A   B   C   D   E
11   A   B   C   D   E
12   A   B   C   D   E
13   A   B   C   D   E
14   A   B   C   D   E
15   A   B   C   D   E

Numeracy (pages 44-47)

Example 1   Practice Question 1

5   4   1

(answer grids 0–9 for Example 1, Practice Question 1, and question 1)

2   **3**   **4**   **5**

(answer grids 0–9 for questions 2, 3, 4, 5)

6   **7**   **8**

(answer grids 0–9 for questions 6, 7, 8)

9   A   B   C   D   E
10   A   B   C   D   E
11   A   B   C   D   E
12   A   B   C   D   E
13   A   B   C   D   E
14   A   B   C   D   E
15   A   B   C   D   E
16   A   B   C   D   E
17   A   B   C   D   E
18   A   B   C   D   E

Pupil's Full Name:

Instructions:
Mark the boxes correctly like this ✏

Please sign your name here:

Comprehension (pages 49-52)

Example 1

| A | B | C | D |

Practice Question 1

| A | B | C | D |

1   A   B   C   D
2   A   B   C   D
3   A   B   C   D
4   A   B   C   D
5   A   B   C   D
6   A   B   C   D
7   A   B   C   D
8   A   B   C   D
9   A   B   C   D
10   A   B   C   D

Shuffled Sentences (pages 53-55)

Example 1

| A | B | C | D | E |

Practice Question 1

| A | B | C | D | E |

1   A   B   C   D   E
2   A   B   C   D   E
3   A   B   C   D   E
4   A   B   C   D   E
5   A   B   C   D   E
6   A   B   C   D   E
7   A   B   C   D   E
8   A   B   C   D   E
9   A   B   C   D   E
10   A   B   C   D   E
11   A   B   C   D   E
12   A   B   C   D   E
13   A   B   C   D   E
14   A   B   C   D   E
15   A   B   C   D   E

Numeracy (pages 56-57)

Example 1　　**Practice Question 1**　　**1**

5 4

(number grids 0–9 for Example 1, Practice Question 1, and 1)

2　　**3**　　**4**　　**5**

(number grids 0–9)

6　　**7**　　**8**　　**9**

(number grids 0–9)

10　　**11**　　**12**

(number grids 0–9)

Continued over page

13   **14**

(number grid boxes 0–9 for questions 13 and 14)

15

(number grid box 0–9 for question 15)

Problem Solving (pages 58-59)

Example 1

   A   B   **C**   D   E

Practice Question 1

   A   B   C   D   E

1   A   B   C   D   E
2   A   B   C   D   E
3   A   B   C   D   E
4   A   B   C   D   E
5   A   B   C   D   E
6   A   B   C   D   E
7   A   B   C   D   E
8   A   B   C   D   E
9   A   B   C   D   E
10   A   B   C   D   E

Synonyms (pages 60-63)

Example 1

   A   **B̶**   C   D   E

Practice Question 1

   A   B   C   D   E

1   A   B   C   D   E
2   A   B   C   D   E
3   A   B   C   D   E
4   A   B   C   D   E
5   A   B   C   D   E

6   A   B   C   D   E
7   A   B   C   D   E
8   A   B   C   D   E
9   A   B   C   D   E
10   A   B   C   D   E
11   A   B   C   D   E
12   A   B   C   D   E
13   A   B   C   D   E
14   A   B   C   D   E
15   A   B   C   D   E
16   A   B   C   D   E
17   A   B   C   D   E
18   A   B   C   D   E
19   A   B   C   D   E
20   A   B   C   D   E
21   A   B   C   D   E
22   A   B   C   D   E
23   A   B   C   D   E
24   A   B   C   D   E

Non-Verbal Reasoning (pages 64-67)

REFLECTION Example 1

   A   B   **C̶**   D

REFLECTION Practice Question 1

   A   B   C   D

LEAST SIMILAR Example 2

   A   **B̶**   C   D   E

LEAST SIMILAR Practice Question 2

   A   B   C   D   E

1   A   B   C   D
2   A   B   C   D
3   A   B   C   D
4   A   B   C   D
5   A   B   C   D
6   A   B   C   D
7   A   B   C   D   E
8   A   B   C   D   E
9   A   B   C   D   E
10   A   B   C   D   E
11   A   B   C   D   E
12   A   B   C   D   E

Pupil's Full Name:

Instructions:
Mark the boxes correctly like this ⬌

Please sign your name here:

Problem Solving (pages 69-71)

Example 1

A B ⊝ D E F G H ⊞ ⊟

Practice Question 1

A B C D E F G H ⊞ ⊟

1 A B C D E F G H ⊞ ⊟
   K L M N O

2 A B C D E F G H ⊞ ⊟
   K L M N O

3 A B C D E F G H ⊞ ⊟
   K L M N O

4 A B C D E F G H ⊞ ⊟
   K L M N O

5 A B C D E F G H ⊞ ⊟
   K L M N O

6 A B C D E F G H ⊞ ⊟
   K L M N O

7 A B C D E F G H ⊞ ⊟
   K L M N O

8 A B C D E F G H ⊞ ⊟
   K L M N O

9 A B C D E F G H ⊞ ⊟
   K L M N O

10 A B C D E F G H ⊞ ⊟
   K L M N O

11 A B C D E F G H ⊞ ⊟
   K L M N O

12 A B C D E F G H ⊞ ⊟
   K L M N O

13 A B C D E F G H ⊞ ⊟
   K L M N O

14 A B C D E F G H ⊞ ⊟
   K L M N O

15 A B C D E F G H ⊞ ⊟
   K L M N O

Cloze (pages 72-74)

Example 1

⬌ B C D E

Practice Question 1

A B C D E

1 A B C D E F G H ⊞ ⊟

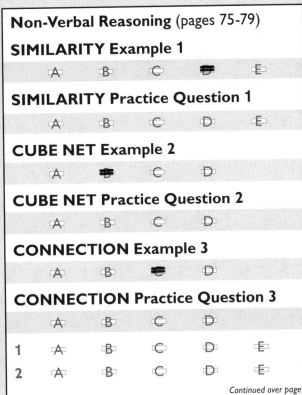

2 A B C D E F G H ⊞ ⊟
3 A B C D E F G H ⊞ ⊟
4 A B C D E F G H ⊞ ⊟
5 A B C D E F G H ⊞ ⊟
6 A B C D E F G H ⊞ ⊟
7 A B C D E F G H ⊞ ⊟
8 A B C D E F G H ⊞ ⊟
9 A B C D E F G H ⊞ ⊟
10 A B C D E F G H ⊞ ⊟
11 A B C D E F G H ⊞ ⊟
12 A B C D E F G H ⊞ ⊟
13 A B C D E F G H ⊞ ⊟
14 A B C D E F G H ⊞ ⊟
15 A B C D E F G H ⊞ ⊟
16 A B C D E F G H ⊞ ⊟
17 A B C D E F G H ⊞ ⊟
18 A B C D E F G H ⊞ ⊟
19 A B C D E F G H ⊞ ⊟
20 A B C D E F G H ⊞ ⊟

Non-Verbal Reasoning (pages 75-79)

SIMILARITY Example 1

A   B   C   ⬌   E

SIMILARITY Practice Question 1

A   B   C   D   E

CUBE NET Example 2

A   ⬌   C   D

CUBE NET Practice Question 2

A   B   C   D

CONNECTION Example 3

A   B   ⬌   D

CONNECTION Practice Question 3

A   B   C   D

1 A   B   C   D   E
2 A   B   C   D   E

Continued over page

3	A	B	C	D	E
4	A	B	C	D	E
5	A	B	C	D	E
6	A	B	C	D	
7	A	B	C	D	
8	A	B	C	D	
9	A	B	C	D	
10	A	B	C	D	
11	A	B	C	D	
12	A	B	C	D	
13	A	B	C	D	
14	A	B	C	D	
15	A	B	C	D	

Antonyms (pages 80-83)

Example 1

	A	B	C	D	E

Practice Question 1

	A	B	C	D	E
1	A	B	C	D	E
2	A	B	C	D	E
3	A	B	C	D	E
4	A	B	C	D	E
5	A	B	C	D	E
6	A	B	C	D	E
7	A	B	C	D	E
8	A	B	C	D	E
9	A	B	C	D	E
10	A	B	C	D	E
11	A	B	C	D	E
12	A	B	C	D	E
13	A	B	C	D	E
14	A	B	C	D	E
15	A	B	C	D	E
16	A	B	C	D	E
17	A	B	C	D	E
18	A	B	C	D	E

Numeracy (pages 84-86)

Example 1   **Practice Question 1**   **1**   **2**

5 4

3   **4**   **5**   **6**

7   **8**   **9**   **10**

11   **12**   **13**   **14**

15   **16**   **17**   **18**

Letts

11+ Success for CEM

Practice Test Papers

4 test papers

- Comprehension
- Verbal Reasoning
- Maths
- Non-Verbal Reasoning

Get test-ready

🎧 Audio

Faisal Nasim

Contents

Guidance notes for parents

What your child will need to sit these papers

- A quiet place to sit the exam
- A clearly visible clock
- A way to play the audio download
- A pencil and an eraser
- A piece of paper

Your child should not use a calculator for any of these papers.

How to invigilate the test papers

It is recommended that your child sits Test A (with a 15-minute break between Papers 1 and 2) and then sits Test B in the same way at a later date. Don't help your child or allow any talking. Review the answers with your child and help improve their weaker areas.

Step 1: Cut out the answers and keep them hidden from your child.

Step 2: Cut out the answer sheet section. Your child should write their full name on top of the first answer sheet. Give them the question paper booklet. They must not open the paper until they are told to do so by the audio instructions.

Step 3: Start the audio.

Step 4: Ask your child to work through the practice questions before the time starts for each section. An example is already marked on each section of the answer sheet. Your child should mark the answer sheet clearly and check that the practice questions are correctly marked.

Step 5: Mark the answer sheet. Then, together with your child, work through the questions that were answered incorrectly. When working through the Non-Verbal Reasoning sections, ensure you have the question papers open to help explain the answers to your child.

How your child should complete the answer sheet

Your child MUST NOT write their answers on the question paper; they must use the answer sheet. They should put a horizontal line through the boxes on the answer sheet. To change an answer, your child should fully erase the incorrect answer and then clearly select a new answer. Any rough workings should be done on a separate piece of paper.

The audio instructions

Both papers have audio instructions in order to prepare your child to listen and act upon them. Audio instructions are at the start, during and at the end of the sections. Audio warnings on the time remaining will be given at varying intervals. Your child should listen out for these warnings.

The symbols at the foot of the page

Written instructions are at the foot of the page. Your child MUST follow these instructions:

Continue working

Stop and wait for instructions

Your child can review questions within the allocated time, but must not move on to the next section until they are allowed to do so.

The instructions and examples at the beginning of the section

In the instructions, your child should look for: the time allowed; how many questions there are; and how to complete the answers.

Examples are at the beginning of every section to show the type of question included in a particular section. The example questions will be worked through as part of the audio instructions.

How to work out your child's overall score for each Test

Each question is worth one mark. For the purpose of marking, each test is split into two subject areas:

1) Maths (which includes Numeracy and Problem Solving) & Non-Verbal Reasoning

2) English (which includes the remaining sections).

For each test follow these steps to calculate your child's overall score:

1) Add up your child's scores for each of the two subject areas in both papers and note them in the blue boxes on the next page.

    For example, Test A Paper 1: 33 for English and 28 for Maths & Non-Verbal Reasoning and in Test A Paper 2: 29 for English and 30 for Maths & Non-Verbal Reasoning.

2) Add together both your child's total scores in English and then add together both your child's total scores in Maths & Non-Verbal Reasoning. Fill in each total in the blue boxes on the next page.

    For example: For English 33 + 29 = 62 and for Maths & Non-Verbal Reasoning 28 + 30 = 58.

3) Take your child's total English score and divide it by the maximum total English score (as shown in the table on the next page) and then multiply that figure by 100 to give you a percentage. Repeat this process for Maths & Non-Verbal Reasoning.

    For example: English: 62 ÷ 92 × 100 = 67%
    Maths & Non-Verbal Reasoning: 58 ÷ 79 × 100 = 73%

4) Now add both percentages together and divide by 2 to give you your child's overall score for one test.

    For example: 67 + 73 = 140 ÷ 2 = 70%

5) Repeat the steps above to calculate your child's overall score for Test B.

Test A	Subject	Your child's score	Maximum score
Test A Paper 1	English		49
Test A Paper 1	Maths & Non-Verbal Reasoning		36
Test A Paper 2	English		43
Test A Paper 2	Maths & Non-Verbal Reasoning		43
		Your child's total English score	Maximum total English score
			92
		Your child's total Maths & Non-Verbal Reasoning score	Maximum total Maths & Non-Verbal Reasoning score
			79

Your child's English percentage score	Your child's Maths & Non-Verbal Reasoning percentage score	Your child's overall score

Test B	Subject	Your child's score	Maximum score
Test B Paper 1	English		49
Test B Paper 1	Maths & Non-Verbal Reasoning		37
Test B Paper 2	English		38
Test B Paper 2	Maths & Non-Verbal Reasoning		48
		Your child's total English score	Maximum total English score
			87
		Your child's total Maths & Non-Verbal Reasoning score	Maximum total Maths & Non-Verbal Reasoning score
			85

Your child's English percentage score	Your child's Maths & Non-Verbal Reasoning percentage score	Your child's overall score

Please note: Your child should be aiming for an overall score of at least 70–75% in each Test. If your child does not score a good mark, focus on the areas where your child did not perform well and continue practising under timed conditions.

As the content varies from year to year in CEM exams, a good score in these papers does not guarantee a pass, and a lower score may not always suggest a fail!

Get Test-Ready
Test A Paper 1

Instructions

1. Ensure you have pencils and an eraser with you.
2. Make sure you are able to see a clock or watch.
3. Write your name on the answer sheet.
4. Do not open the question booklet until you are told to do so by the audio instructions.
5. Listen carefully to the audio instructions given.
6. Mark your answers on the answer sheet only.
7. All workings must be completed on a separate piece of paper.
8. You should not use a calculator, dictionary or thesaurus at any point in this paper.
9. Move through the papers as quickly as possible and with care.
10. Follow the instructions at the foot of each page.
11. You should mark your answers with a horizontal line, as shown on the answer sheet.
12. If you want to change your answer, ensure that you rub out your first answer and that your second answer is clearly more visible.
13. You can go back and review any questions that are within the section you are working on only. You must await further instructions before moving on to another section.

Symbols and Phrases used in the Tests

 Instructions
 Time allowed for this section
 Stop working and await instructions
 Continue working

Comprehension

 ## INSTRUCTIONS

 YOU HAVE 9 MINUTES TO COMPLETE THE FOLLOWING SECTION.

YOU HAVE 10 QUESTIONS TO COMPLETE WITHIN THE TIME GIVEN.

EXAMPLES

Comprehension Example

South Africa is becoming an increasingly popular holiday destination. People from all over the world are attracted by its natural beauty, cosmopolitan cities and diverse wildlife. Cape Town, the capital of South Africa, is especially popular. The city is dynamic, exciting and has a rich history and culture. It is also home to the stunning Table Mountain, which you can ascend on foot or by cable car.

Example 1

Which of the following is not mentioned as a reason why people are attracted to South Africa?

A   Natural beauty
B   Excellent food
C   Cosmopolitan cities
D   Diverse wildlife

The correct answer is B. This has already been marked in Example 1 in the Comprehension section of your answer sheet.

Practice Question 1

What is the name of the mountain in Cape Town?

A   Cape Mountain
B   Africa Mountain
C   Table Mountain
D   Leopard Mountain

The correct answer is C. Please mark this in Practice Question 1 in the Comprehension section of your answer sheet.

STOP AND WAIT FOR FURTHER INSTRUCTIONS ⊗

Read the passage below and then answer the questions that follow.

An extract from: **The End of the Party**
by Graham Greene

Peter Morton woke with a start to face the first light. Rain tapped against the glass. It was January the fifth.

He looked across a table on which a night-light had guttered into a pool of water, at the other bed. Francis Morton was still asleep, and Peter lay down again with his eyes on his brother. It amused him to imagine it was himself whom he watched, the same hair, the same eyes, the same lips and line of cheek. But the thought palled, and the mind went back to the fact which lent the day importance. It was the fifth of January. He could hardly believe a year had passed since Mrs Henne-Falcon had given her last children's party.

Francis turned suddenly upon his back and threw an arm across his face, blocking his mouth. Peter's heart began to beat fast, not with pleasure now but with uneasiness. He sat up and called across the table, "Wake up." Francis's shoulders shook and he waved a clenched fist in the air, but his eyes remained closed. To Peter Morton the whole room seemed to darken, and he had the impression of a great bird swooping. He cried again, "Wake up," and once more there was silver light and the touch of rain on the windows.

Francis rubbed his eyes. "Did you call out?" he asked.

"You are having a bad dream," Peter said. Already experience had taught him how far their minds reflected each other. But he was the elder, by a matter of minutes, and that brief extra interval of light, while his brother still struggled in pain and darkness, had given him self-reliance and an instinct of protection towards the other who was afraid of so many things.

"I dreamed that I was dead," Francis said.

"What was it like?" Peter asked.

"I can't remember," Francis said.

"You dreamed of a big bird."

"Did I?"

The two lay silent in bed facing each other, the same green eyes, the same nose tilting at the tip, the same firm lips, and the same premature modelling of the chin. The fifth of January, Peter thought again, his mind drifting idly from the image of cakes to the prizes which might be won. Egg-and-spoon races, spearing apples in basins of water, blind man's buff.

"I don't want to go," Francis said suddenly. "I suppose Joyce will be there…Mabel Warren." Hateful to him, the thought of a party shared with those two. They were older than he. Joyce was eleven and Mabel Warren thirteen. The long pigtails swung superciliously to a masculine stride. Their sex humiliated him, as they watched him fumble with his egg, from under lowered scornful lids. And last year…he turned his face away from Peter, his cheeks scarlet.

CONTINUE WORKING

"What's the matter?" Peter asked.

"Oh, nothing. I don't think I'm well. I've got a cold. I oughtn't to go to the party."

Peter was puzzled. "But Francis, is it a bad cold?"

"It will be a bad cold if I go to the party. Perhaps I shall die."

"Then you mustn't go," Peter said, prepared to solve all difficulties with one plain sentence, and Francis let his nerves relax, ready to leave everything to Peter. But though he was grateful he did not turn his face towards his brother. His cheeks still bore the badge of a shameful memory, of the game of hide and seek last year in the darkened house, and of how he had screamed when Mabel Warren put her hand suddenly upon his arm. He had not heard her coming. Girls were like that. Their shoes never squeaked. No boards whined under the tread. They slunk like cats on padded claws.

When the nurse came in with hot water Francis lay tranquil leaving everything to Peter. Peter said, "Nurse, Francis has got a cold."

The tall starched woman laid the towels across the cans and said, without turning, "The washing won't be back till tomorrow. You must lend him some of your handkerchiefs."

"But, Nurse," Peter asked, "hadn't he better stay in bed?"

"We'll take him for a good walk this morning," the nurse said. "Wind'll blow away the germs. Get up now, both of you," and she closed the door behind her.

---

(1) At what time of year does this story take place?

    A   Summer
    B   Spring
    C   Autumn
    D   Winter

(2) How were Francis and Peter related to each other?

    A   They were cousins
    B   They were brothers-in-law
    C   They were siblings
    D   They were not related to each other

(3) What event was planned for the fifth of January?

    A   A birthday party
    B   A carol service
    C   A swimming gala
    D   A children's party

CONTINUE WORKING ⇨

(4) Which of the following best describe Peter's attitude towards Francis?

Option 1: Dismissive
Option 2: Protective
Option 3: Jealous
Option 4: Callous

A   Options 1 and 3 only
B   Options 2 and 4 only
C   Option 2 only
D   Options 3 and 4 only

(5) How old could Peter be?

A   Ten
B   Eleven
C   Twelve
D   Thirteen

(6) Why did Francis not turn towards Peter?

A   He was annoyed with Peter
B   He was too exhausted to do so
C   He was too embarrassed to do so
D   He was in too much physical pain to do so

(7) Which word best describes the nurse's character?

A   Pragmatic
B   Belligerent
C   Ambivalent
D   Wicked

(8) What type of word is 'superciliously'?

A   Common noun
B   Adverb
C   Pronoun
D   Preposition

(9) What does the word 'tranquil' mean?

A   Frozen
B   Serene
C   Jittery
D   Fastidious

(10) What literary technique is used in the phrase 'They slunk like cats on padded claws'?

A   Alliteration
B   Metaphor
C   Simile
D   Personification

STOP AND WAIT FOR FURTHER INSTRUCTIONS ⊗

Shuffled Sentences

 INSTRUCTIONS

 YOU HAVE 8 MINUTES TO COMPLETE THE FOLLOWING SECTION.

YOU HAVE 15 QUESTIONS TO COMPLETE WITHIN THE TIME GIVEN.

EXAMPLES

Example 1

The following sentence is shuffled and also contains one unnecessary word. Rearrange the sentence correctly in order to identify the unnecessary word.

wake under before must sunrise up we.

A	B	C	D	E
up	before	under	wake	sunrise

The correct answer is C. This has already been marked in Example 1 in the Shuffled Sentences section of your answer sheet.

Practice Question 1

The following sentence is shuffled and also contains one unnecessary word. Rearrange the sentence correctly in order to identify the unnecessary word.

very girl quickly the ran throw.

A	B	C	D	E
quickly	girl	the	ran	throw

The correct answer is E. Please mark this in Practice Question 1 in the Shuffled Sentences section of your answer sheet.

STOP AND WAIT FOR FURTHER INSTRUCTIONS

Each sentence below is shuffled and also contains one unnecessary word.
Rearrange each sentence correctly in order to identify the unnecessary word.

1 free that wood animals insisted were to roam farmer his the.

A	B	C	D	E
animals	wood	roam	farmer	free

2 have was sold the that auctioneer antique the mirror to thrilled.

A	B	C	D	E
antique	thrilled	was	that	mirror

3 audience the final is enjoyed the watching gripping.

A	B	C	D	E
is	enjoyed	audience	final	watching

4 it burn dry wood in order be yellow kept must to for effectively.

A	B	C	D	E
kept	order	burn	effectively	yellow

5 at to liked closing open night leave her Sheena window.

A	B	C	D	E
closing	leave	window	liked	at

6 his be and unkind and behaviour found to I uncharitable.

A	B	C	D	E
unkind	I	be	his	and

7 one majority momentous as are this few as occasions.

A	B	C	D	E
momentous	majority	this	as	occasions

CONTINUE WORKING ⬛➡

(8) bough quest the tree progressed the sloth the of along lazily.

A	B	C	D	E
tree	bough	the	along	quest

(9) several and in sent up were of jail rounded to the protesters.

A	B	C	D	E
in	rounded	sent	were	protesters

(10) your think from you decisions for make own yourself must and learn to.

A	B	C	D	E
think	to	from	own	yourself

(11) was twice as new television old as one expensive the the through.

A	B	C	D	E
television	through	one	expensive	as

(12) territory slowly encroached with have into snakes the gigantic.

A	B	C	D	E
with	have	slowly	encroached	territory

(13) survival to fundamental human is partial water.

A	B	C	D	E
survival	to	fundamental	water	partial

(14) health deteriorate slide of old the the man rapidly began to.

A	B	C	D	E
began	to	slide	of	rapidly

(15) an sauce unbiased source find the to found it reporter hard.

A	B	C	D	E
sauce	find	unbiased	found	reporter

STOP AND WAIT FOR FURTHER INSTRUCTIONS ⊗

Numeracy

 YOU HAVE 6 MINUTES TO COMPLETE THE FOLLOWING SECTION.

YOU HAVE 13 QUESTIONS TO COMPLETE WITHIN THE TIME GIVEN.

EXAMPLES

The questions within this section are not multiple choice. Write the answer to each question on the answer sheet by selecting the correct digits from the columns provided.

Example 1

Calculate the answer to the following:

12 + 42

The correct answer is 54. This has already been marked in Example 1 in the Numeracy section of your answer sheet.

Practice Question 1

Calculate the answer to the following:

55 − 47

The correct answer is 8. Please mark this in Practice Question 1 in the Numeracy section of your answer sheet. Note that a single-digit answer should be marked with a 0 in the left-hand column, so mark 08 on your answer sheet.

STOP AND WAIT FOR FURTHER INSTRUCTIONS

(1) Calculate the answer to the following:

456 + 1,238

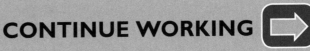
CONTINUE WORKING

(2) Calculate the answer to the following:

$507 \div 13$

(3) Calculate the answer to the following:

$134 + 123 - 221 + 12$

(4) Calculate the median of the following data:

8, 7, 17, 17, 9, 21, 34, 51, 48, 12, 7

(5) Which number should replace the '?' in the following sequence?

67, 58, 50, 43, ?, 32

(6) How many more centimetres are there in 2·45 km than in 2,448 metres?

(7) What is the value of *B* in this equation?

$4B - 7 = 2B + 15$

(8) Multiply the third lowest factor of 18 by 73.

(9) How many fewer eighths are there in $3\frac{1}{4}$ than in $4\frac{3}{4}$?

(10) Triangle A has a base of 9 cm and a height of 9 cm. Triangle B has a base of 3 cm and a height of 3 cm.

How many times greater is the area of Triangle A than the area of Triangle B?

(11) Tina draws 7 crosses on each face of a cube.

How many crosses does Tina draw?

(12) There are 9 apple trees in a field. Last year, each apple tree produced 82 apples. This year, the 9 trees produced a total of 927 apples.

On average, how many more apples did each tree produce this year?

(13) The ratio of pens to pencils in a crate is 5:7.

If there are 203 pencils in the crate, how many pens and pencils are there in total in the crate?

STOP AND WAIT FOR FURTHER INSTRUCTIONS

Problem Solving

 YOU HAVE 8 MINUTES TO COMPLETE THE FOLLOWING SECTION.

YOU HAVE 10 QUESTIONS TO COMPLETE WITHIN THE TIME GIVEN.

EXAMPLES

Example 1

Calculate the answer to the following:

Tom buys a chocolate bar for £1·50. He pays with a £5 note.
How much change does he receive?

A £1·50	**B** £3	**C** £3·50
D £4	**E** £5	

The correct answer is C. This has already been marked in Example 1 in the Problem Solving section of your answer sheet.

Practice Question 1

Sarah eats $\frac{1}{4}$ of a pizza.

What fraction of the pizza remains?

A $\frac{1}{2}$	**B** $\frac{1}{3}$	**C** $\frac{2}{5}$
D $\frac{3}{4}$	**E** $\frac{5}{6}$	

The correct answer is D. Please mark this in Practice Question 1 in the Problem Solving section of your answer sheet.

STOP AND WAIT FOR FURTHER INSTRUCTIONS ⊗

Calculate the answers to the following.

(1) 3 angles in a quadrilateral are 55°, 134° and 109°.

What is the measure of the 4th angle?

   A 62°   **B** 81°   **C** 45°
   D 120°   **E** 109°

(2) 350 people attend a concert. 50% of them have black hair. $\frac{2}{5}$ of those with black hair wear glasses and 0·2 of those with black hair and glasses are left-handed.

How many left-handed people who wear glasses and have black hair attended the concert?

   A 84   **B** 70   **C** 175
   D 245   **E** 14

(3) A cube has a surface area of 24 cm². What is the volume of the cube?

   A 2 cm³   **B** 4 cm³   **C** 8 cm³
   D 10 cm³   **E** 12 cm³

(4) Linda cuts 2 identical equilateral triangles out of the corners of a square to form Figure A.

How many lines of symmetry does Figure A have?

Figure A

   A 0   **B** 1   **C** 2
   D 3   **E** 4

(5) Figure B is made of 2 identical squares. Figure B has an area of 162 cm².

What is the perimeter of Figure B?

Not drawn to scale

Figure B

   A 10 cm   **B** 24 cm   **C** 82 cm
   D 54 cm   **E** 109 cm

CONTINUE WORKING ⇨

(6) For every 2 leopards in a zoo, there are 9 lions.

If there are Y leopards in the zoo, which expression represents the number of lions in the zoo?

A $Y + 9$

B $4Y + 1$

C $9 - Y$

D $2Y - 9$

E $9Y \div 2$

(7) The table below shows the hourly departure times of the city bus. The city bus runs 24 hours per day.

How many departures are there in 3 days?

Departure times (minutes past the hour)

07
16
43
58

A 24

B 4

C 3

D 12

E 288

(8) How many more days were there in the first decade of this millennium (2000 – 2009) than there are in the second decade (2010 – 2019) of this millennium?

A 0

B 1

C 2

D 3

E 4

(9) $\oslash X = 3(X + 1) - 2X$

If $X = 9$, what is the value of $\oslash 9$?

A 12

B 3

C 15

D 27

E 18

(10) Each term in a sequence is 7 times bigger than the previous term.

How many times bigger is the the 8th term than the 4th term?

A 4

B 49

C 7

D 2,401

E 18

STOP AND WAIT FOR FURTHER INSTRUCTIONS

Synonyms

 YOU HAVE 7 MINUTES TO COMPLETE THE FOLLOWING SECTION.

YOU HAVE 24 QUESTIONS TO COMPLETE WITHIN THE TIME GIVEN.

EXAMPLES

Example 1

Select the word that is most similar in meaning to the following word:

push

A	B	C	D	E
shallow	shove	tug	hollow	cry

The correct answer is B. This has already been marked in Example 1 in the Synonyms section of your answer sheet.

Practice Question 1

Select the word that is most similar in meaning to the following word:

imitate

A	B	C	D	E
cover	copy	grow	live	irritate

The correct answer is B. Please mark this in Practice Question 1 in the Synonyms section of your answer sheet.

STOP AND WAIT FOR FURTHER INSTRUCTIONS

For each row, select the word from the table that is most similar in meaning to the word above the table.

1 hoax

A	B	C	D	E
jump	spring	ruse	bread	hex

2 prohibit

A	B	C	D	E
promise	forbid	ignore	summarise	counter

3 stern

A	B	C	D	E
rig	boat	melancholic	joyful	severe

4 disperse

A	B	C	D	E
scatter	brave	burst	coin	disrupt

5 resolve

A	B	C	D	E
resolute	puzzle	greedy	settle	martial

6 extract

A	B	C	D	E
upper	grade	tact	dig	remove

7 deceive

A	B	C	D	E
delete	private	swindle	jest	waste

8 margin

A	B	C	D	E
line	leeway	poll	error	paper

CONTINUE WORKING ⇨

9 employ

A	B	C	D	E
law	under	frozen	improve	engage

10 abandon

A	B	C	D	E
box	relinquish	hurry	mark	abate

11 condemn

A	B	C	D	E
control	cast	chastise	crow	cover

12 reveal

A	B	C	D	E
threat	manner	original	summary	disclose

13 comprehend

A	B	C	D	E
comprise	sent	grasp	appeal	computer

14 insert

A	B	C	D	E
search	grow	partner	even	supplement

15 proclaim

A	B	C	D	E
assert	hover	produce	figure	find

16 oblige

A	B	C	D	E
respect	entertain	obey	fester	compel

CONTINUE WORKING ⇨

17 seize

A	B	C	D	E
occupy	cover	cease	polite	divine

18 revive

A	B	C	D	E
resuscitate	negate	through	revel	utmost

19 lament

A	B	C	D	E
mend	laser	summon	destroy	wail

20 abode

A	B	C	D	E
abstain	wonder	boat	home	gun

21 adhere

A	B	C	D	E
human	bond	appeal	across	here

22 contract

A	B	C	D	E
connive	case	diminish	treat	legal

23 haven

A	B	C	D	E
pond	respite	lever	refuge	post

24 pioneer

A	B	C	D	E
progress	kite	parity	train	instigate

STOP AND WAIT FOR FURTHER INSTRUCTIONS ⊗

Non-Verbal Reasoning

 INSTRUCTIONS

 YOU HAVE 7 MINUTES TO COMPLETE THE FOLLOWING SECTION.

YOU HAVE 13 QUESTIONS TO COMPLETE WITHIN THE TIME GIVEN.

EXAMPLES

COMPLETE THE SQUARE Example 1

Which figure on the right should replace the blank square in the pattern?

   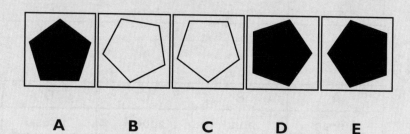

A   **B**   **C**   **D**   **E**

The correct answer is D. This has already been marked in Example 1 in the Non-Verbal Reasoning section of your answer sheet.

COMPLETE THE SQUARE Practice Question 1

Which figure on the right should replace the blank square in the pattern?

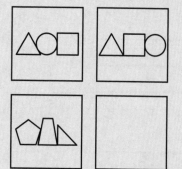   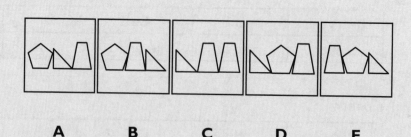

A   **B**   **C**   **D**   **E**

The correct answer is A. Please mark this in Practice Question 1 in the Non-Verbal Reasoning section of your answer sheet.

CONTINUE WORKING

REFLECTION Example 2

Select how the following shape or pattern would appear when reflected in the dashed line.

                                             A   B   C   D

The correct answer is C. This has already been marked in Example 2 in the Non-Verbal Reasoning section of your answer sheet.

REFLECTION Practice Question 2

Select how the following shape or pattern would appear when reflected in the dashed line.

                                             A   B   C   D

The correct answer is C. Please mark this in Practice Question 2 in the Non-Verbal Reasoning section of your answer sheet.

DIMENSION Example 3

Select how the following 3D figure would appear in a top-down, plan view.

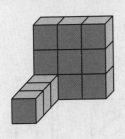   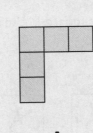   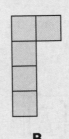   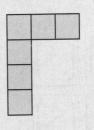   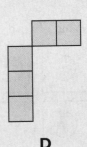

                                           A   B   C   D

The correct answer is C. This has already been marked in Example 3 in the Non-Verbal Reasoning section of your answer sheet.

DIMENSION Practice Question 3

Select how the following 3D figure would appear in a top-down, plan view.

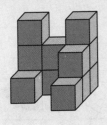   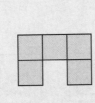   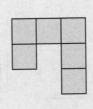   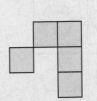   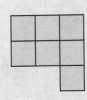

                                           A   B   C   D

The correct answer is B. Please mark this in Practice Question 3 in the Non-Verbal Reasoning section of your answer sheet.

STOP AND WAIT FOR FURTHER INSTRUCTIONS

1 Which figure on the right should replace the blank square in the pattern?

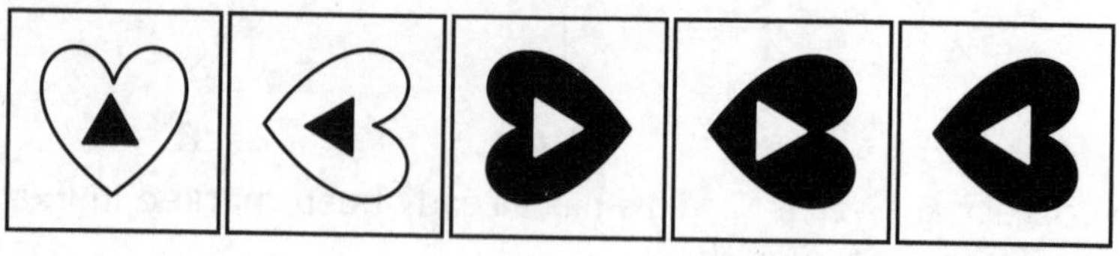

A   B   C   D   E

2 Which figure on the right should replace the blank square in the pattern?

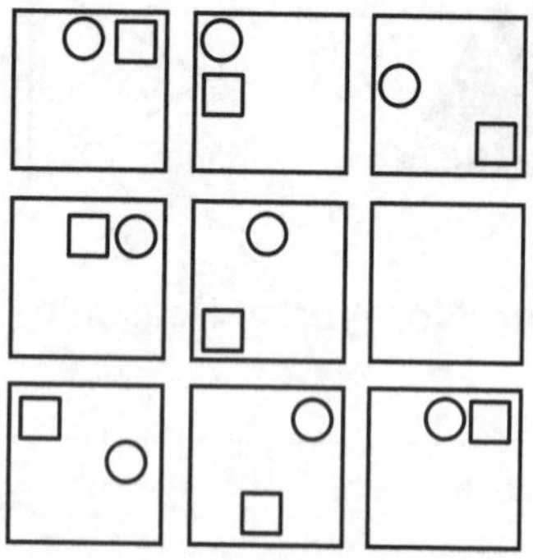

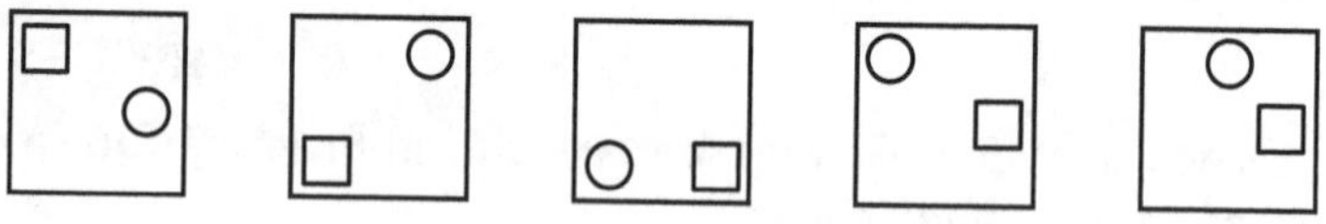

A   B   C   D   E

3 Which figure on the right should replace the blank square in the pattern?

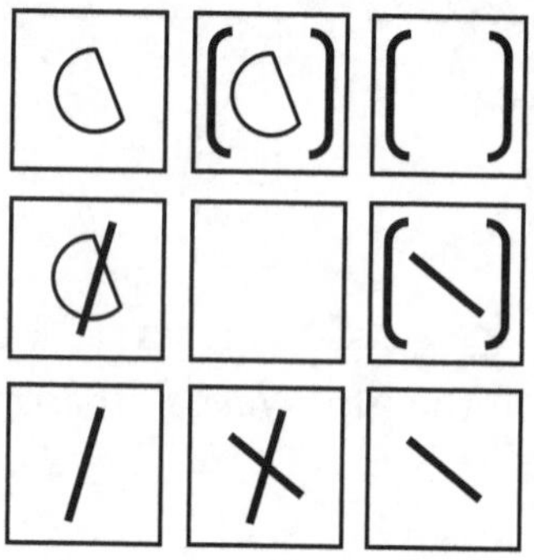

A   B   C   D   E

4 Which figure on the right should replace the blank square in the pattern?

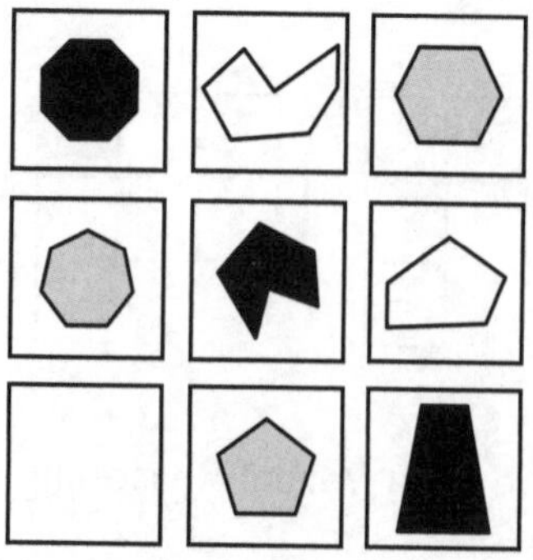

A   B   C   D   E

CONTINUE WORKING ➡

(5) Select how the following shape or pattern would appear when reflected in the dashed line.

A   **B**   **C**   **D**

(6) Select how the following shape or pattern would appear when reflected in the dashed line.

   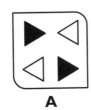         

A   **B**   **C**   **D**

(7) Select how the following shape or pattern would appear when reflected in the dashed line.

A   **B**   **C**   **D**

(8) Select how the following shape or pattern would appear when reflected in the dashed line.

A   **B**   **C**   **D**

(9) Select how the following 3D figure would appear in a top-down, plan view.

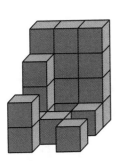   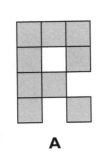   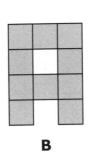   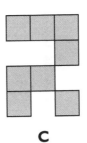   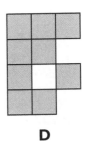

A   **B**   **C**   **D**

CONTINUE WORKING ⬜➡

(10) Select how the following 3D figure would appear in a top-down, plan view.

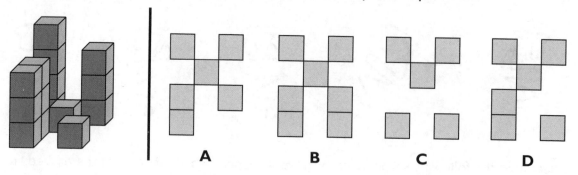

A   **B**   **C**   **D**

(11) Select how the following 3D figure would appear in a top-down, plan view.

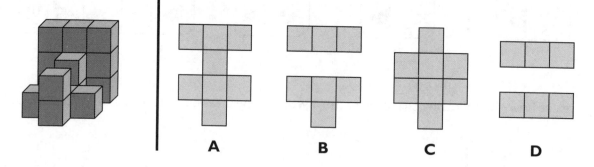

A   **B**   **C**   **D**

(12) Select how the following 3D figure would appear in a top-down, plan view.

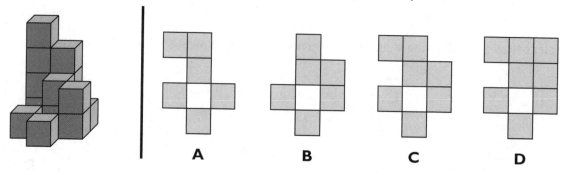

A   **B**   **C**   **D**

(13) Select how the following 3D figure would appear in a top-down, plan view.

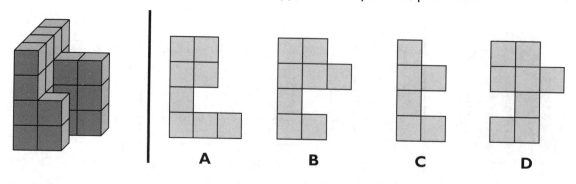

A   **B**   **C**   **D**

END OF PAPER

Get Test-Ready
Test A Paper 2

Instructions

1. Ensure you have pencils and an eraser with you.

2. Make sure you are able to see a clock or watch.

3. Write your name on the answer sheet.

4. Do not open the question booklet until you are told to do so by the audio instructions.

5. Listen carefully to the audio instructions given.

6. Mark your answers on the answer sheet only.

7. All workings must be completed on a separate piece of paper.

8. You should not use a calculator, dictionary or thesaurus at any point in this paper.

9. Move through the papers as quickly as possible and with care.

10. Follow the instructions at the foot of each page.

11. You should mark your answers with a horizontal line, as shown on the answer sheet.

12. If you want to change your answer, ensure that you rub out your first answer and that your second answer is clearly more visible.

13. You can go back and review any questions that are within the section you are working on only. You must await further instructions before moving on to another section.

Symbols and Phrases used in the Tests

 Instructions

 Time allowed for this section

 Stop working and await instructions

 Continue working

Problem Solving

 YOU HAVE 8 MINUTES TO COMPLETE THE FOLLOWING SECTION.

YOU HAVE 10 QUESTIONS TO COMPLETE WITHIN THE TIME GIVEN.

EXAMPLES

A $\dfrac{1}{2}$	B £3	C £3·50	D $\dfrac{3}{4}$	E $\dfrac{1}{3}$
F £1·50	G £5	H $\dfrac{2}{5}$	I £4	J $\dfrac{5}{6}$

Example 1

Select an answer to the question from the 10 different possible answers in the table above.

Tom buys a chocolate bar for £1·50. He pays with a £5 note.
How much change does he receive?

The correct answer is C. This has already been marked in Example 1 in the Problem Solving section of your answer sheet.

Practice Question 1

Sarah eats $\dfrac{1}{4}$ of a pizza.

What fraction of the pizza remains?

The correct answer is D. Please mark this in Practice Question 1 in the Problem Solving section of your answer sheet.

STOP AND WAIT FOR FURTHER INSTRUCTIONS

A	£775	B	113·3 km	C	$\frac{1}{4}$	D	10:25 a.m.	E	7
F	10:10 a.m.	G	9		H	96 km	I	£2,269	J	$\frac{2}{3}$

Several questions will follow for you to answer. Select an answer to each question from the 10 different possible answers in the table above. You may use an answer for more than one question.

(1) A football team plays 35 matches per season. They win $\frac{3}{5}$ of them and draw 20% of them.

How many matches do they lose?

(2) In 1 match, the 11 players on the team run for an average of 10·3 km each.

What is the total distance covered by the 11 players?

(3) The range in the weekly salaries of the football players is £1,231.

If the best paid player earns £3,500 per week, how much does the worst paid player earn?

(4) The squad contains 24 players. 8 of the players weigh more than 90 kg.

What fraction of the players weigh 90 kg or less?

(5) Daily training begins 75 minutes before noon. All players must arrive 5 minutes before training begins.

If Player A lives $\frac{1}{2}$ an hour from the training venue, what is the latest time she can leave home and arrive on time?

(6) The team travels 32 km by bus to an away match. A diversion forces them to take a route that is twice as long on the return journey.

What is the total distance covered in the round trip?

(7) Football tickets cost £25 for adults and half as much for children.

What is the total cost of 13 adult tickets and 3 dozen child tickets?

(8) Player B wakes up 20 minutes before daily training starts.

At what time does Player B wake up?

CONTINUE WORKING

(9) Over the course of a season of matches, the team uses 315 balls.

On average how many balls do they use per match?

(10) The football stadium has a capacity of 22,000.

If 16,500 fans attend a match, what fraction of the stadium is empty?

STOP AND WAIT FOR FURTHER INSTRUCTIONS

Cloze

INSTRUCTIONS

 YOU HAVE 10 MINUTES TO COMPLETE THE FOLLOWING SECTION.

YOU HAVE 20 QUESTIONS TO COMPLETE WITHIN THE TIME GIVEN.

EXAMPLES

Example 1

Read the sentence below and select the most appropriate word from the table.

A	B	C	D	E
defeated	heaved	master	flow	politely

The skilful chess player easily (Q1) _____ his opponent.

Please select your answer to go in the place of (Q1) in the above sentence.

The correct answer is A. This has already been marked in Example 1 in the Cloze section of your answer sheet.

Practice Question 1

Read the sentence below and select the most appropriate word from the table.

A	B	C	D	E
crunching	eating	dreading	reading	shining

The sun was (Q2) _____ and there was not a single cloud in the sky.

Please select your answer to go in the place of (Q2) in the above sentence.

The correct answer is E. Please mark the answer E in Practice Question 1 in the Cloze section of your answer sheet.

STOP AND WAIT FOR FURTHER INSTRUCTIONS

Read the passage and select the most appropriate word from the table below by choosing the letter above the word. There are 10 questions. For example, Q1 is where you should put your answer to Question 1 on your answer sheet.

A	B	C	D	E
coconut	crackle	towards	bathing	fine

F	G	H	I	J
wandered	coloured	clusters	deck	rubber

Man from the South

It was getting on (Q1) _____ six o'clock so I thought I'd buy myself a beer and go out and sit in a (Q2) _____ chair by the swimming pool and have a little evening sun.

I went to the bar and got the beer and carried it outside and (Q3) _____ down the garden toward the pool.

It was a (Q4) _____ garden with lawns and beds of azaleas and tall (Q5) _____ palms, and the wind was blowing strongly through the tops of the palm trees making the leaves hiss and (Q6) _____ as though they were on fire. I could see the (Q7) _____ of big brown nuts hanging down underneath the leaves.

There were plenty of deck chairs around the swimming pool and there were white tables and huge brightly (Q8) _____ umbrellas and sunburned men and women sitting around in (Q9) _____ suits. In the pool itself there were three or four girls and about a dozen boys, all splashing about and making a lot of noise and throwing a large (Q10) _____ ball at one another.

An extract from: **Someone Like You**
by Roald Dahl

CONTINUE WORKING ⏵

Read the passage and select the most appropriate word from the table below by choosing the letter above the word. There are 10 questions. For example, Q11 is where you should put your answer to Question 11 on your answer sheet.

A	B	C	D	E
travelled	absence	twisted	intangible	excusing

F	G	H	I	J
steep	flung	broken	undulations	peep

To Build a Fire

Day had (Q11) _____ cold and grey, exceedingly cold and grey, when the man turned aside from the main Yukon trail and climbed the high earth-bank, where a dim and little (Q12) _____ trail led eastward through the fat spruce timberland. It was a (Q13) _____ bank, and he paused for breath at the top, (Q14) _____ the act to himself by looking at his watch. It was nine o'clock. There was no sun nor hint of sun, though there was not a cloud in the sky. It was a clear day, and yet there seemed an (Q15) _____ pall over the face of things, a subtle gloom that made the day dark, and that was due to the (Q16) _____ of sun. This fact did not worry the man. He was used to the lack of sun. It had been days since he had seen the sun, and he knew that a few more days must pass before that cheerful orb, due south, would just (Q17) _____ above the sky-line and dip immediately from view.

The man (Q18) _____ a look back along the way he had come. The Yukon lay a mile wide and hidden under three feet of ice. On top of this ice were as many feet of snow. It was all pure white, rolling in gentle (Q19) _____ where the ice jams of the freeze-up had formed. North and south, as far as his eye could see, it was unbroken white, save for a dark hairline that curved and (Q20) _____ from around the spruce-covered island to the south, and that curved and twisted away into the north, where it disappeared behind another spruce-covered island.

An extract from: **To Build a Fire**
by Jack London

STOP AND WAIT FOR FURTHER INSTRUCTIONS ⊗

Non-Verbal Reasoning

  INSTRUCTIONS

 YOU HAVE 8 MINUTES TO COMPLETE THE FOLLOWING SECTION.

YOU HAVE 15 QUESTIONS TO COMPLETE WITHIN THE TIME GIVEN.

EXAMPLES

SIMILARITY Example 1

The three figures given are similar in some way.

Work out how they are similar and select the figure that goes with them.

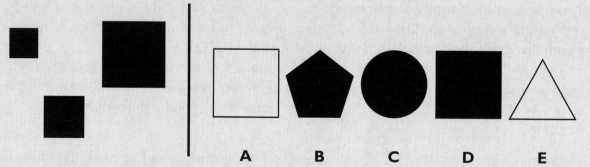

The correct answer is D. This has already been marked in Example 1 in the Non-Verbal Reasoning section of your answer sheet.

SIMILARITY Practice Question 1

The three figures given are similar in some way.

Work out how they are similar and select the figure that goes with them.

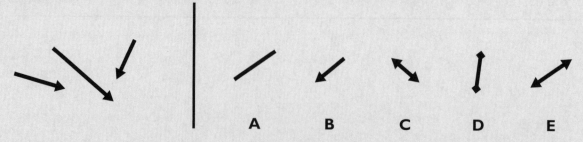

The correct answer is B. Please mark this in Practice Question 1 in the Non-Verbal Reasoning section of your answer sheet.

CONTINUE WORKING

CUBE NET Example 2

Look at the cube net below. Select the only cube that could be formed from the net.

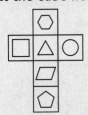

A   **B**   **C**   **D**

The correct answer is B. This has already been marked in Example 2 in the Non-Verbal Reasoning section of your answer sheet.

CUBE NET Practice Question 2

Look at the cube net below. Select the only cube that could be formed from the net.

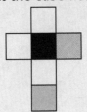 

A   **B**   **C**   **D**

The correct answer is C. Please mark this in Practice Question 2 in the Non-Verbal Reasoning section of your answer sheet.

COMPLETE THE SEQUENCE Example 3

Select the correct picture from the row on the right in order to finish the incomplete sequence on the left.

A   **B**   **C**   **D**   **E**

The correct answer is A. This has already been marked in Example 3 in the Non-Verbal Reasoning section of your answer sheet.

COMPLETE THE SEQUENCE Practice Question 3

Select the correct picture from the row on the right in order to finish the incomplete sequence on the left.

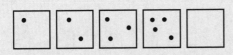

A   **B**   **C**   **D**   **E**

The correct answer is D. Please mark this in Practice Question 3 in the Non-Verbal Reasoning section of your answer sheet.

STOP AND WAIT FOR FURTHER INSTRUCTIONS

1. The three figures given are similar in some way. Work out how they are similar and select the figure that goes with them.

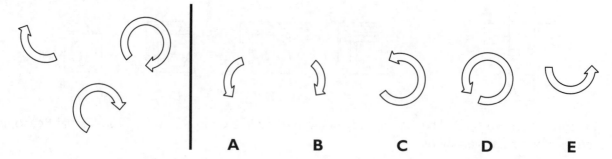

A   B   C   D   E

2. The three figures given are similar in some way. Work out how they are similar and select the figure that goes with them.

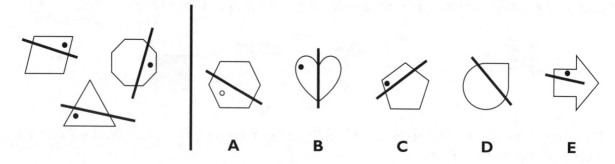

A   B   C   D   E

3. The three figures given are similar in some way. Work out how they are similar and select the figure that goes with them.

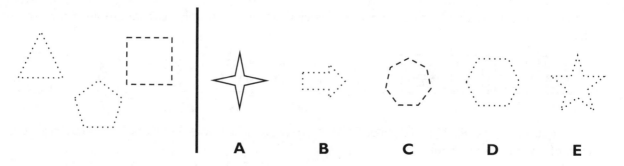

A   B   C   D   E

4. The three figures given are similar in some way. Work out how they are similar and select the figure that goes with them.

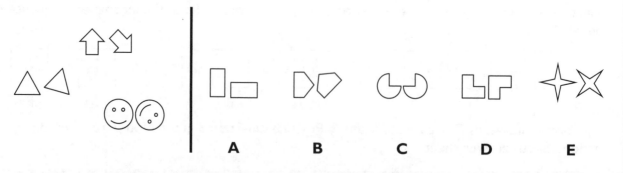

A   B   C   D   E

CONTINUE WORKING ⇨

5 The three figures given are similar in some way. Work out how they are similar and select the figure that goes with them.

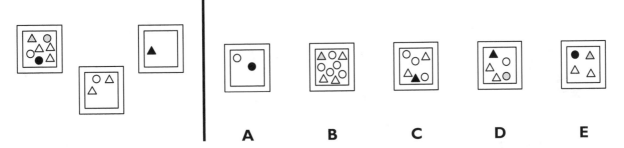

A   B   C   D   E

6 Look at the cube net below. Select the only cube that could be formed from the net.

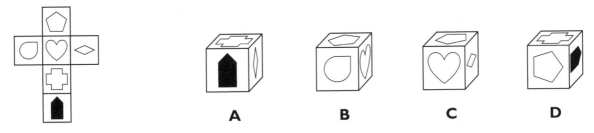

A   B   C   D

7 Look at the cube net below. Select the only cube that could be formed from the net.

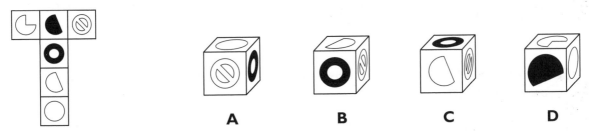

A   B   C   D

8 Look at the cube net below. Select the only cube that could be formed from the net.

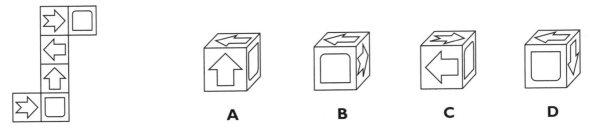

A   B   C   D

9 Look at the cube net below. Select the only cube that could be formed from the net.

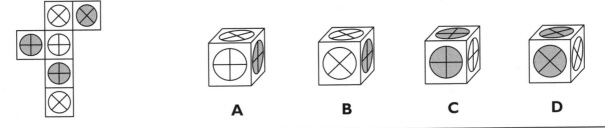

A   B   C   D

CONTINUE WORKING ⏩

(10) Look at the cube net below. Select the only cube that could be formed from the net.

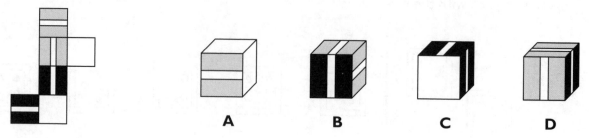

(11) Select the correct picture from the row on the right in order to finish the incomplete sequence on the left.

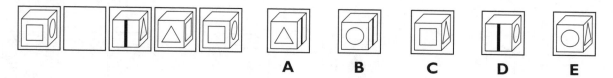

(12) Select the correct picture from the row on the right in order to finish the incomplete sequence on the left.

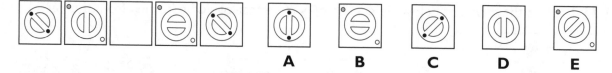

(13) Select the correct picture from the row on the right in order to finish the incomplete sequence on the left.

(14) Select the correct picture from the row on the right in order to finish the incomplete sequence on the left.

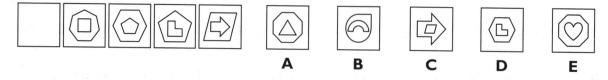

(15) Select the correct picture from the row on the right in order to finish the incomplete sequence on the left.

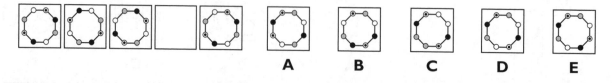

STOP AND WAIT FOR FURTHER INSTRUCTIONS

Grammar & Spelling

INSTRUCTIONS

 YOU HAVE 5 MINUTES TO COMPLETE THE FOLLOWING SECTION.

YOU HAVE 8 QUESTIONS TO COMPLETE WITHIN THE TIME GIVEN.

EXAMPLES

Example 1

Identify a homophone of the word 'night' from the words below.

A	B	C	D	E
knight	dark	bright	summer	light

The correct answer is A. This has already been marked in Example 1 in the Grammar & Spelling section of your answer sheet.

Practice Question 1

Select the correct prefix to give the opposite of the word 'believable'.

A	B	C	D	E
in	un	on	mis	pro

The correct answer is B. Please mark the answer B in Practice Question 1 in the Grammar & Spelling section of your answer sheet.

STOP AND WAIT FOR FURTHER INSTRUCTIONS

1 Identify a homophone of the word 'rye' from the words below.

A	B	C	D	E
high	rile	wry	eye	bread

2 Select the correct prefix to give the opposite of the word 'activate'.

A	B	C	D	E
mis	un	dis	de	non

3 Select the word below that is misspelt.

A	B	C	D	E
supreme	inappropriate	wierd	melancholy	easily

4 Select the word below that is misspelt.

A	B	C	D	E
suffering	acommodate	summarise	flavourful	immediate

5 Select the word below that is misspelt.

A	B	C	D	E
colourful	eager	grateful	urn	hankerchief

6 Select the word below that is misspelt.

A	B	C	D	E
typically	cemetary	hubris	jokingly	frustrating

7 Select the word below that is misspelt.

A	B	C	D	E
rythm	calamity	sinister	subtle	artful

8 Select the word below that is misspelt.

A	B	C	D	E
hovering	demise	aplomb	capability	opress

STOP AND WAIT FOR FURTHER INSTRUCTIONS

Antonyms

 YOU HAVE 5 MINUTES TO COMPLETE THE FOLLOWING SECTION.

YOU HAVE 15 QUESTIONS TO COMPLETE WITHIN THE TIME GIVEN.

EXAMPLES

Example 1

Which word is most opposite in meaning to the following word?

hot

A	B	C	D	E
follow	cold	freeze	ice	jelly

The correct answer is B. This has already been marked in Example 1 in the Antonyms section of your answer sheet.

Practice Question 1

Which word is most opposite in meaning to the following word?

below

A	B	C	D	E
attack	deep	lower	above	before

The correct answer is D. Please mark the answer D in Practice Question 1 in the Antonyms section of your answer sheet.

STOP AND WAIT FOR FURTHER INSTRUCTIONS

For each row, select the word from the table that is most opposite in meaning to the word above the table.

(1) hasty

A	B	C	D	E
considered	tasty	fast	aid	hat

(2) perish

A	B	C	D	E
prevent	grave	anonymous	attack	survive

(3) disreputable

A	B	C	D	E
reputation	foolhardy	decent	ravine	abridged

(4) sow

A	B	C	D	E
cheese	reap	harvest	seed	piglet

(5) stout

A	B	C	D	E
tout	breeze	barrel	hunger	thin

(6) temperate

A	B	C	D	E
peaceful	excessive	tree	emergency	climate

(7) destitute

A	B	C	D	E
delivered	dealings	prosperous	parody	tutor

CONTINUE WORKING ⬛➡

8 gratitude

A	B	C	D	E
thanklessness	singular	gander	grater	appeasement

9 obstinate

A	B	C	D	E
observation	grovel	approach	compliant	donkey

10 evade

A	B	C	D	E
inertia	invade	embrace	succumb	conglomerate

11 accustomed

A	B	C	D	E
customer	unfamiliar	habit	people	forthright

12 absurd

A	B	C	D	E
confusing	abrasive	totally	rational	frenetic

13 burden

A	B	C	D	E
sack	weight	boon	neck	pain

14 original

A	B	C	D	E
dictionary	oak	bible	signed	duplicate

15 wither

A	B	C	D	E
flourish	whiter	root	bravado	writer

STOP AND WAIT FOR FURTHER INSTRUCTIONS ⊗

Numeracy

 INSTRUCTIONS

 YOU HAVE 9 MINUTES TO COMPLETE THE FOLLOWING SECTION.

YOU HAVE 18 QUESTIONS TO COMPLETE WITHIN THE TIME GIVEN.

EXAMPLES

Some questions within this section are not multiple choice. For these write the answer to each question on the answer sheet by selecting the correct digits from the columns provided.

Example 1

Calculate the answer to the following:

12 + 42

The correct answer is 54. This has already been marked in Example 1 in the Numeracy section of your answer sheet.

Practice Question 1

Calculate the answer to the following:

55 – 47

The correct answer is 8. Please mark this in Practice Question 1 in the Numeracy section of your answer sheet. Note that a single-digit answer should be marked with a 0 in the left-hand column, so mark 08 on your answer sheet.

STOP AND WAIT FOR FURTHER INSTRUCTIONS ⊗

(1) Calculate the answer to the following:

2,085 − 1,965

(2) Which number comes next in the following sequence?

54, 60, 65, 71, 76, ?

(3) Which of these numbers is not divisible by 9?

18, 63, 108, 153, 171, 207, 278

(4) How many ninths are there in $21\frac{8}{36}$?

(5) Calculate the value of X in the equation below.

$0{\cdot}5X = \dfrac{50}{X}$

(6) What is the remainder when 321 is divided by 17?

(7) 1 km = $\dfrac{5}{8}$ mile

How many metres are there in 5 miles?

(8) How much greater is 13% of 300 than $\dfrac{1}{9}$ of 45?

(9) A basket contains 3 kiwis, 4 bananas, 5 oranges, 6 cherries and 1 pineapple.

Tim selects 1 piece of fruit at random. Each piece has an equal chance of being selected.

What is the probability that Tim selects neither a cherry nor a pineapple?

A	B	C	D	E
$\dfrac{2}{3}$	$\dfrac{4}{19}$	$\dfrac{12}{19}$	$\dfrac{15}{19}$	$\dfrac{7}{19}$

(10) A five-cent coin has a weight of 1·2 g.

What is the total weight of 80 cents' worth of five-cent coins?

A	B	C	D	E
18 g	36 g	120 g	44 g	19·2 g

CONTINUE WORKING ⇨

(11) Calculate the mode of the following numbers:

1, 2, 1, 1, 5, 7, 6, 1, 7, 7, 2, 1, 5, 4, 1, 6, 2, 5, 1, 5, 5, 5

A	B	C	D	E
1	5	6	2	7

(12) The angles in a triangle are $3X°$, $5X°$ and $10X°$.

What is the measure of the smallest angle in the triangle?

A	B	C	D	E
30°	50°	15°	90°	10°

(13) The coordinates of 3 vertices of a rectangle are (−2, 4), (−2, 10) and (−8, 4).

What are the coordinates of the 4th vertex of the rectangle?

A	B	C	D	E
(10, −10)	(10, −8)	(−8, 10)	(−8, −10)	(−8, 8)

(14) Calculate the answer to the following:

$$1\frac{2}{3} + 3\frac{2}{7}$$

A	B	C	D	E
$4\frac{6}{7}$	$5\frac{4}{21}$	$4\frac{8}{9}$	$4\frac{2}{3}$	$4\frac{20}{21}$

(15) Calculate the answer to the following:

$$\frac{3}{11} \times \frac{11}{9}$$

A	B	C	D	E
$\frac{3}{12}$	$\frac{4}{9}$	$\frac{8}{11}$	$\frac{1}{3}$	$\frac{44}{99}$

CONTINUE WORKING ⇨

(16) Calculate the answer to the following:

$$\frac{1}{8} \div \frac{3}{9}$$

A	B	C	D	E
$\frac{3}{8}$	$\frac{1}{5}$	$\frac{1}{8}$	$\frac{5}{8}$	$\frac{4}{9}$

(17) I think of a number, square it, add 2, divide by 3 and then subtract 9.

My answer is 0.

Which number did I think of?

A	B	C	D	E
0	3	5	9	7

(18) I mix 4 litres of blue paint with 2 litres of red paint.

I use 50% of the mixture to paint my bedroom and $\frac{1}{3}$ of the remainder to paint my kitchen.

How much paint do I have left?

A	B	C	D	E
1 litre	2 litres	2·5 litres	3 litres	3·5 litres

END OF PAPER

Get Test-Ready

Test B Paper 1

Instructions

1. Ensure you have pencils and an eraser with you.

2. Make sure you are able to see a clock or watch.

3. Write your name on the answer sheet.

4. Do not open the question booklet until you are told to do so by the audio instructions.

5. Listen carefully to the audio instructions given.

6. Mark your answers on the answer sheet only.

7. All workings must be completed on a separate piece of paper.

8. You should not use a calculator, dictionary or thesaurus at any point in this paper.

9. Move through the papers as quickly as possible and with care.

10. Follow the instructions at the foot of each page.

11. You should mark your answers with a horizontal line, as shown on the answer sheet.

12. If you want to change your answer, ensure that you rub out your first answer and that your second answer is clearly more visible.

13. You can go back and review any questions that are within the section you are working on only. You must await further instructions before moving on to another section.

Symbols and Phrases used in the Tests

 Instructions   Time allowed for this section   Stop working and await instructions   Continue working

Comprehension

 INSTRUCTIONS

 YOU HAVE 9 MINUTES TO COMPLETE THE FOLLOWING SECTION.

YOU HAVE 10 QUESTIONS TO COMPLETE WITHIN THE TIME GIVEN.

EXAMPLES

Comprehension Example

South Africa is becoming an increasingly popular holiday destination. People from all over the world are attracted by its natural beauty, cosmopolitan cities and diverse wildlife. Cape Town, the capital of South Africa, is especially popular. The city is dynamic, exciting and has a rich history and culture. It is also home to the stunning Table Mountain, which you can ascend on foot or by cable car.

Example 1

Which of the following is not mentioned as a reason why people are attracted to South Africa?

A　Natural beauty
B　Excellent food
C　Cosmopolitan cities
D　Diverse wildlife

The correct answer is B. This has already been marked in Example 1 in the Comprehension section of your answer sheet.

Practice Question 1

What is the name of the mountain in Cape Town?

A　Cape Mountain
B　Africa Mountain
C　Table Mountain
D　Leopard Mountain

The correct answer is C. Please mark this in Practice Question 1 in the Comprehension section of your answer sheet.

STOP AND WAIT FOR FURTHER INSTRUCTIONS

Read the passage below and then answer the questions that follow.

An extract from: **The Open Window**
by H. H. Munro (Saki)

"My aunt will be down presently, Mr. Nuttel," said a very self-possessed young lady of fifteen; "in the meantime you must try and put up with me."

Framton Nuttel endeavoured to say the correct something which should duly flatter the niece of the moment without unduly discounting the aunt that was to come. Privately he doubted more than ever whether these formal visits on a succession of total strangers would do much towards helping the nerve cure which he was supposed to be undergoing.

"I know how it will be," his sister had said when he was preparing to migrate to this rural retreat; "you will bury yourself down there and not speak to a living soul, and your nerves will be worse than ever from moping. I shall just give you letters of introduction to all the people I know there. Some of them, as far as I can remember, were quite nice."

Framton wondered whether Mrs. Sappleton, the lady to whom he was presenting one of the letters of introduction, came into the nice division.

"Do you know many of the people round here?" asked the niece, when she judged that they had had sufficient silent communion.

"Hardly a soul," said Framton. "My sister was staying here, at the rectory, you know, some four years ago, and she gave me letters of introduction to some of the people here."

He made the last statement in a tone of distinct regret.

"Then you know practically nothing about my aunt?" pursued the self-possessed young lady.

"Only her name and address," admitted the caller. He was wondering whether Mrs. Sappleton was in the married or widowed state. An undefinable something about the room seemed to suggest masculine habitation.

"Her great tragedy happened just three years ago," said the child; "that would be since your sister's time."

"Her tragedy?" asked Framton; somehow in this restful country spot tragedies seemed out of place.

"You may wonder why we keep that window wide open on an October afternoon," said the niece, indicating a large French window that opened on to a lawn.

"It is quite warm for the time of the year," said Framton; "but has that window got anything to do with the tragedy?"

CONTINUE WORKING

"Out through that window, three years ago to a day, her husband and her two young brothers went off for their day's shooting. They never came back. In crossing the moor to their favourite snipe-shooting ground they were all three engulfed in a treacherous piece of bog. It had been that dreadful wet summer, you know, and places that were safe in other years gave way suddenly without warning. Their bodies were never recovered. That was the dreadful part of it." Here the child's voice lost her self-possessed note and became falteringly human. "Poor aunt always thinks that they will come back some day, they and the little brown spaniel that was lost with them, and walk in at that window just as they used to do. That is why the window is kept open every evening till it is quite dusk. Poor dear aunt, she has often told me how they went out, her husband with his white waterproof coat over his arm, and Ronnie, her youngest brother, singing 'Bertie, why do you bound?' as he always did to tease her, because she said it got on her nerves. Do you know, sometimes on still, quiet evenings like this, I almost get a creepy feeling that they will all walk in through that window –"

She broke off with a little shudder. It was a relief to Framton when the aunt bustled into the room with a whirl of apologies for being late in making her appearance.

"I hope Vera has been amusing you?" she said.

"She has been very interesting," said Framton.

① Why was Framton Nuttel visiting Mrs. Sappleton?

   A   Framton was hoping to seek a cure for his illness from Mrs. Sappleton
   B   Framton hoped to find work at Mrs. Sappleton's house
   C   Framton's sister had recommended that he visit Mrs. Sappleton
   D   Framton had been invited for tea by Mrs. Sappleton

② Why had Framton moved to a rural area?

   A   To help him focus while writing his new novel
   B   To help him recover from an affliction
   C   To begin a new life on a farm
   D   To live closer to his friends and family

③ Why did Framton think there was a man living at the house?

   A   He could see a man's boots in the hall
   B   He had seen a man passing by the kitchen
   C   There were photos of a man on the mantelpiece
   D   We do not know

CONTINUE WORKING

(4) Which word best describes Vera?

   A   Confident
   B   Aloof
   C   Frenetic
   D   Insecure

(5) Why was the French window left open?

   A   It was unusually warm
   B   Mrs. Sappleton liked the afternoon breeze
   C   Mrs. Sappleton was hoping for the return of her husband and brothers
   D   Vera had forgotten to close it

(6) What tragedy had befallen the brown spaniel?

   A   It had become very ill and passed away
   B   It had drowned on the moor
   C   It had become lost and was struck by a car
   D   It had lost its sense of smell

(7) How did Framton feel about visiting Mrs. Sappleton?

   Option 1: Unsure
   Option 2: Grateful
   Option 3: Excited
   Option 4: Regretful

   A   Options 2 and 3 only
   B   Options 2 and 4 only
   C   Options 1, 2 and 4 only
   D   Options 1 and 4 only

(8) What type of word is 'quite'?

   A   Adverb
   B   Adjective
   C   Noun
   D   Pronoun

(9) What does the word 'falteringly' mean?

   A   Falsely
   B   Hesitantly
   C   Passionately
   D   Considerably

(10) Which of the following is an antonym for 'distinct'?

   A   Pain
   B   Disbelieve
   C   Distinction
   D   Indefinite

STOP AND WAIT FOR FURTHER INSTRUCTIONS ⊗

Shuffled Sentences

INSTRUCTIONS

 YOU HAVE 8 MINUTES TO COMPLETE THE FOLLOWING SECTION.

YOU HAVE 15 QUESTIONS TO COMPLETE WITHIN THE TIME GIVEN.

EXAMPLES

Example 1

The following sentence is shuffled and also contains one unnecessary word. Rearrange the sentence correctly in order to identify the unnecessary word.

wake under before must sunrise up we.

A	B	C	D	E
up	before	under	wake	sunrise

The correct answer is C. This has already been marked in Example 1 in the Shuffled Sentences section of your answer sheet.

Practice Question 1

The following sentence is shuffled and also contains one unnecessary word. Rearrange the sentence correctly in order to identify the unnecessary word.

very girl quickly the ran throw.

A	B	C	D	E
quickly	girl	the	ran	throw

The correct answer is E. Please mark this in Practice Question 1 in the Shuffled Sentences section of your answer sheet.

STOP AND WAIT FOR FURTHER INSTRUCTIONS

Each sentence below is shuffled and also contains one unnecessary word.
Rearrange each sentence correctly in order to identify the unnecessary word.

1 making in kept mistakes same he the on.

A	B	C	D	E
making	kept	in	same	he

2 of was severity lawyer by the crime the the deterred not joy.

A	B	C	D	E
lawyer	the	crime	joy	deterred

3 were currant voters with disillusioned the president many current.

A	B	C	D	E
voters	with	were	currant	president

4 use necks toes trees tall to giraffes long leaves on their reach.

A	B	C	D	E
toes	to	reach	giraffes	reach

5 upset of outcome on with women the the both were.

A	B	C	D	E
on	upset	both	of	women

6 mystery the illness the legal contracted show of star a.

A	B	C	D	E
illness	star	of	show	legal

7 are no arguments some hypothesis there against this.

A	B	C	D	E
arguments	hypothesis	against	there	no

8 the for yellow bought daughter man bag his a her.

A	B	C	D	E
yellow	man	bought	bag	her

CONTINUE WORKING ⇨

9 blistering pace a at the hiker blister ascended the mountain.

A	B	C	D	E
pace	blister	at	ascended	mountain

10 the was in the orchard half eaten stolen fruit of.

A	B	C	D	E
orchard	half	was	fruit	eaten

11 the above sewers a emanated from city below smell the vile.

A	B	C	D	E
above	sewers	city	emanated	smell

12 was sold business booming young for entrepreneur the.

A	B	C	D	E
young	for	business	sold	entrepreneur

13 on daily endangered are basis plentiful extinct a becoming species.

A	B	C	D	E
basis	plentiful	are	becoming	species

14 below on loved eager rower the time spend to the water.

A	B	C	D	E
rower	time	spend	water	below

15 whether black I to red not or could my police room paint decide.

A	B	C	D	E
police	could	paint	room	red

STOP AND WAIT FOR FURTHER INSTRUCTIONS ⊗

Numeracy

 ## INSTRUCTIONS

 YOU HAVE 7 MINUTES TO COMPLETE THE FOLLOWING SECTION.

YOU HAVE 15 QUESTIONS TO COMPLETE WITHIN THE TIME GIVEN.

EXAMPLES

The questions within this section are not multiple choice. Write the answer to each question on the answer sheet by selecting the correct digits from the columns provided.

Example 1

Calculate the answer to the following: 12 + 42

The correct answer is 54. This has already been marked in Example 1 in the Numeracy section of your answer sheet.

Practice Question 1

Calculate the answer to the following: 55 – 47

The correct answer is 8. Please mark this in Practice Question 1 in the Numeracy section of your answer sheet. Note that a single-digit answer should be marked with a 0 in the left-hand column, so mark 08 on your answer sheet.

STOP AND WAIT FOR FURTHER INSTRUCTIONS

(**1**) What is $\frac{7}{9}$ of 99?

(**2**) Bob runs at a speed of 15 kph (kilometres per hour).

How many kilometres will Bob have covered in 40 minutes?

CONTINUE WORKING

(3) How many cubes with a side length of 2 cm can fit inside a cube with a side length of 8 cm?

(4) X is $2\frac{1}{3}$ times larger than Y.

If Y equals 27, what is the value of X?

(5) Which number should replace the '?' in the following sequence?

18, 3, 16, ?, 14, 9, 12, 12

(6) Neil washes his car 4 times in July and 3 times in August.

Each wash takes $\frac{1}{6}$ of an hour.

How many minutes does Neil spend washing his car in July and August?

(7) How much greater is 4,330 rounded to the nearest 50 than 4,330 rounded to the nearest 20?

(8) Last year, Tina was 5 years old. In 3 years' time, Alex will be three times older than Tina's current age.

How old will Alex be next year?

(9) 41 Fobs have the same value as 1 Fib. 92 Fibs have the same value as 2 Fabs.

How many Fobs have the same value as 1 Fab?

(10) How many more edges than faces does a hexagonal prism have?

(11) Subtract one thousand, eight hundred and eighty-one from two thousand, nine hundred and fifty.

(12) The hens on a farm produce 80 eggs per week.

How many eggs do they produce in half a year?

(13) A cup holds 220 ml of water.

How many identical cups can I fill completely with a jug that holds 2·02 litres of water?

(14) Calculate the answer to the following:

$14 + 19(4 - 2) + 7(6 + 7)$

(15) Jason shares 180 sweets equally between himself and 5 of his friends.

How many sweets do they each receive?

STOP AND WAIT FOR FURTHER INSTRUCTIONS

Problem Solving

 INSTRUCTIONS

 YOU HAVE 8 MINUTES TO COMPLETE THE FOLLOWING SECTION.

YOU HAVE 10 QUESTIONS TO COMPLETE WITHIN THE TIME GIVEN.

EXAMPLES

Example 1

Calculate the answer to the following:

Tom buys a chocolate bar for £1·50. He pays with a £5 note.
How much change does he receive?

A   £1·50   **B**   £3   **C**   £3·50   **D**   £4   **E**   £5

The correct answer is C. This has already been marked in Example 1 in the Problem Solving section of your answer sheet.

Practice Question 1

Sarah eats $\frac{1}{4}$ of a pizza.

What fraction of the pizza remains?

A $\frac{1}{2}$ **B** $\frac{1}{3}$ **C** $\frac{2}{5}$ **D** $\frac{3}{4}$ **E** $\frac{5}{6}$

The correct answer is D. Please mark this in Practice Question 1 in the Problem Solving section of your answer sheet.

STOP AND WAIT FOR FURTHER INSTRUCTIONS

Calculate the answers to the following.

(1) How many different combinations of coin values make a total of 7 pence?

    A 2   **B** 3   **C** 4   **D** 5   **E** 6

CONTINUE WORKING

(2) The ratio of rainy days to non-rainy days in April is 3:7.

How many fewer rainy days than non-rainy days were there in April?

    A   10   **B**   3   **C**   5   **D**   7   **E**   12

(3) Which of the following is not equal to 14?

    A $\frac{1}{2}$ of 28   **B**   0·2 of 70   **C** $3(107 - 101) - 4$ **D** $252 \div 18$ **E** $\frac{3}{4}$ of 21

(4) What is the value of the digit 8 in the number 3,487,612·096?

    A   80,000,000   **B**   800   **C**   80,000   **D**   8,000   **E**   8

(5) Fred earns £6·50 an hour. On Tuesday, he begins work at 8:30 a.m. and ends at 6 p.m. (including an unpaid half-hour lunch break).

How much money does Fred earn on Tuesday?

    A   £6·50   **B**   £58·50   **C**   £9·75   **D**   £61·75   **E**   £65

(6) In 1 week, Shiv consumes an average of 325 ml of cola per day. The table below shows how much he consumed each day.

How much cola did Shiv consume on Tuesday?

Cola consumed in ml

Monday	350
Tuesday	?
Wednesday	280
Thursday	100
Friday	175
Saturday	480
Sunday	450

    A   60 ml   **B**   80 ml   **C**   325 ml   **D**   500 ml   **E**   440 ml

(7) George has 40 red pens, twice as many green pens and 80 blue pens.

What percentage of George's pens are green?

    A   60%   **B**   80%   **C**   30%   **D**   40%   **E**   10%

(8) What is the sum of the largest 3-digit prime number and the largest 3-digit square number?

    A   1,958   **B**   1,998   **C**   1,897   **D**   1,956   **E**   1,980

(9) If $7T + 8 = 85$, what is the value of $6T - 8$?

    A   58   **B**   22   **C**   66   **D**   10   **E**   18

(10) 2 machines take 3 hours to clear 80 m of ditch.

How long will it take 3 machines to clear 160 m of ditch?

    A   6 hours   **B**   12 hours   **C**   3 hours   **D**   4 hours   **E**   5 hours

STOP AND WAIT FOR FURTHER INSTRUCTIONS

Synonyms

INSTRUCTIONS

 YOU HAVE 7 MINUTES TO COMPLETE THE FOLLOWING SECTION.

YOU HAVE 24 QUESTIONS TO COMPLETE WITHIN THE TIME GIVEN.

EXAMPLES

Example 1

Select the word that is most similar in meaning to the following word:

push

A	B	C	D	E
shallow	shove	tug	hollow	cry

The correct answer is B. This has already been marked in Example 1 in the Synonyms section of your answer sheet.

Practice Question 1

Select the word that is most similar in meaning to the following word:

imitate

A	B	C	D	E
cover	copy	grow	live	irritate

The correct answer is B. Please mark this in Practice Question 1 in the Synonyms section of your answer sheet.

STOP AND WAIT FOR FURTHER INSTRUCTIONS

For each row, select the word from the table that is most similar in meaning to the word above the table.

(1) liable

A	B	C	D	E
lonely	liar	hopeful	believable	accountable

(2) virtuous

A	B	C	D	E
upright	virtual	urn	happy	ignorant

(3) banish

A	B	C	D	E
bear	expel	disgrace	spell	vanish

(4) torment

A	B	C	D	E
total	jovial	candid	distress	bent

(5) immerse

A	B	C	D	E
imply	submerge	ocean	callous	cold

(6) plunder

A	B	C	D	E
power	return	hearing	thunder	loot

(7) charred

A	B	C	D	E
community	scorched	earth	soil	raw

(8) conspire

A	B	C	D	E
collude	huddle	various	super	perspire

CONTINUE WORKING ⏵

9 quiver

A	B	C	D	E
quite	burden	implore	arrow	quake

10 robust

A	B	C	D	E
slender	vigorous	boisterous	great	robot

11 nimble

A	B	C	D	E
needy	hurdle	agile	progress	suffocate

12 elude

A	B	C	D	E
vanquish	borrow	huge	nude	escape

13 depot

A	B	C	D	E
lorry	criminal	warehouse	window	bar

14 object

A	B	C	D	E
vital	yesterday	pin	cloak	oppose

15 coax

A	B	C	D	E
cox	cajole	train	winter	knife

16 linger

A	B	C	D	E
laced	hinder	grape	loiter	dream

CONTINUE WORKING ⟶

(17) peril

A	B	C	D	E
pile	safety	brine	climb	danger

(18) lethargic

A	B	C	D	E
summer	late	age	showman	torpid

(19) devote

A	B	C	D	E
elect	impose	complain	dedicate	unite

(20) stoop

A	B	C	D	E
crouch	crunch	venal	stop	flow

(21) deceit

A	B	C	D	E
dastardly	delete	receipt	crumble	fraud

(22) suspend

A	B	C	D	E
social	hang	heave	alter	breeze

(23) peculiar

A	B	C	D	E
bizarre	valiant	provide	capsule	guarantee

(24) curb

A	B	C	D	E
stone	empower	restrain	aggravate	curt

STOP AND WAIT FOR FURTHER INSTRUCTIONS ⊗

Non-Verbal Reasoning

INSTRUCTIONS

 YOU HAVE 6 MINUTES TO COMPLETE THE FOLLOWING SECTION.

YOU HAVE 12 QUESTIONS TO COMPLETE WITHIN THE TIME GIVEN.

EXAMPLES

REFLECTION Example 1

Select how the following shape or pattern would appear when reflected in the dashed line.

The correct answer is C. This has already been marked in Example 1 in the Non-Verbal Reasoning section of your answer sheet.

REFLECTION Practice Question 1

Select how the following shape or pattern would appear when reflected in the dashed line.

The correct answer is C. Please mark this in Practice Question 1 in the Non-Verbal Reasoning section of your answer sheet.

CONTINUE WORKING

LEAST SIMILAR Example 2

Select the figure that is least similar to other figures.

A   **B**   **C**   **D**   **E**

The correct answer is B. This has already been marked in Example 2 in the Non-Verbal Reasoning section of your answer sheet.

LEAST SIMILAR Practice Question 2

Select the figure that is least similar to other figures.

 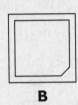 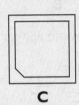 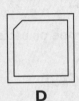 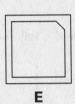

A   **B**   **C**   **D**   **E**

The correct answer is A. Please mark this in Practice Question 2 in the Non-Verbal Reasoning section of your answer sheet.

STOP AND WAIT FOR FURTHER INSTRUCTIONS

① Select how the following shape or pattern would appear when reflected in the dashed line.

 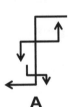 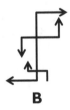 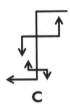 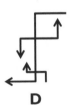

               A   **B**   **C**   **D**

② Select how the following shape or pattern would appear when reflected in the dashed line.

 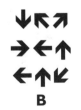

               A   **B**   **C**   **D**

CONTINUE WORKING

③ Select how the following shape or pattern would appear when reflected in the dashed line.

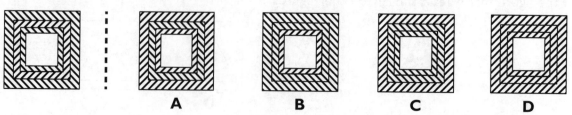

A   **B**   **C**   **D**

④ Select how the following shape or pattern would appear when reflected in the dashed line.

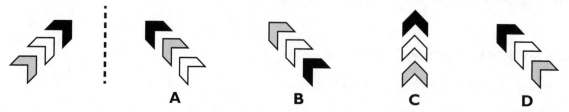

A   **B**   **C**   **D**

⑤ Select how the following shape or pattern would appear when reflected in the dashed line.

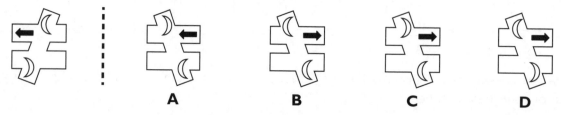

A   **B**   **C**   **D**

⑥ Select how the following shape or pattern would appear when reflected in the dashed line.

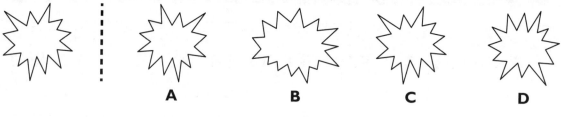

A   **B**   **C**   **D**

⑦ Select the figure that is least similar to other figures.

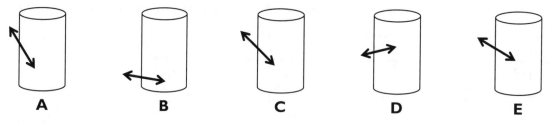

A   **B**   **C**   **D**   **E**

⑧ Select the figure that is least similar to other figures.

A   **B**   **C**   **D**   **E**

CONTINUE WORKING ▷

9 Select the figure that is least similar to other figures.

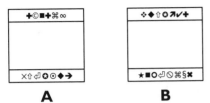

    A   **B**   **C**   **D**   **E**

10 Select the figure that is least similar to other figures.

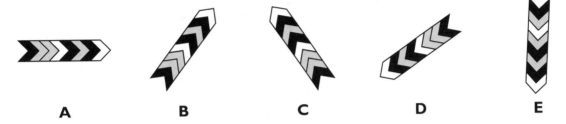

    A   **B**   **C**   **D**   **E**

11 Select the figure that is least similar to other figures.

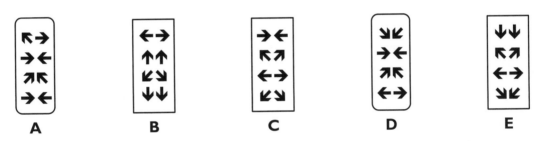

    A   **B**   **C**   **D**   **E**

12 Select the figure that is least similar to other figures.

$+-\times\div+-\times\div$　　$-\times\div+-\times\div-$　　$\div+-\div\times+-\times\div$　　$\times\div+-\times\div+-\times$　　$\div+-\times\div+-\times\div$

    A   **B**   **C**   **D**   **E**

END OF PAPER

Get Test-Ready
Test B Paper 2

Instructions

1. Ensure you have pencils and an eraser with you.

2. Make sure you are able to see a clock or watch.

3. Write your name on the answer sheet.

4. Do not open the question booklet until you are told to do so by the audio instructions.

5. Listen carefully to the audio instructions given.

6. Mark your answers on the answer sheet only.

7. All workings must be completed on a separate piece of paper.

8. You should not use a calculator, dictionary or thesaurus at any point in this paper.

9. Move through the papers as quickly as possible and with care.

10. Follow the instructions at the foot of each page.

11. You should mark your answers with a horizontal line, as shown on the answer sheet.

12. If you want to change your answer, ensure that you rub out your first answer and that your second answer is clearly more visible.

13. You can go back and review any questions that are within the section you are working on only. You must await further instructions before moving on to another section.

Symbols and Phrases used in the Tests

 Instructions
 Time allowed for this section
 Stop working and await instructions
 Continue working

Problem Solving

 INSTRUCTIONS

 YOU HAVE 12 MINUTES TO COMPLETE THE FOLLOWING SECTION.

YOU HAVE 15 QUESTIONS TO COMPLETE WITHIN THE TIME GIVEN.

EXAMPLES

A $\frac{1}{2}$	B £3	C £3·50	D $\frac{3}{4}$	E $\frac{1}{3}$
F £1·50	G £5	H $\frac{2}{5}$	I £4	J $\frac{5}{6}$

Example 1

Select an answer to the question from the 10 different possible answers in the table above.

Tom buys a chocolate bar for £1·50. He pays with a £5 note.
How much change does he receive?

The correct answer is C. This has already been marked in Example 1 in the Problem Solving section of your answer sheet.

Practice Question 1

Sarah eats $\frac{1}{4}$ of a pizza.

What fraction of the pizza remains?

The correct answer is D. Please mark this in Practice Question 1 in the Problem Solving section of your answer sheet.

STOP AND WAIT FOR FURTHER INSTRUCTIONS

A	18	B	35	C	54	D	3	E	534
F	288	G	455	H	200	I	999	J	400
K	324	L	4,989	M	21	N	6,600	O	48

Several questions will follow for you to answer. Select an answer to each question from the 15 different possible answers in the table above. You may use an answer for more than one question.

(1) What number is twice as large as triple 89?

(2) Subtract the smallest factor of 70 from the largest factor of 1,000.

(3) A train passes through Station A every 5 minutes.

How many trains pass through Station A in 24 hours?

(4) Which number comes next in the following sequence?

999   1,998   2,996   3,993   ?

(5) The mean of a set of 5 numbers is 12. When a 6th number is added to the set, the mean increases to 13.

What is the 6th number?

(6) When X is divided by 7, the remainder is 5.

What is the value of X?

(7) 7 apples cost £1·75.

How many apples can be bought for £8·95?

(8) Calculate the answer to the following:

200 ÷ 0·5

(9) Calculate 18^2

CONTINUE WORKING

(10) Set D consists of all even 2-digit square numbers.

How many numbers are in Set D?

(11) Ron picks a blue card from a deck of 320 cards.

The probability of picking a blue card is $\frac{5}{8}$.

How many blue cards are in the deck?

(12) Martin travels to work 5 days per week. 20% of the time, he travels to work by bicycle.

Martin takes 4 weeks of holiday per year during which he does not travel to work.

How many times does Martin cycle to work per year?

(13) Jon has X pairs of socks. Harry has twice as many pairs of socks as Jon. Peter has 3 more pairs of socks than Harry. In total, they have 48 pairs of socks.

How many pairs of socks does Peter have?

(14) 1,200 guests attend a party. 30% of the guests are children and the rest are adults.

On average, each child eats 9 sweets at the party and each adult eats 4 sweets at the party.

How many sweets are eaten at the party in total?

(15) Calculate the answer to the following:

$65 \times 0 \cdot 07 \times 100$

STOP AND WAIT FOR FURTHER INSTRUCTIONS ⊗

Cloze

 INSTRUCTIONS

 YOU HAVE 10 MINUTES TO COMPLETE THE FOLLOWING SECTION.

YOU HAVE 20 QUESTIONS TO COMPLETE WITHIN THE TIME GIVEN.

EXAMPLES

Example 1

Read the sentence below and select the most appropriate word from the table.

A	B	C	D	E
defeated	heaved	master	flow	politely

The skilful chess player easily (Q1) _____ his opponent.

Please select your answer to go in the place of (Q1) in the above sentence.

The correct answer is A. This has already been marked in Example 1 in the Cloze section of your answer sheet.

Practice Question 1

Read the sentence below and select the most appropriate word from the table.

A	B	C	D	E
crunching	eating	dreading	reading	shining

The sun was (Q2) _____ and there was not a single cloud in the sky.

Please select your answer to go in the place of (Q2) in the above sentence.

The correct answer is E. Please mark the answer E in Practice Question 1 in the Cloze section of your answer sheet.

STOP AND WAIT FOR FURTHER INSTRUCTIONS ✖

Read the passage and select the most appropriate word from the table below by choosing the letter above the word. There are 10 questions. For example, Q1 is where you should put your answer to Question 1 on your answer sheet.

A	B	C	D	E
aunt	sultry	another	attentions	occupants

F	G	H	I	J
opposite	reluctantly	emphatically	protested	window

The Storyteller

It was a hot afternoon, and the railway carriage was correspondingly (Q1) _____, and the next stop was at Templecombe, nearly an hour ahead. The (Q2) _____ of the carriage were a small girl, and a smaller girl, and a small boy. An aunt belonging to the children occupied one corner seat, and the further corner seat on the (Q3) _____ side was occupied by a bachelor who was a stranger to their party, but the small girls and the small boy (Q4) _____ occupied the compartment. Both the aunt and the children were conversational in a limited, persistent way, reminding one of the (Q5) _____ of a housefly that refused to be discouraged. Most of the aunt's remarks seemed to begin with "Don't," and nearly all of the children's remarks began with "Why?" The bachelor said nothing out loud.

"Don't, Cyril, don't," exclaimed the (Q6) _____, as the small boy began smacking the cushions of the seat, producing a cloud of dust at each blow.

"Come and look out of the (Q7) _____," she added.

The child moved (Q8) _____ to the window. "Why are those sheep being driven out of that field?" he asked.

"I expect they are being driven to (Q9) _____ field where there is more grass," said the aunt weakly.

"But there is lots of grass in that field," (Q10) _____ the boy; "there's nothing else but grass there. Aunt, there's lots of grass in that field."

An extract from: **The Storyteller**
by H. H. Munro (Saki)

CONTINUE WORKING

Read the passage and select the most appropriate word from the table below by choosing the letter above the word. There are 10 questions. For example, Q11 is where you should put your answer to Question 11 on your answer sheet.

A	B	C	D	E
treacherous	study	climate	species	landscape

F	G	H	I	J
rare	important	state	number	population

Bhutan

Bhutan is a landlocked, sovereign (Q11) _____ in the Eastern Himalayas in South Asia. Its (Q12) _____ ranges from lush tropical plains in the south to mountainous regions in the north, filled with (Q13) _____ peaks that remain unclimbed by man.

The (Q14) _____ varies with elevation, with warm weather in the south and a cold, polar climate in the north. The country is home to many (Q15) _____ and endangered animal (Q16) _____ such as the golden langur, the Bengal tiger and the clouded leopard.

Buddhism is the state religion and it plays an (Q17) _____ role in the everyday lives of the Bhutanese. However, there is a relatively large Hindu (Q18) _____ too.

The country's official language is Bhutanese but a recent (Q19) _____ found there to be a diverse (Q20) _____ of spoken languages in the country, perhaps as many as twenty-four.

STOP AND WAIT FOR FURTHER INSTRUCTIONS ⊗

Non-Verbal Reasoning

 YOU HAVE 8 MINUTES TO COMPLETE THE FOLLOWING SECTION.

YOU HAVE 15 QUESTIONS TO COMPLETE WITHIN THE TIME GIVEN.

EXAMPLES

SIMILARITY Example 1

The three figures given are similar in some way.

Work out how they are similar and select the figure that goes with them.

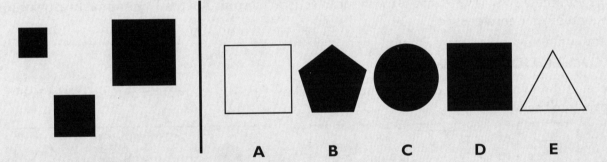

The correct answer is D. This has already been marked in Example 1 in the Non-Verbal Reasoning section of your answer sheet.

SIMILARITY Practice Question 1

The three figures given are similar in some way.

Work out how they are similar and select the figure that goes with them.

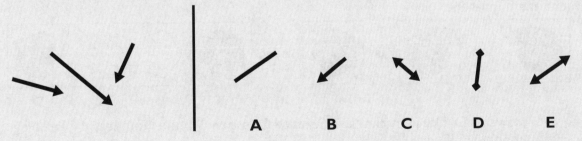

The correct answer is B. Please mark this in Practice Question 1 in the Non-Verbal Reasoning section of your answer sheet.

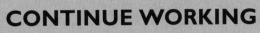 **CONTINUE WORKING**

CUBE NET Example 2

Look at the cube net below. Select the only cube that could be formed from the net.

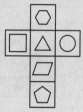

A   B   C   D

The correct answer is B. This has already been marked in Example 2 in the Non-Verbal Reasoning section of your answer sheet.

CUBE NET Practice Question 2

Look at the cube net below. Select the only cube that could be formed from the net.

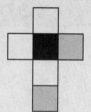

A   B   C   D

The correct answer is C. Please mark this in Practice Question 2 in the Non-Verbal Reasoning section of your answer sheet.

CONNECTION Example 3

Look at the two shapes on the left immediately below. Find the connection between them and apply it to the third shape.

 is to as is to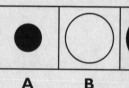

A   B   C   D

The correct answer is C. This has already been marked in Example 3 in the Non-Verbal Reasoning section of your answer sheet.

CONNECTION Practice Question 3

Look at the two shapes on the left immediately below. Find the connection between them and apply it to the third shape.

 is to as is to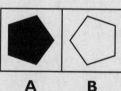

A   B   C   D

The correct answer is D. Please mark this in Practice Question 3 in the Non-Verbal Reasoning section of your answer sheet.

STOP AND WAIT FOR FURTHER INSTRUCTIONS

① The three figures given are similar in some way. Work out how they are similar and select the figure that goes with them.

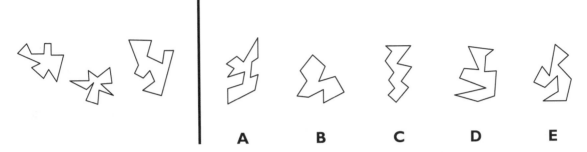

   A   **B**   **C**   **D**   **E**

② The three figures given are similar in some way. Work out how they are similar and select the figure that goes with them.

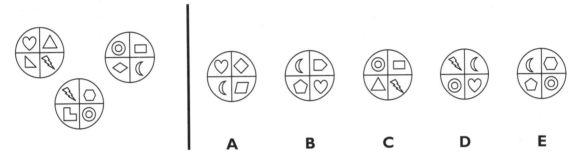

   A   **B**   **C**   **D**   **E**

③ The three figures given are similar in some way. Work out how they are similar and select the figure that goes with them.

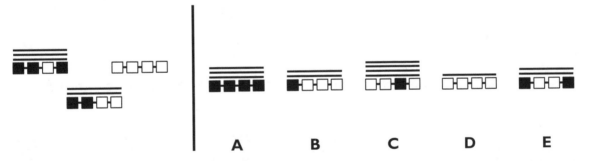

   A   **B**   **C**   **D**   **E**

④ The three figures given are similar in some way. Work out how they are similar and select the figure that goes with them.

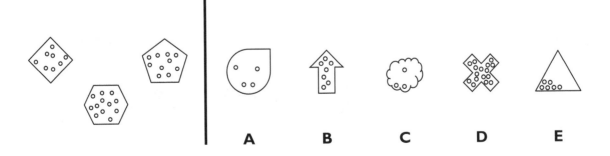

   A   **B**   **C**   **D**   **E**

CONTINUE WORKING ⮕

5 The three figures given are similar in some way. Work out how they are similar and select the figure that goes with them.

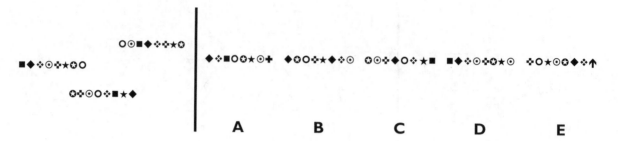

           A   **B**   **C**   **D**   **E**

6 Look at the cube net below. Select the only cube that could be formed from the net.

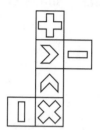

           A   **B**   **C**   **D**

7 Look at the cube net below. Select the only cube that could be formed from the net.

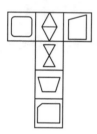

           A   **B**   **C**   **D**

8 Look at the cube net below. Select the only cube that could be formed from the net.

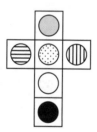

           A   **B**   **C**   **D**

9 Look at the cube net below. Select the only cube that could be formed from the net.

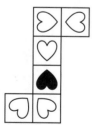

           A   **B**   **C**   **D**

CONTINUE WORKING

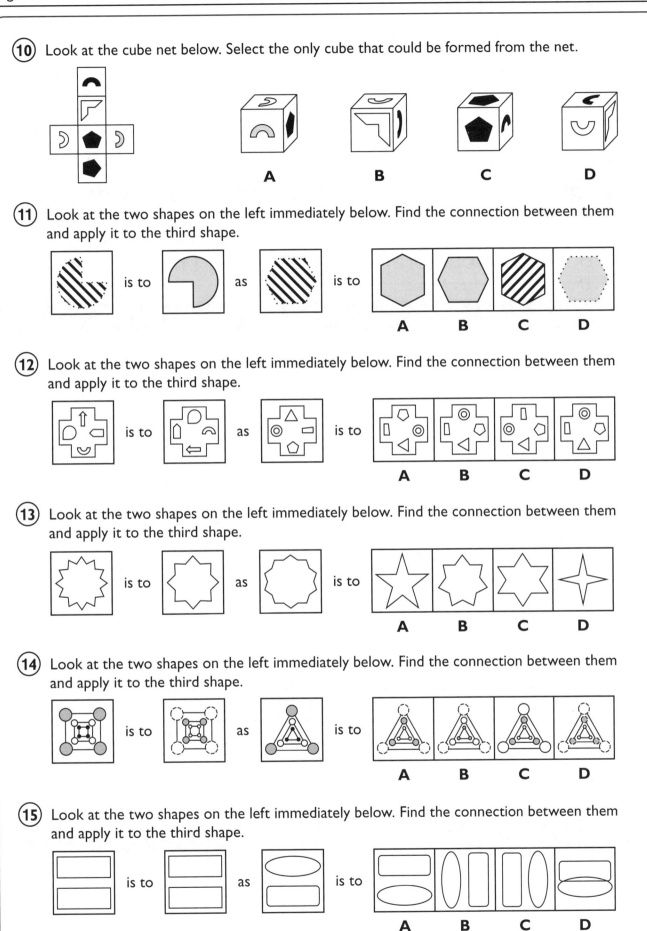

10) Look at the cube net below. Select the only cube that could be formed from the net.

A   B   C   D

11) Look at the two shapes on the left immediately below. Find the connection between them and apply it to the third shape.

is to   as   is to   A   B   C   D

12) Look at the two shapes on the left immediately below. Find the connection between them and apply it to the third shape.

is to   as   is to   A   B   C   D

13) Look at the two shapes on the left immediately below. Find the connection between them and apply it to the third shape.

is to   as   is to   A   B   C   D

14) Look at the two shapes on the left immediately below. Find the connection between them and apply it to the third shape.

is to   as   is to   A   B   C   D

15) Look at the two shapes on the left immediately below. Find the connection between them and apply it to the third shape.

is to   as   is to   A   B   C   D

STOP AND WAIT FOR FURTHER INSTRUCTIONS

Antonyms

 INSTRUCTIONS

 YOU HAVE 6 MINUTES TO COMPLETE THE FOLLOWING SECTION.

YOU HAVE 18 QUESTIONS TO COMPLETE WITHIN THE TIME GIVEN.

EXAMPLES

Example 1

Which word is most opposite in meaning to the following word?

hot

A	B	C	D	E
follow	cold	freeze	ice	jelly

The correct answer is B. This has already been marked in Example 1 in the Antonyms section of your answer sheet.

Practice Question 1

Which word is most opposite in meaning to the following word?

below

A	B	C	D	E
attack	deep	lower	above	before

The correct answer is D. Please mark the answer D in Practice Question 1 in the Antonyms section of your answer sheet.

STOP AND WAIT FOR FURTHER INSTRUCTIONS

For each row, select the word from the table that is most opposite in meaning to the word above the table.

(1) convalesce

A	B	C	D	E
convince	sugar	attempt	recover	deteriorate

(2) harass

A	B	C	D	E
hate	bother	creep	support	cool

(3) confine

A	B	C	D	E
marry	horse	unease	cope	unleash

(4) devise

A	B	C	D	E
hurry	improvise	coordinate	yelp	develop

(5) quaint

A	B	C	D	E
figure	queer	generous	old	common

(6) remedy

A	B	C	D	E
reel	oppose	hunger	worsen	medicine

CONTINUE WORKING ➡

7 provoke

A	B	C	D	E
tinder	allay	desert	never	lock

8 confront

A	B	C	D	E
utter	often	severe	oppose	avoid

9 bore

A	B	C	D	E
tower	entertain	defend	hole	boar

10 earnest

A	B	C	D	E
earned	fellow	honest	gripe	insincere

11 humiliate

A	B	C	D	E
terrorise	dream	dignify	politicise	suck

12 nourish

A	B	C	D	E
deprive	demand	nurture	heap	neutral

CONTINUE WORKING ➡

(13) bolster

A	B	C	D	E
alleviate	even	uphold	itemise	undermine

(14) taciturn

A	B	C	D	E
tactical	outgoing	solemn	fortunate	taper

(15) rebellious

A	B	C	D	E
seemly	riled	heathen	rotten	acquiescent

(16) passionate

A	B	C	D	E
indifferent	pastry	pages	courageous	ardent

(17) violent

A	B	C	D	E
placid	crime	viola	blood	murderous

(18) supplement

A	B	C	D	E
medicine	desire	pill	deduct	supple

STOP AND WAIT FOR FURTHER INSTRUCTIONS ⊗

Numeracy

 INSTRUCTIONS

 YOU HAVE 9 MINUTES TO COMPLETE THE FOLLOWING SECTION.

YOU HAVE 18 QUESTIONS TO COMPLETE WITHIN THE TIME GIVEN.

EXAMPLES

The questions within this section are not multiple choice. Write the answer to each question on the answer sheet by selecting the correct digits from the columns provided.

Example 1

Calculate the answer to the following:

12 + 42

The correct answer is 54. This has already been marked in Example 1 in the Numeracy section of your answer sheet.

Practice Question 1

Calculate the answer to the following:

55 − 47

The correct answer is 8. Please mark this in Practice Question 1 in the Numeracy section of your answer sheet. Note that a single-digit answer should be marked with a 0 in the left-hand column, so mark 08 on your answer sheet.

STOP AND WAIT FOR FURTHER INSTRUCTIONS

(1) Calculate the answer to the following:

77,898 − 77,778

(2) Calculate the value of X in the following equation:

$5X − 8 = 2X + 7$

(3) Calculate the next term in the following sequence:

470, 440, 400, 350, ?

(4) What number is 18 less than half of 726?

(5) What is the area of this triangle in cm²?

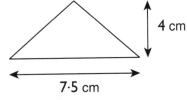

7·5 cm

Not drawn to scale

(6) How many square tiles, each with an area of 0·15 m², are needed to fully cover a rectangular surface measuring 1·5 m by 1·5 m?

(7) What is the total number of days in the months of the year that have more than 30 days each?

(8) How many minutes are there in 3·9 hours?

(9) The ratio 2·5:7·5 is equivalent to the ratio H:81.

What is the value of H?

(10) Vera earns £35 per week. She manages to save 15% of her earnings.

How many weeks will it take Vera to save £50?

(11) Calculate the product of 75 and half of 22.

CONTINUE WORKING

(12) This table shows the number of books read by a group of children over the summer holidays.

How many books did the children read in total?

Number of children	Number of books read
12	0
11	1
7	2
8	3
3	4
1	5

(13) Shape A is made from 2 identical quadrilaterals. The area of each quadrilateral is 27·25 m².

Shape B is four times as large as 1 of the quadrilaterals.

How many times bigger is Shape B than Shape A?

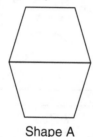

Shape A

Not drawn to scale

(14) David spends $\frac{2}{5}$ of a day at work.

How many hours does David spend at work in 5 days?

(15) How many ninths are there in $3\frac{1}{3}$?

(16) 18 is 2·5% of *U*.

What is the value of *U*?

(17) Ella can complete a lap of a running track in 50 seconds.

Jill is 10% faster than Ella.

How many seconds does it take Jill to complete a lap of the running track?

(18) Omar is standing 7th from the back of a queue and 8th from the front of the queue.

What is the probability that Omar is standing in the first half of the queue?

END OF PAPER

Key abbreviations: *cm: centimetre, g: gram, kg: kilogram, km: kilometre, m: metre, ml: millilitre, R: remainder*

Answers to *Get Test-Ready* Test A Paper 1

Comprehension (pages 8-9)

Q1 D
Winter (the passage says 'It was January the fifth.')

Q2 C
They were siblings (the passage says 'Peter lay down again with his eyes on his brother.')

Q3 D
A children's party

Q4 C
Option 2 only (the passage says 'had given him self-reliance and an instinct of protection towards the other who was afraid of so many things')

Q5 A
Ten (the passage says 'They were older than he. Joyce was eleven and Mabel Warren thirteen.')
Francis and Peter are the same age (the passage says 'But he was the elder, by a matter of minutes')

Q6 C
He was too embarrassed to do so (the passage says 'His cheeks still bore the badge of a shameful memory')

Q7 A
Pragmatic (the passage describes how she offers sensible and practical suggestions and is not drawn in by the boys' excuses)

Q8 B
Adverb

Q9 B
Serene

Q10 C
Simile

Shuffled Sentences (pages 11-12)

Q1 B
wood *The farmer insisted that his animals were free to roam.*

Q2 D
that *The auctioneer was thrilled to have sold the antique mirror.*

Q3 A
is *The audience enjoyed watching the gripping final.*

Q4 E
yellow *Wood must be kept dry in order for it to burn effectively.*

Q5 A
closing *Sheena liked to leave her window open at night.*

Q6 E
and *I found his behaviour to be unkind and uncharitable. OR I found his behaviour to be uncharitable and unkind.*

Q7 B
majority *Few occasions are as momentous as this one.*

Q8 E
quest *The sloth lazily progressed along the bough of the tree. OR The sloth progressed lazily along the bough of the tree.*

Q9 A
in *Several of the protesters were rounded up and sent to jail.*

Q10 C
from *You must learn to think for yourself and make your own decisions. OR You must learn to make your own decisions and think for yourself.*

Q11 B
through *The new television was twice as expensive as the old one.*

Q12 A
with *Gigantic snakes have slowly encroached into the territory.*

Q13 E
partial *Water is fundamental to human survival.*

Q14 C
slide *The health of the old man began to deteriorate rapidly. OR The health of the old man began to rapidly deteriorate OR The health of the old man rapidly began to deteriorate.*

Q15 *A*

> *sauce* The reporter found it hard to find an unbiased source.

Numeracy (pages 13-14)

Q1 *1,694*

$456 + 1,238 = 1,694$

Q2 *39*

$507 \div 13 = 39$

Q3 *48*

$134 + 123 - 221 + 12 = 48$

Q4 *17*

Rearrange in ascending order:
7, 7, 8, 9, 12, 17, 17, 21, 34, 48, 51
Therefore, median is 17

Q5 *37*

Sequence is $-9, -8, -7, -6, -5$
So missing term is $43 - 6 = 37$

Q6 *200*

$2 \cdot 45$ km $= 2,450$ m $= 245,000$ cm
$2,448$ m $= 244,800$ cm
$245,000$ cm $- 244,800$ cm $= 200$ cm

Q7 *11*

$4B - 7 = 2B + 15$
$4B - 2B = 15 + 7$
$2B = 22$
$B = 11$

Q8 *219*

Factors of 18: 1, 2, 3, 6, 9, 18
Third lowest factor is 3
$73 \times 3 = 219$

Q9 *12*

$4\frac{3}{4} - 3\frac{1}{4} = 1\frac{2}{4} = 1\frac{4}{8} = \frac{12}{8}$

Q10 *9*

Area of Triangle A $=$
9 cm $\times 9$ cm $\times \frac{1}{2} = 40 \cdot 5$ cm^2
Area of Triangle B $=$
3 cm $\times 3$ cm $\times \frac{1}{2} = 4 \cdot 5$ cm^2
$40 \cdot 5$ cm$^2 \div 4 \cdot 5$ cm$^2 = 9$

Q11 *42*

Cube has 6 faces
$6 \times 7 = 42$

Q12 *21*

Total apples produced last year $=$
$82 \times 9 = 738$
Extra apples produced this year $=$
$927 - 738 = 189$
Average extra per tree $= 189 \div 9 = 21$

Q13 *348*

$203 \div 7 = 29$
Number of pens $= 29 \times 5 = 145$
Total $= 145 + 203 = 348$

Problem Solving (pages 16-17)

Q1 *A*

Sum of angles in a quadrilateral $= 360°$
4th angle $=$
$360° - 55° - 134° - 109° = 62°$

Q2 *E*

Number with black hair $= 50\%$ of $350 = 175$
Number with black hair and glasses
$= \frac{2}{5} \times 175 = 70$
Number with black hair, glasses and left-handed $= 0 \cdot 2 \times 70 = 14$

Q3 *C*

Area of 1 face $= 24$ cm$^2 \div 6 = 4$ cm^2
Each face is a square so side length of cube $= 2$ cm
Volume of cube $=$
2 cm $\times 2$ cm $\times 2$ cm $= 8$ cm^3

Q4 *B*

1

Q5 *D*

Area of 1 square $= 162$ cm$^2 \div 2 = 81$ cm^2
So side length of 1 square $= 9$ cm
Perimeter of Figure B consists of 6 of these sides
9 cm $\times 6 = 54$ cm

Q6 *E*

The ratio of lions to leopards is 9:2
$9 \div 2 = 4 \cdot 5$
So there are $4 \cdot 5$ times more lions than leopards
So if there are Y leopards, there must be $4 \cdot 5Y$ lions
The expression that shows this number of lions is $9Y \div 2$

Q7 *E*

Departures per hour $= 4$
Departures per day $= 24 \times 4 = 96$
Departures in 3 days $= 96 \times 3 = 288$

Q8 *B*

All years have 365 days, except leap years, which have 366
Leap years in first decade: 2000, 2004 and 2008
Leap years in second decade: 2012 and 2016
So there was 1 extra day in the first decade.

Q9 A

$\oslash 9 = 3(9 + 1) - (2 \times 9) = 30 - 18 = 12$

Q10 D

Four terms separate the 4th and 8th term
Each term is 7 times bigger than the
previous one so 8th term must be 7^4 times
bigger than 4th term:

$7 \times 7 \times 7 \times 7 = 2{,}401$

Synonyms (pages 19-21)

Q1	**C** ruse		**Q13**	**C** grasp
Q2	**B** forbid		**Q14**	**E** supplement
Q3	**E** severe		**Q15**	**A** assert
Q4	**A** scatter		**Q16**	**E** compel
Q5	**D** settle		**Q17**	**A** occupy
Q6	**E** remove		**Q18**	**A** resuscitate
Q7	**C** swindle		**Q19**	**E** wail
Q8	**B** leeway		**Q20**	**D** home
Q9	**E** engage		**Q21**	**B** bond
Q10	**B** relinquish		**Q22**	**C** diminish
Q11	**C** chastise		**Q23**	**D** refuge
Q12	**E** disclose		**Q24**	**E** instigate

Non-Verbal Reasoning (pages 24-26)

Q1 E

The figure in the top left consists of an inner
and an outer shape.
To form the figure in the top right, the outer
shape rotates 90° clockwise and the inner
shape rotates 90° anticlockwise. Also, the
shading of the two shapes switches.
These changes must be applied to the figure
in the bottom left to form the figure in the
bottom right.
Therefore, the answer is E.

Q2 D

In each figure, the small circle moves one place
clockwise and the small square moves one
place anticlockwise to form the figure below it.
Therefore, these rules should be applied to
the figure in the top right to form the figure
below.
Therefore, the answer is D.

Q3 B

In each row, the figure in the centre is a
combination of the figures on the left and
the right.
Therefore, the answer is B.

Q4 A

Each column contains three figures. One is
shaded white, one is shaded black and one is
shaded grey.
Each figure has one side less than the figure
above it.
Therefore, the answer is A.

Q5 D

Q6 B

Q7 B

Q8 C

Q9 A

Q10 D

Q11 A

Q12 C

Q13 B

Answers to Get Test-Ready Test A Paper 2

Problem Solving (pages 29-30)

Q1 E

Matches won $= \dfrac{3}{5} \times 35 = 21$
Matches drawn $= 20\%$ of $35 = 7$
Matches lost $= 35 - 21 - 7 = 7$

Q2 B

$11 \times 10{\cdot}3$ km $= 113{\cdot}3$ km

Q3 I

Worst paid player salary
$= £3{,}500 - £1{,}231 = £2{,}269$

Q4 J

Number of players weighing 90 kg
or less $= 24 - 8 = 16$
$\dfrac{16}{24} = \dfrac{2}{3}$

Q5 F

Training begins at 10:45 a.m.

Players must arrive by 10:40 a.m.

$\frac{1}{2}$ an hour before 10:40 a.m. is 10:10 a.m.

Q6 H

Return journey distance = 32 km × 2 = 64 km

Round trip distance = 32 km + 64 km

= 96 km

Q7 A

Adult tickets cost = 13 × £25 = £325

Child tickets cost = 36 × £12·50 = £450

Total ticket costs = £325 + £450 = £775

Q8 D

Training starts at 10:45 a.m.

20 minutes before 10:45 a.m. is 10:25 a.m.

Q9 G

35 matches per season

Average number of balls used per match

= 315 ÷ 35 = 9

Q10 C

$$\frac{16,500}{22,000} = \frac{3}{4}$$

Fraction of stadium that is empty

$$= 1 - \frac{3}{4} = \frac{1}{4}$$

Cloze (pages 32-33)

Q1	**C** towards		**Q11**	**H** broken
Q2	**I** deck		**Q12**	**A** travelled
Q3	**F** wandered		**Q13**	**F** steep
Q4	**E** fine		**Q14**	**E** excusing
Q5	**A** coconut		**Q15**	**D** intangible
Q6	**B** crackle		**Q16**	**B** absence
Q7	**H** clusters		**Q17**	**J** peep
Q8	**G** coloured		**Q18**	**G** flung
Q9	**D** bathing		**Q19**	**I** undulations
Q10	**J** rubber		**Q20**	**C** twisted

Non-Verbal Reasoning (pages 36-38)

Q1 B

The arrows in each of the figures on the left point in a clockwise direction.

Therefore, the answer is B.

Q2 C

The figures on the left are each divided into two unequal parts by a black line that passes through two sides of the figure.

The smaller part of each figure on the left contains a black circle.

Therefore, the answer is C.

Q3 B

If a figure on the left has an even number of sides, it has dashed sides.

If a figure on the left has an odd number of sides, it has dotted sides.

Therefore, the answer is B.

Q4 E

The figures on the left each consist of two of the same shape. The right-hand of these two shapes is a 135° clockwise rotation of the left-hand shape.

Therefore, the answer is E.

Q5 D

The figures on the left each contain one more triangle than than they do circles.

Therefore, the answer is D.

Q6 B

Q7 D

Q8 A

Q9 C

Q10 A

Q11 B

From left to right, the cube turns one face to the left from one box to the next.

Therefore, the answer is B.

Q12 C

From left to right, the circular figure rotates 45° clockwise from one box to the next.

From left to right, the two circles alternate from being within the shape to outside the shape. The circles are black within the shape and white or grey outside the shape.

Therefore, the answer is C.

Q13 B

Each figure consists of two shapes.

From left to right, the outer shape alternates between two positions.

From left to right, the inner shape rotates 90° clockwise from one box to the next.

Therefore, the answer is B.

Q14 A

Each figure consists of two shapes.

From left to right, the outer shape has one side less from one box to the next.

From left to right, the inner shape has one side more from one box to the next.

Therefore, the answer is A.

Q15 D

From left to right, the colour of circles in each figure change from one box to the next as follows:

Black circles turn grey. White circles turn black. Dot circles turn white. Grey circles turn to a dot.

Therefore, the answer is D.

Grammar & Spelling (page 40)

Q1 C wry
Q2 D deactivate
Q3 C wierd (should be weird)
Q4 B acommodate (should be accommodate)
Q5 E hankerchief (should be handkerchief)
Q6 B cemetary (should be cemetery)
Q7 A rythm (should be rhythm)
Q8 E opress (should be oppress)

Antonyms (pages 42-43)

Q1 A considered
Q2 E survive
Q3 C decent
Q4 B reap
Q5 E thin
Q6 B excessive
Q7 C prosperous
Q8 A thanklessness
Q9 D compliant
Q10 C embrace
Q11 B unfamiliar
Q12 D rational
Q13 C boon
Q14 E duplicate
Q15 A flourish

Numeracy (pages 45-47)

Q1 120
$2{,}085 - 1{,}965 = 120$

Q2 82
Sequence is $+6, +5, +6, +5$
So next term is $+6$; $76 + 6 = 82$

Q3 278
$278 \div 9 = 30 \text{ R } 8$

Q4 191
Ninths in $21 = 21 \times 9 = 189$
$\frac{8}{36} = \frac{2}{9}$
So ninths in $21\frac{8}{36} = 2 + 189 = 191$

Q5 10
Multiply both sides by 2: $X = \frac{100}{X}$
Multiply both sides by X: $X^2 = 100$
So X must equal 10

Q6 15
$321 \div 17 = 18 \text{ R } 15$

Q7 8,000
$5 \text{ miles} = (5 \div \frac{5}{8}) \text{ km}$
$= (5 \times \frac{8}{5}) \text{ km} = (\frac{40}{5}) \text{ km} = 8 \text{ km}$
$8 \text{ km} = 8{,}000 \text{ metres}$

Q8 34
13% of $300 = 39$
$\frac{1}{9}$ of $45 = 5$
$39 - 5 = 34$

Q9 C
Probability of picking a cherry or a pineapple
$= \frac{6}{19} + \frac{1}{19} = \frac{7}{19}$
Probability of picking neither a cherry nor a pineapple $= 1 - \frac{7}{19} = \frac{12}{19}$

Q10 E
80 cents $\div 5 = 16$
Total weight $= 16 \times 1\cdot2 \text{ g} = 19\cdot2 \text{ g}$

Q11 A
1 is the most common number

Q12 A
$3X° + 5X° + 10X° = 18X°$
$18X° = 180°$
$X° = 10°$
Smallest angle $= 3X° = 3 \times 10° = 30°$

Q13 C
The coordinates of the 4th vertex must be the missing combination of possible x and y values: $(-8, 10)$

Q14 E
$1\frac{2}{3} + 3\frac{2}{7} = 1\frac{14}{21} + 3\frac{6}{21} = 4\frac{20}{21}$

Q15 D
$\frac{3}{11} \times \frac{11}{9} = \frac{33}{99} = \frac{1}{3}$

Q16 A
$\frac{1}{8} \div \frac{3}{9} = \frac{1}{8} \times \frac{9}{3} = \frac{9}{24} = \frac{3}{8}$

Q17 C
Work backwards: $0 + 9 = 9$; $3 \times 9 = 27$;
$27 - 2 = 25$
Square root of 25 is 5

Q18 B
Total mixture $= 6$ litres
50% of 6 litres $= 3$ litres so 3 litres remain
$\frac{1}{3}$ of 3 litres $= 1$ litre
Remaining paint $= 3$ litres $- 1$ litre $= 2$ litres

Answers to *Get Test-Ready* Test B Paper 1

Comprehension (pages 51-52)

Q1 C

Framton's sister had recommended that he visit Mrs. Sappleton (the passage says 'My sister was staying here, at the rectory, you know, some four years ago, and she gave me letters of introduction to some of the people here')

Q2 B

To help him recover from an affliction (the passage says 'the nerve cure which he was supposed to be undergoing')

Q3 D

We do not know (the passage says 'An undefinable something about the room seemed to suggest masculine habitation.')

Q4 A

Confident (the passage says 'a very self-possessed young lady of fifteen')

Q5 C

Mrs. Sappleton was hoping for the return of her husband and brothers (the passage says 'Poor aunt always thinks that they will come back some day… That is why the window is kept open every evening till it is quite dusk.')

Q6 B

It had drowned on the moor (the passage says 'engulfed in a treacherous piece of bog… and the little brown spaniel that was lost with them')

Q7 D

Options 1 and 4 only (the passage says 'Privately he doubted more than ever whether these formal visits on a succession of total strangers would do much towards helping' and 'He made the last statement in a tone of distinct regret.')

Q8 A

Adverb

Q9 B

Hesitantly

Q10 D

Indefinite

Shuffled Sentences (pages 54-55)

Q1 C

in He kept on making the same mistakes.

Q2 D

joy The lawyer was not deterred by the severity of the crime.

Q3 D

currant Many voters were disillusioned with the current president.

Q4 A

toes Giraffes use their long necks to reach leaves on tall trees.

Q5 A

on Both of the women were upset with the outcome.

Q6 E

legal The star of the show contracted a mystery illness.

Q7 E

no There are some arguments against this hypothesis.

Q8 E

her The man bought a yellow bag for his daughter.

Q9 B

blister The hiker ascended the mountain at a blistering pace.

Q10 E

eaten Half of the fruit in the orchard was stolen.

Q11 A

above A vile smell emanated from the sewers below the city.

Q12 D

sold Business was booming for the young entrepreneur.

Q13 B

plentiful Endangered species are becoming extinct on a daily basis.

Q14 E

below The eager rower loved to spend time on the water.

Q15 A

police I could not decide whether to paint my room red or black. OR I could not decide whether to paint my room black or red.

Numeracy (pages 56-57)

Q1 77

$\frac{1}{9}$ of 99 = 99 ÷ 9 = 11

$\frac{7}{9}$ of 99 = 7 × 11 = 77

Q2 10

40 minutes is $\frac{2}{3}$ of 1 hour

$\frac{2}{3}$ of 15 km = 10 km

Q3 64

Volume of cube with side length of 2 cm
= 2 cm × 2 cm × 2 cm = 8 cm³
Volume of cube with side length of 8 cm
= 8 cm × 8 cm × 8 cm = 512 cm³
512 cm³ ÷ 8 cm³ = 64

Q4 63

$X = 27 \times 2\frac{1}{3} = 63$

Q5 6

Difference between the 1st, 3rd, 5th and 7th
terms in sequence is −2
Difference between the 2nd, 4th, 6th and 8th
terms in sequence is +3
So missing term is +3; 3 + 3 = 6

Q6 70

$\frac{1}{6}$ of an hour = 10 minutes

10 minutes × 7 = 70 minutes

Q7 10

4,330 rounded to the nearest 50 = 4,350
4,330 rounded to the nearest 20 = 4,340
4,350 − 4,340 = 10

Q8 16

Tina's age this year = 6
Alex's age in 3 years' time = 3 × 6 = 18
Alex's current age = 18 − 3 = 15
Alex's age next year = 15 + 1 = 16

Q9 1,886

92 Fibs = 2 Fabs so 46 Fibs = 1 Fab
41 Fobs = 1 Fib so (41 × 46) Fobs = 1 Fab
41 × 46 = 1,886

Q10 10

Number of faces = 8
Number of edges = 18
18 − 8 = 10

Q11 1,069

2,950 − 1,881 = 1,069

Q12 2,080

Half a year = 26 weeks
Total eggs produced = 26 × 80 = 2,080

Q13 9

2·02 litres = 2,020 ml
2,020 ÷ 220 = 9 R 40
So 9 cups can be filled completely

Q14 143

14 + 19(4 − 2) + 7(6 + 7) = 14 + 38 + 91
= 143

Q15 30

180 ÷ 6 = 30

Problem Solving (pages 58-59)

Q1 E

Possible combinations:
1) 1p 1p 1p 1p 1p 1p 1p
2) 1p 1p 1p 1p 1p 2p
3) 1p 1p 1p 2p 2p
4) 1p 2p 2p 2p
5) 5p 1p 1p
6) 5p 2p

Q2 E

April has 30 days

$\frac{3}{10}$ are rainy: 9 days

$\frac{7}{10}$ are non-rainy: 21 days

21 − 9 = 12

Q3 E

$\frac{3}{4}$ of 21 ≠ 14

Q4 C

8 is in the tens of thousands column
so 80,000

Q5 B

8:30 a.m. to 6 p.m. is 9·5 hours
9·5 hours minus half-hour lunch break
= 9 hours; 9 × £6·50 = £58·50

Q6 E

Total consumed in 1 week
= 325 ml × 7 = 2,275 ml
Total consumed on Tuesday = 2,275 − 350
− 280 − 100 − 175 − 480 − 450 = 440 ml

Q7 D

40 red pens; 80 green pens; 80 blue pens
Percentage of green pens
= $\frac{80}{200} \times 100 = 40\%$

Q8 A

Largest 3-digit prime number = 997
Largest 3-digit square number = 961
997 + 961 = 1,958

Q9 A

$7T + 8 = 85; 7T = 77; T = 11$

$6T - 8 = 66 - 8 = 58$

Q10 D

6 hours of machine work to clear 80 m
of ditch

160 m is double 80 m so double the number
of hours required: $6 \times 2 = 12$ hours

12 hours of work shared between
3 machines: $12 \div 3 = 4$ hours

Synonyms (pages 61-63)

Q1	**E** accountable	**Q13**	**C** warehouse
Q2	**A** upright	**Q14**	**E** oppose
Q3	**B** expel	**Q15**	**B** cajole
Q4	**D** distress	**Q16**	**D** loiter
Q5	**B** submerge	**Q17**	**E** danger
Q6	**E** loot	**Q18**	**E** torpid
Q7	**B** scorched	**Q19**	**D** dedicate
Q8	**A** collude	**Q20**	**A** crouch
Q9	**E** quake	**Q21**	**E** fraud
Q10	**B** vigorous	**Q22**	**B** hang
Q11	**C** agile	**Q23**	**A** bizarre
Q12	**E** escape	**Q24**	**C** restrain

Non-Verbal Reasoning (pages 65-67)

Q1 D

Q2 B

Q3 A

Q4 D

Q5 C

Q6 A

Q7 D

In all the other figures, the right-hand arrow
is lower than the left-hand arrow.

Q8 E

All the other figures are rotations of the
same shape.

Q9 D

In all the other figures, the bottom row
contains one more symbol than the top row.

Q10 E

All the other figures are rotations of the
same shape.

Q11 A

In all the other figures, the four arrows on the
left are reflected through a vertical mirror
line to form the four arrows on the right.

Q12 C

All the other figures consist of part of a loop
of the sequence $+-\times\div$

Answers to Get Test-Ready Test B Paper 2

Problem Solving (pages 70-71)

Q1 E

$2(89 \times 3) = 534$

Q2 I

Smallest factor of 70 is 1

Largest factor of 1,000 is 1,000

$1,000 - 1 = 999$

Q3 F

60 minutes in an hour so 12 trains pass
through per hour

$12 \times 24 = 288$

Q4 L

Sequence is $+999, +998, +997$

So next term is $+996; 3,993 + 996 = 4,989$

Q5 A

Sum of 5 numbers $= 12 \times 5 = 60$

Sum of 6 numbers $= 13 \times 6 = 78$

So 6th number $= 78 - 60 = 18$

Q6 C

$54 \div 7 = 7 \text{ R } 5$

Q7 B

Cost of 1 apple $= £1·75 \div 7 = £0·25$

$£8·95 \div £0·25 = 35 \text{ R } £0·20$

So 35 apples can be bought with £8·95

Q8 J

$200 \div 0·5 = 400$

Q9 K

$18 \times 18 = 324$

Q10 *D*

Numbers in Set D: 16, 36, 64

So there are 3 numbers in Set D

Q11 *H*

Number of blue cards is $\frac{5}{8} \times 320 = 200$

Q12 *O*

20% of 5 days per week is 1 day per week

So Martin cycles 1 day per week

He takes 4 weeks' holiday so he travels to

work for 48 weeks per year

$48 \times 1 = 48$

Q13 *M*

Jon = X; Harry = 2X; Peter = 2X + 3

$X + 2X + 2X + 3 = 48$; $5X = 45$; $X = 9$

Peter = 2X + 3 = 18 + 3 = 21

Q14 *N*

Number of children = 30% of 1,200 = 360

Number of adults = 1,200 − 360 = 840

Sweets eaten by children = $360 \times 9 = 3,240$

Sweets eaten by adults = $840 \times 4 = 3,360$

Total number of sweets eaten

$= 3,240 + 3,360 = 6,600$

Q15 *G*

$65 \times 0\cdot07 \times 100 = 65 \times 7 = 455$

Cloze (pages 73-74)

Q1	**B**	sultry	**Q11**	**H**	state
Q2	**E**	occupants	**Q12**	**E**	landscape
Q3	**F**	opposite	**Q13**	**A**	treacherous
Q4	**H**	emphatically	**Q14**	**C**	climate
Q5	**D**	attentions	**Q15**	**F**	rare
Q6	**A**	aunt	**Q16**	**D**	species
Q7	**J**	window	**Q17**	**G**	important
Q8	**G**	reluctantly	**Q18**	**J**	population
Q9	**C**	another	**Q19**	**B**	study
Q10	**I**	protested	**Q20**	**I**	number

Non-Verbal Reasoning (pages 77-79)

Q1 *C*

The figures on the left each have thirteen sides.

Therefore, the answer is C.

Q2 *B*

The shapes in the top right and bottom left

quarters of each figure on the left have the

same number of sides.

Therefore, the answer is B.

Q3 *E*

In each figure on the left, the number

of black squares equals the number of

horizontal lines above the squares.

Therefore, the answer is E.

Q4 *E*

In each figure on the left, the number of

circles is twice the number of sides of the

shape they are in.

Therefore, the answer is E.

Q5 *C*

The figures on the left each consist of the

same eight symbols, each appearing once.

Therefore, the answer is C.

Q6 *B*

Q7 *C*

Q8 *D*

Q9 *A*

Q10 *D*

Q11 *B*

The shading of the figure changes from

striped to grey.

The border of the shape changes from

dotted to solid and the shape rotates 180°.

Therefore, the answer is B.

Q12 *B*

The four shapes within the cross shape move

and rotate as follows:

The shape at the top rotates 90°

anticlockwise and moves to the bottom.

The shape on the left moves to the top.

The shape at the bottom rotates 180° and

moves to the right.

The shape on the right rotates 90° clockwise

and moves to the left.

Therefore, the answer is B.

Q13 *C*

The number of points on the star

decreases by 4.

Therefore, the answer is C.

Q14 *A*

The outer grey circles turn white and their

border changes from solid to dashed.

The middle white circles turn grey.

The inner black circles turn white.

Therefore, the answer is A.

Q15 *A*

The two shapes in the square switch places.

Therefore, the answer is A.

Antonyms (pages 81-83)

Q1 **E** *deteriorate*   **Q10** **E** *insincere*
Q2 **D** *support*   **Q11** **C** *dignify*
Q3 **E** *unleash*   **Q12** **A** *deprive*
Q4 **B** *improvise*   **Q13** **E** *undermine*
Q5 **E** *common*   **Q14** **B** *outgoing*
Q6 **D** *worsen*   **Q15** **E** *acquiescent*
Q7 **B** *allay*   **Q16** **A** *indifferent*
Q8 **E** *avoid*   **Q17** **A** *placid*
Q9 **B** *entertain*   **Q18** **D** *deduct*

Numeracy (pages 85-86)

Q1 *120*
$77,898 - 77,778 = 120$

Q2 *5*
$5X - 8 = 2X + 7; 5X - 2X = 7 + 8;$
$3X = 15; X = 5$

Q3 *290*
Sequence is −30, −40, −50
So next term is −60; 350 − 60 = 290

Q4 *345*
Half of 726 = 363
$363 - 18 = 345$

Q5 *15*
Area = 7·5 cm × 4 cm × 0·5 = 15 cm²

Q6 *15*
Area of surface = 1·5 m x 1·5 m = 2·25 m²
$2·25 \text{ m}^2 \div 0·15 \text{ m}^2 = 15$

Q7 *217*
7 months with 31 days: Jan, Mar, May, Jul, Aug, Oct, Dec
$31 \times 7 = 217$

Q8 *234*
3 hours = 180 minutes
0·9 hours = 0·9 of 60 minutes = 54 minutes
180 minutes + 54 minutes = 234 minutes

Q9 *27*
2·5:7·5 = 1:3
$81 \div 3 = 27$

Q10 *10*
Savings per week = 15% of £35 = £5·25
$9 \times £5·25 = £47·25$
$10 \times £5·25 = £52·50$
So 10 weeks are needed

Q11 *825*
Half of 22 = 11
$75 \times 11 = 825$

Q12 *66*
Number of books read = (12 × 0) +
(11 × 1) + (7 × 2) + (8 × 3) + (3 × 4) +
(1 × 5) = 11 + 14 + 24 + 12 + 5 = 66

Q13 *2*
Shape B is four times as large as half of Shape A so Shape B must be two times as large as Shape A.

Q14 *48*
Time spent at work in 5 days is $\frac{2}{5} \times 5 = \frac{10}{5}$
= 2 days
= 2 × 24 hours = 48 hours

Q15 *30*
$1 = \frac{9}{9}$ *so* $3 = \frac{27}{9}$
$\frac{1}{3} = \frac{3}{9}$
So $3\frac{3}{9} = \frac{27}{9} + \frac{3}{9} = \frac{30}{9}$
So there are 30 ninths in $3\frac{3}{9}$

Q16 *720*
2·5% of U = 18
So 1% of U = 18 ÷ 2·5 = 7·2
So 100% of U = 7·2 × 100 = 720

Q17 *45*
10% of 50 seconds = 5 seconds
Jill's time = 50 seconds − 5 seconds
= 45 seconds

Q18 *0*
There 7 people in front of Omar and 6 people behind him.
So he stands 8th out of 14, so he is in the 2nd half of the queue.
So there is zero probability that he is in the first half of the queue.

Pupil's Full Name:

Instructions:
Mark the boxes correctly like this ▰

Please sign your name here:

Comprehension (pages 6-9)

Example 1

Ⓐ　~~Ⓑ~~　Ⓒ　Ⓓ

Practice Question 1

Ⓐ　Ⓑ　Ⓒ　Ⓓ

1　Ⓐ　Ⓑ　Ⓒ　Ⓓ
2　Ⓐ　Ⓑ　Ⓒ　Ⓓ
3　Ⓐ　Ⓑ　Ⓒ　Ⓓ
4　Ⓐ　Ⓑ　Ⓒ　Ⓓ
5　Ⓐ　Ⓑ　Ⓒ　Ⓓ
6　Ⓐ　Ⓑ　Ⓒ　Ⓓ
7　Ⓐ　Ⓑ　Ⓒ　Ⓓ
8　Ⓐ　Ⓑ　Ⓒ　Ⓓ
9　Ⓐ　Ⓑ　Ⓒ　Ⓓ
10　Ⓐ　Ⓑ　Ⓒ　Ⓓ

Shuffled Sentences (pages 10-12)

Example 1

Ⓐ　Ⓑ　~~Ⓒ~~　Ⓓ　Ⓔ

Practice Question 1

Ⓐ　Ⓑ　Ⓒ　Ⓓ　Ⓔ

1　Ⓐ　Ⓑ　Ⓒ　Ⓓ　Ⓔ
2　Ⓐ　Ⓑ　Ⓒ　Ⓓ　Ⓔ
3　Ⓐ　Ⓑ　Ⓒ　Ⓓ　Ⓔ
4　Ⓐ　Ⓑ　Ⓒ　Ⓓ　Ⓔ
5　Ⓐ　Ⓑ　Ⓒ　Ⓓ　Ⓔ
6　Ⓐ　Ⓑ　Ⓒ　Ⓓ　Ⓔ
7　Ⓐ　Ⓑ　Ⓒ　Ⓓ　Ⓔ
8　Ⓐ　Ⓑ　Ⓒ　Ⓓ　Ⓔ
9　Ⓐ　Ⓑ　Ⓒ　Ⓓ　Ⓔ
10　Ⓐ　Ⓑ　Ⓒ　Ⓓ　Ⓔ
11　Ⓐ　Ⓑ　Ⓒ　Ⓓ　Ⓔ
12　Ⓐ　Ⓑ　Ⓒ　Ⓓ　Ⓔ
13　Ⓐ　Ⓑ　Ⓒ　Ⓓ　Ⓔ
14　Ⓐ　Ⓑ　Ⓒ　Ⓓ　Ⓔ
15　Ⓐ　Ⓑ　Ⓒ　Ⓓ　Ⓔ

Numeracy (pages 13-14)

Example 1　　**Practice Question 1**　　**1**

5 4

Answer grids for Example 1, Practice Question 1, and questions 1–13, each with digit columns 0–9.

2　　**3**　　**4**　　**5**

6　　**7**　　**8**　　**9**

10　　**11**　　**12**　　**13**

Problem Solving (pages 15-17)

Example 1

   A   B   C̶   D   E

Practice Question 1

   A   B   C   D   E

	A	B	C	D	E
1	A	B	C	D	E
2	A	B	C	D	E
3	A	B	C	D	E
4	A	B	C	D	E
5	A	B	C	D	E
6	A	B	C	D	E
7	A	B	C	D	E
8	A	B	C	D	E
9	A	B	C	D	E
10	A	B	C	D	E

Synonyms (pages 18-21)

Example 1

   A   B̶   C   D   E

Practice Question 1

   A   B   C   D   E

	A	B	C	D	E
1	A	B	C	D	E
2					
3	A	B	C	D	E
4	A	B	C	D	E
5	A	B	C	D	E
6	A	B	C	D	E
7	A	B	C	D	E
8	A	B	C	D	E
9	A	B	C	D	E
10	A	B	C	D	E
11	A	B	C	D	E
12	A	B	C	D	E
13	A	B	C	D	E
14	A	B	C	D	E
15	A	B	C	D	E
16	A	B	C	D	E
17	A	B	C	D	E
18	A	B	C	D	E
19	A	B	C	D	E
20	A	B	C	D	E
21	A	B	C	D	E
22	A	B	C	D	E

23	A	B	C	D	E
24	A	B	C	D	E

Non-Verbal Reasoning (pages 22-26)

COMPLETE THE SQUARE Example 1

   A   B   C   D̶   E

COMPLETE THE SQUARE Practice Question 1

   A   B   C   D   E

REFLECTION Example 2

   A   B   C̶   D

REFLECTION Practice Question 2

   A   B   C   D

DIMENSION Example 3

   A   B   C̶   D

DIMENSION Practice Question 3

   A   B   C   D

	A	B	C	D	E
1	A	B	C	D	E
2	A	B	C	D	E
3	A	B	C	D	E
4	A	B	C	D	E
5	A	B	C	D	
6	A	B	C	D	
7	A	B	C	D	
8	A	B	C	D	
9	A	B	C	D	
10	A	B	C	D	
11	A	B	C	D	
12	A	B	C	D	
13	A	B	C	D	

Pupil's Full Name:

Instructions:
Mark the boxes correctly like this ▬

Please sign your name here:

Problem Solving (pages 28-30)

Example 1

Ⓐ Ⓑ ⊖ Ⓓ Ⓔ Ⓕ Ⓖ Ⓗ ⊞ ⊟

Practice Question 1

Ⓐ Ⓑ Ⓒ Ⓓ Ⓔ Ⓕ Ⓖ Ⓗ ⊞ ⊟

1   Ⓐ Ⓑ Ⓒ Ⓓ Ⓔ Ⓕ Ⓖ Ⓗ ⊞ ⊟
2   Ⓐ Ⓑ Ⓒ Ⓓ Ⓔ Ⓕ Ⓖ Ⓗ ⊞ ⊟
3   Ⓐ Ⓑ Ⓒ Ⓓ Ⓔ Ⓕ Ⓖ Ⓗ ⊞ ⊟
4   Ⓐ Ⓑ Ⓒ Ⓓ Ⓔ Ⓕ Ⓖ Ⓗ ⊞ ⊟
5   Ⓐ Ⓑ Ⓒ Ⓓ Ⓔ Ⓕ Ⓖ Ⓗ ⊞ ⊟
6   Ⓐ Ⓑ Ⓒ Ⓓ Ⓔ Ⓕ Ⓖ Ⓗ ⊞ ⊟
7   Ⓐ Ⓑ Ⓒ Ⓓ Ⓔ Ⓕ Ⓖ Ⓗ ⊞ ⊟
8   Ⓐ Ⓑ Ⓒ Ⓓ Ⓔ Ⓕ Ⓖ Ⓗ ⊞ ⊟
9   Ⓐ Ⓑ Ⓒ Ⓓ Ⓔ Ⓕ Ⓖ Ⓗ ⊞ ⊟
10   Ⓐ Ⓑ Ⓒ Ⓓ Ⓔ Ⓕ Ⓖ Ⓗ ⊞ ⊟

Cloze (pages 31-33)

Example 1

▬ Ⓑ Ⓒ Ⓓ Ⓔ

Practice Question 1

Ⓐ Ⓑ Ⓒ Ⓓ Ⓔ

1   Ⓐ Ⓑ Ⓒ Ⓓ Ⓔ Ⓕ Ⓖ Ⓗ ⊞ ⊟
2   Ⓐ Ⓑ Ⓒ Ⓓ Ⓔ Ⓕ Ⓖ Ⓗ ⊞ ⊟
3   Ⓐ Ⓑ Ⓒ Ⓓ Ⓔ Ⓕ Ⓖ Ⓗ ⊞ ⊟
4   Ⓐ Ⓑ Ⓒ Ⓓ Ⓔ Ⓕ Ⓖ Ⓗ ⊞ ⊟
5   Ⓐ Ⓑ Ⓒ Ⓓ Ⓔ Ⓕ Ⓖ Ⓗ ⊞ ⊟
6   Ⓐ Ⓑ Ⓒ Ⓓ Ⓔ Ⓕ Ⓖ Ⓗ ⊞ ⊟
7   Ⓐ Ⓑ Ⓒ Ⓓ Ⓔ Ⓕ Ⓖ Ⓗ ⊞ ⊟
8   Ⓐ Ⓑ Ⓒ Ⓓ Ⓔ Ⓕ Ⓖ Ⓗ ⊞ ⊟
9   Ⓐ Ⓑ Ⓒ Ⓓ Ⓔ Ⓕ Ⓖ Ⓗ ⊞ ⊟
10   Ⓐ Ⓑ Ⓒ Ⓓ Ⓔ Ⓕ Ⓖ Ⓗ ⊞ ⊟
11   Ⓐ Ⓑ Ⓒ Ⓓ Ⓔ Ⓕ Ⓖ Ⓗ ⊞ ⊟
12   Ⓐ Ⓑ Ⓒ Ⓓ Ⓔ Ⓕ Ⓖ Ⓗ ⊞ ⊟
13   Ⓐ Ⓑ Ⓒ Ⓓ Ⓔ Ⓕ Ⓖ Ⓗ ⊞ ⊟
14   Ⓐ Ⓑ Ⓒ Ⓓ Ⓔ Ⓕ Ⓖ Ⓗ ⊞ ⊟

15   Ⓐ Ⓑ Ⓒ Ⓓ Ⓔ Ⓕ Ⓖ Ⓗ ⊞ ⊟
16   Ⓐ Ⓑ Ⓒ Ⓓ Ⓔ Ⓕ Ⓖ Ⓗ ⊞ ⊟
17   Ⓐ Ⓑ Ⓒ Ⓓ Ⓔ Ⓕ Ⓖ Ⓗ ⊞ ⊟
18   Ⓐ Ⓑ Ⓒ Ⓓ Ⓔ Ⓕ Ⓖ Ⓗ ⊞ ⊟
19   Ⓐ Ⓑ Ⓒ Ⓓ Ⓔ Ⓕ Ⓖ Ⓗ ⊞ ⊟
20   Ⓐ Ⓑ Ⓒ Ⓓ Ⓔ Ⓕ Ⓖ Ⓗ ⊞ ⊟

Non-Verbal Reasoning (pages 34-38)

SIMILARITY Example 1

Ⓐ Ⓑ Ⓒ ⊖ Ⓔ

SIMILARITY Practice Question 1

Ⓐ Ⓑ Ⓒ Ⓓ Ⓔ

CUBE NET Example 2

Ⓐ ⊟ Ⓒ Ⓓ

CUBE NET Practice Question 2

Ⓐ Ⓑ Ⓒ Ⓓ

COMPLETE THE SEQUENCE Example 3

▬ Ⓑ Ⓒ Ⓓ Ⓔ

COMPLETE THE SEQUENCE Practice Question 3

Ⓐ Ⓑ Ⓒ Ⓓ Ⓔ

1   Ⓐ Ⓑ Ⓒ Ⓓ Ⓔ
2   Ⓐ Ⓑ Ⓒ Ⓓ Ⓔ
3   Ⓐ Ⓑ Ⓒ Ⓓ Ⓔ
4   Ⓐ Ⓑ Ⓒ Ⓓ Ⓔ
5   Ⓐ Ⓑ Ⓒ Ⓓ Ⓔ
6   Ⓐ Ⓑ Ⓒ Ⓓ
7   Ⓐ Ⓑ Ⓒ Ⓓ
8   Ⓐ Ⓑ Ⓒ Ⓓ
9   Ⓐ Ⓑ Ⓒ Ⓓ
10   Ⓐ Ⓑ Ⓒ Ⓓ
11   Ⓐ Ⓑ Ⓒ Ⓓ Ⓔ
12   Ⓐ Ⓑ Ⓒ Ⓓ Ⓔ
13   Ⓐ Ⓑ Ⓒ Ⓓ Ⓔ
14   Ⓐ Ⓑ Ⓒ Ⓓ Ⓔ
15   Ⓐ Ⓑ Ⓒ Ⓓ Ⓔ

Grammar & Spelling (page 39-40)

Example 1

| ~~A~~ | B | C | D | E |

Practice Question 1

| A | B | C | D | E |

	A	B	C	D	E
1	A	B	C	D	E
2	A	B	C	D	E
3	A	B	C	D	E
4	A	B	C	D	E
5	A	B	C	D	E
6	A	B	C	D	E
7	A	B	C	D	E
8	A	B	C	D	E

Antonyms (pages 41-43)

Example 1

| A | ~~B~~ | C | D | E |

Practice Question 1

| A | B | C | D | E |

	A	B	C	D	E
1	A	B	C	D	E
2	A	B	C	D	E
3	A	B	C	D	E
4	A	B	C	D	E
5	A	B	C	D	E
6	A	B	C	D	E
7	A	B	C	D	E
8	A	B	C	D	E
9	A	B	C	D	E
10	A	B	C	D	E
11	A	B	C	D	E
12	A	B	C	D	E
13	A	B	C	D	E
14	A	B	C	D	E
15	A	B	C	D	E

Numeracy (pages 44-47)

Example 1　　**Practice**

5 4　　　　**Question 1**　　1

(numeracy grid columns: digits 0–9)

2　　**3**　　**4**　　**5**

(numeracy grid columns: digits 0–9)

6　　**7**　　**8**

(numeracy grid columns: digits 0–9)

	A	B	C	D	E
9	A	B	C	D	E
10	A	B	C	D	E
11	A	B	C	D	E
12	A	B	C	D	E
13	A	B	C	D	E
14	A	B	C	D	E
15	A	B	C	D	E
16	A	B	C	D	E
17	A	B	C	D	E
18	A	B	C	D	E

Pupil's Full Name:

Instructions:
Mark the boxes correctly like this ▬

Please sign your name here:

Comprehension (pages 49-52)

Example 1

| | A | ~~B~~ | C | D |

Practice Question 1

| | A | B | C | D |

1	A	B	C	D
2	A	B	C	D
3	A	B	C	D
4	A	B	C	D
5	A	B	C	D
6	A	B	C	D
7	A	B	C	D
8	A	B	C	D
9	A	B	C	D
10	A	B	C	D

Shuffled Sentences (pages 53-55)

Example 1

| | A | B | ~~C~~ | D | E |

Practice Question 1

| | A | B | C | D | E |

1	A	B	C	D	E
2	A	B	C	D	E
3	A	B	C	D	E
4	A	B	C	D	E
5	A	B	C	D	E
6	A	B	C	D	E
7	A	B	C	D	E
8	A	B	C	D	E
9	A	B	C	D	E
10	A	B	C	D	E
11	A	B	C	D	E
12	A	B	C	D	E
13	A	B	C	D	E
14	A	B	C	D	E
15	A	B	C	D	E

Numeracy (pages 56-57)

Example 1 — 5 4

Practice Question 1

Questions 1–5 and 6–12 each provide number-entry grids with digits 0–9.

Continued over page

13   **14**   **15**

Columns of numbered bubbles (0–9) for questions 13, 14 and 15.

13	A	B	C	D	E
14	A	B	C	D	E
15	A	B	C	D	E
16	A	B	C	D	E
17	A	B	C	D	E
18	A	B	C	D	E
19	A	B	C	D	E
20	A	B	C	D	E
21	A	B	C	D	E
22	A	B	C	D	E
23	A	B	C	D	E
24	A	B	C	D	E

Problem Solving (pages 58-59)

Example 1

A   B   **C**   D   E

Practice Question 1

A   B   C   D   E

1	A	B	C	D	E
2	A	B	C	D	E
3	A	B	C	D	E
4	A	B	C	D	E
5	A	B	C	D	E
6	A	B	C	D	E
7	A	B	C	D	E
8	A	B	C	D	E
9	A	B	C	D	E
10	A	B	C	D	E

Non-Verbal Reasoning (pages 64-67)

REFLECTION Example 1

A   B   **C**   D

REFLECTION Practice Question 1

A   B   C   D

LEAST SIMILAR Example 2

A   **B**   C   D   E

LEAST SIMILAR Practice Question 2

A   B   C   D   E

1	A	B	C	D	
2	A	B	C	D	
3	A	B	C	D	
4	A	B	C	D	
5	A	B	C	D	
6	A	B	C	D	
7	A	B	C	D	E
8	A	B	C	D	E
9	A	B	C	D	E
10	A	B	C	D	E
11	A	B	C	D	E
12	A	B	C	D	E

Synonyms (pages 60-63)

Example 1

A   **B**   C   D   E

Practice Question 1

A   B   C   D   E

1	A	B	C	D	E
2	A	B	C	D	E
3	A	B	C	D	E
4	A	B	C	D	E
5	A	B	C	D	E
6	A	B	C	D	E
7	A	B	C	D	E
8	A	B	C	D	E
9	A	B	C	D	E
10	A	B	C	D	E
11	A	B	C	D	E
12	A	B	C	D	E

Pupil's Full Name:

Instructions:
Mark the boxes correctly like this ▬

Please sign your name here:

Problem Solving (pages 69-71)

Example 1

A   B   ⊖   D   E   F   G   H   I   J

Practice Question 1

A   B   C   D   E   F   G   H   I   J

1   A B C D E F G H I J
    K L M N O

2   A B C D E F G H I J
    K L M N O

3   A B C D E F G H I J
    K L M N O

4   A B C D E F G H I J
    K L M N O

5   A B C D E F G H I J
    K L M N O

6   A B C D E F G H I J
    K L M N O

7   A B C D E F G H I J
    K L M N O

8   A B C D E F G H I J
    K L M N O

9   A B C D E F G H I J
    K L M N O

10 A B C D E F G H I J
    K L M N O

11 A B C D E F G H I J
    K L M N O

12 A B C D E F G H I J
    K L M N O

13 A B C D E F G H I J
    K L M N O

14 A B C D E F G H I J
    K L M N O

15 A B C D E F G H I J
    K L M N O

Cloze (pages 72-74)

Example 1

▬ B C D E

Practice Question 1

A B C D E

1   A B C D E F G H I J

---

2   A B C D E F G H I J
3   A B C D E F G H I J
4   A B C D E F G H I J
5   A B C D E F G H I J
6   A B C D E F G H I J
7   A B C D E F G H I J
8   A B C D E F G H I J
9   A B C D E F G H I J
10 A B C D E F G H I J
11 A B C D E F G H I J
12 A B C D E F G H I J
13 A B C D E F G H I J
14 A B C D E F G H I J
15 A B C D E F G H I J
16 A B C D E F G H I J
17 A B C D E F G H I J
18 A B C D E F G H I J
19 A B C D E F G H I J
20 A B C D E F G H I J

Non-Verbal Reasoning (pages 75-79)

SIMILARITY Example 1

A   B   C   ⊖   E

SIMILARITY Practice Question 1

A   B   C   D   E

CUBE NET Example 2

A   ⊕   C   D

CUBE NET Practice Question 2

A   B   C   D

CONNECTION Example 3

A   B   ⊖   D

CONNECTION Practice Question 3

A   B   C   D

1   A   B   C   D   E
2   A   B   C   D   E

Continued over page

3	A	B	C	D	E
4	A	B	C	D	E
5	A	B	C	D	E
6	A	B	C	D	
7	A	B	C	D	
8	A	B	C	D	
9	A	B	C	D	
10	A	B	C	D	
11	A	B	C	D	
12	A	B	C	D	
13	A	B	C	D	
14	A	B	C	D	
15	A	B	C	D	

Antonyms (pages 80-83)

Example 1

A	B	C	D	E

Practice Question 1

A	B	C	D	E

1	A	B	C	D	E
2	A	B	C	D	E
3	A	B	C	D	E
4	A	B	C	D	E
5	A	B	C	D	E
6	A	B	C	D	E
7	A	B	C	D	E
8	A	B	C	D	E
9	A	B	C	D	E
10	A	B	C	D	E
11	A	B	C	D	E
12	A	B	C	D	E
13	A	B	C	D	E
14	A	B	C	D	E
15	A	B	C	D	E
16	A	B	C	D	E
17	A	B	C	D	E
18	A	B	C	D	E

Numeracy (pages 84-86)

Example 1 — **Practice Question 1**

5 4

Numeracy answer grids for Example 1, Practice Question 1, and Questions 1–18, each with columns of digits 0–9.